Integrating and Applying Science

A *practical handbook for effective coastal ecosystem assessment*

Edited by
**B.J. Longstaff • T.J.B. Carruthers • W.C. Dennison
T.R. Lookingbill • J.M. Hawkey • J.E. Thomas
E.C. Wicks • J. Woerner**

Additional science communication provided by
Emily Nauman

University of Maryland
CENTER FOR ENVIRONMENTAL SCIENCE

WWW.UMCES.EDU

Integration &
Application
Network

WWW.IAN.UMCES.EDU

CHESAPEAKE
ECOCHECK
Assessing and forecasting ecosystem status

WWW.ECO-CHECK.ORG

Preferred citation: Longstaff, B.J., T.J.B. Carruthers, W.C. Dennison, T.R. Lookingbill, J.M. Hawkey, J.E. Thomas, E.C. Wicks, and J. Woerner (eds) (2010) Integrating and applying science: A handbook for effective coastal ecosystem assessment. IAN Press, Cambridge, Maryland.

PO Box 775
Cambridge, MD 21613
U.S.A.
www.ian.umces.edu
ianpress@umces.edu

Disclaimer: The information in this book was current at the time of publication. While the book was prepared with care by the authors, UMCES accepts no liability from any matters arising from its contents.

ISBN 978-0-9822305-2-7
UMCES contribution 4353
First published in 2010
Set in Minion Pro

PRESS

University of Maryland
CENTER FOR ENVIRONMENTAL SCIENCE

IAN Press is committed to producing practical, user-centered communications that foster a better understanding of science and enable readers to pursue new opportunities in research, education, and environmental problem-solving. IAN Press is the publication division of the Integration and Application Network at the University of Maryland Center for Environmental Science (UMCES). Visit *www.ian.umces.edu* for information on our publications and access to downloadable PDFs of our reports, newsletters, posters, and presentations. Contact IAN Press at *ianpress@umces.edu*.

The Integration and Application Network (IAN) is a collection of scientists interested in solving, not just studying environmental problems. IAN seeks to inspire, manage, and produce timely syntheses and assessments on key environmental issues, with a special emphasis on Chesapeake Bay and its watershed. IAN is an initiative of the University of Maryland Center for Environmental Science, but links with other academic institutions, resource management agencies, and non-governmental organizations.

Beginning as a small college laboratory and a state research and education agency, UMCES has developed into a multi-campus institution of Maryland's university system. UMCES continues its rich tradition of discovery, integration, application, and teaching at its three laboratories: Chesapeake Biological Laboratory (1925), Appalachian Laboratory (1962), and Horn Point Laboratory (1973), as well as Maryland Sea Grant in College Park and the Annapolis Synthesis Center in downtown Annapolis. The Integration and Application Network was established in 2002 to allow UMCES to apply the scientific knowledge of its faculty and staff to the environmental challenges we face today. The Integration and Application Network was established in 2002 to allow UMCES to apply the scientific knowledge of its faculty and staff to the environmental challenges we face today.

Integrating and Applying Science

A *practical handbook for effective coastal ecosystem assessment*

Editors:

Ben J. Longstaff[1,2], Tim J.B. Carruthers[3], William C. Dennison[3], Todd Lookingbill[4,5], Jane M. Hawkey[3], Jane E. Thomas[3], E. Caroline Wicks[1], and Joanna Woerner[3]

[1]*EcoCheck (National Oceanic and Atmospheric Administration–University of Maryland Center for Environmental Science Partnership), Cooperative Oxford Laboratory, Oxford, Maryland, U.S.A.*
[2]*Lake Simcoe Region Conservation Authority, Newmarket, Ontario, Canada*
[3]*Integration and Application Network, University of Maryland Center for Environmental Science, Cambridge, Maryland, U.S.A.*
[4]*Appalachian Laboratory, University of Maryland Center for Environmental Science, Frostburg, Maryland, U.S.A.*
[5]*University of Richmond, Richmond, VA*

Additional science communication:

Emily Nauman, *EcoCheck (NOAA-UMCES Partnership)*

Chapter authors:

Ben Best, *Duke University*
Tim J.B. Carruthers, *Integration and Application Network, UMCES*
Shawn Carter, *U.S. National Park Service*
Christopher S. Conner, *University of Maryland Center for Environmental Science*
William C. Dennison, *Integration and Application Network, UMCES*
Benjamin Fertig, *Integration and Application Network, UMCES*
Lisa Florkowski, *Integration and Application Network, UMCES*
Jane M. Hawkey, *Integration and Application Network, UMCES*
David Jasinski, *Chesapeake Research Consortium*
Adrian B. Jones, *Integration and Application Network, UMCES*
R. Heath Kelsey, *EcoCheck (NOAA-UMCES Partnership)*
David Kimmel, *Horn Point Laboratory, UMCES; East Carolina University*
Benjamin J. Longstaff, *EcoCheck (NOAA-UMCES Partnership); Lake Simcoe Region Conservation Authority*
Todd R. Lookingbill, *Appalachian Laboratory, UMCES; University of Richmond*
Emily Nauman, *EcoCheck (NOAA-UMCES Partnership)*
William Nuttle, *Eco-hydrology*
Stuart Phinn, *University of Queensland*
Chris Roelfsema, *University of Queensland*
Geoff Sanders, *U.S. National Park Service*
Gary Shenk, *Chesapeake Bay Program, U.S. Environmental Protection Agency*
Richard P. Stumpf, *National Oceanic and Atmospheric Administration*
Mario Tamburri, *Chesapeake Biological Laboratory, UMCES*
Jeremy Testa, *Horn Point Laboratory, UMCES*
Jane E. Thomas, *Integration and Application Network, UMCES*
Howard Townsend, *NOAA Chesapeake Bay Office*
Mark Trice, *Maryland Department of Natural Resources*
E. Caroline Wicks, *EcoCheck (NOAA-UMCES Partnership)*
Michael Williams, *Integration and Application Network, UMCES*
Joanna Woerner, *Integration and Application Network, UMCES*

ACKNOWLEDGEMENTS

We would like to thank the reviewers of this book for all their comments and helpful edits. The external review process was a key step to ensure accurate information was provided and to make this book a useful handbook for practitioners.

Jon Anderson	Andrew Elmore	Travis Loop	Nick Salafsky
Jude Apple	Barry Hart	Paul Maxwell	Don Scavia
Kate Boicourt	Kirk Havens	Conor McGowan	Britta Schaffelke
Suzanne Bricker	David Haynes	Alice Newton	Robert Twilley
Jana Davis	Gary Kendrick	Elgin Perry	Dave Wilson
Michelle Devlin	Fred Lipschultz	Dwayne Potter	

We especially appreciate Alice Newton's contribution as she reviewed and provided valuable feedback on the entire book.

We would also like to thank NOAA and Packard Foundation who provided funds necessary to complete this book. NOAA's Chesapeake Bay Office provides funding for EcoCheck, which spearheaded this effort. Without funding from NCBO, this book would not have been written. Packard Foundation provided funds for Integration and Application Network staff to work on the book. Thanks is also given to LOICZ and the International Riverfoundation who played an important role in data synthesis and integration.

Support from Ken Barton and Dottie Samonisky was invaluable throughout the entire process and production of the book.

For Chapter 13: Remote sensing, funding and support was through ARC Discovery Project—Innovative Coral Reef Mapping, University of South Pacific, World Bank GEF Coral Reef Target Research—Remote Sensing Working Group. We would like to acknowledgement the support and assistance by staff and students of the University of the South Pacific, especially Bill Aalbersberg, James Comley, Leon Zann and Meo Simisi; the people of Navakavu Qoliqoli; and D. Kleine.

CONTENTS

FOREWORD

Alice Newton
Chair, Scientific Steering Committee, Land-Ocean Interactions in the Coastal Zone (LOICZ)
Professor, University of Algarve, Portugal

Our coasts are a hotspot of global change. Coastal systems throughout the world are subject to multiple pressures and stressors: pollution, eutrophication, acidification, erosion, sea level rise, tsunamis, and storms. However, more and more humans choose to live by the coast or spend their leisure time on the coast. Forty-five percent of the world's population now lives in coastal zones that represent only 5% of the land surface. The growth of coastal cities is accompanied by a decline in the quality of life of the people, which was the reason they moved to the coastal zone. Coastal "squeeze" traps the inhabitants between the land and the sea where the resources of the coastal environments and the opportunities for the sustainable utilization of coastal ecosystems are being squandered by overexploitation. Thus, a handbook focused on coastal ecosystem assessment is timely and much needed.

Innovation is needed to solve the widespread problems of our coasts if we are to turn the tide of losses, and this book, "Integrating and Applying Science: A Practical Handbook for Effective Coastal Ecosystem Assessment," is an example of innovative thinking and creative treatment of a well-known problem. In fact, this book turns the problem around, starting with community engagement and working backward to show the science basis that is fundamental for the communication products to be of high quality. Many books and scientific papers partly address the problems and solutions covered in "Integrating and Applying Science: A Practical Handbook for Effective Coastal Ecosystem Assessment," but this book uniquely integrates them and provides a holistic framework.

The book draws on hard-earned lessons from leaders in the field and these are based on real life case studies. However, it is also a very practical handbook mainly aimed at practitioners, coastal managers, and post-graduate students. Nevertheless, the rich graphics make this book approachable to a wide audience including stakeholders, end users, decision makers, and policymakers who are involved in the governance of the coastal zone. The variety of coastal watersheds used as examples and the multi-agency approach make it applicable to coastal ecosystems in both the developing and developed world. "Integrating and Applying Science: A Practical Handbook for Effective Coastal Ecosystem Assessment" provides a global context of assessment that is appropriate for all coasts, which are on the frontline of global change.

INTRODUCTION
DELVING INTO THIS BOOK

In all things of nature there is something of the marvelous.

　　　　　　　　　　　　　　　　　－Aristotle

A global problem

Vast areas of the globe's coastal zone have experienced significant declines in ecosystem health. Deteriorating water quality, loss and alteration of vital habitats, and reduced populations of fish and shellfish are some of the major changes recorded. As approximately half the world's population lives within the coastal zone (three billion people within 200 km of a coastline),[1] it is perhaps not surprising that this region is in trouble. Population impacts on the coastal zone include pollution, development, climate change (including sea level rise), and degradation of habitat and marine resources. The coastal zone is important from both an economic and environmental standpoint, with most of

Coastal zone

The narrow region that is the transition between land and the surrounding seas and oceans

the global fisheries and a large fraction of the biological productivity occurring in the zone. With the constant pressure on the coastal zone, effective coastal management that aims to halt and reverse human impacts is needed. The coastal zone exhibits strong gradients and variability in physical parameters (e.g., salinity and temperature), and is a place where sediments and nutrients are captured, and intense cycling occurs. The physical, chemical, and biological complexity of the coastal zone combined with increasing human pressure as populations grow, makes the task of effectively managing coastal zone ecosystem health a formidable, but achievable, challenge.

Development in the coastal zone has occurred throughout the world, leading to declines in ecosystem health. Managing these impacts is a challenge for coastal assessment programs. Photo credits clockwise: Jane Hawkey, Atlantic City Convention & Visitors Authority, Adrian Jones, Joanna Woerner.

While environmental degradation is a global problem, the solutions are found at local and regional levels, and thus, within this book, we attempt to articulate some of the basic principles that can be applied in a variety of coastal ecosystem types across the globe.

Program framework

Regardless of the differences between cultures, climate regions, and population pressures, integrated management and science is required to solve coastal environmental problems. Establishing and running an effective coastal management program is a complex process that necessitates strategic collaboration and partnerships between many individuals and agencies. Navigating the varied institutional affiliations and management structures, political climates, individual backgrounds, and personal agendas and beliefs can make the process challenging to say the least. These types of challenges, which can be overcome

through some of the ideas presented in this book, partially explain why many programs are failing, or making little headway. Overall, it can be stated that the process of restoring a coastal region "is not rocket science, it's a lot harder." - Don Boesch

Book organization

Data is not information, Information is not knowledge, knowledge is not understanding, understanding is not wisdom.
                                    —Chris Stoll and Gary Shubert

We have written this book to make the process of running a coastal management program easier and the outcomes more effective. It provides a step by step approach from data collection and information management to synthesis and application and draws on the knowledge of a variety of coastal scientists and managers. The book is divided into four sections that represent the four major steps needed to apply data within a coastal management

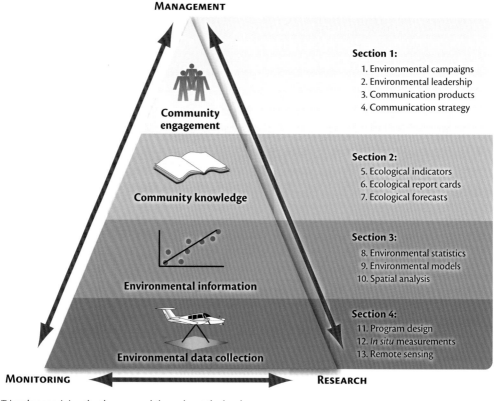

Triangle containing the themes used throughout the book.

program (community engagement, community knowledge, environmental information, and environmental data collection). These steps are represented with a triangle that: (a) depicts the continued reduction of data as it is synthesized, analyzed, and interpreted into products that are used to engage the community, and (b) places the process of engaging the community at the apex in recognition that this step is the most important, and should help direct the tasks and activities in all other steps. The other feature illustrated in the triangle is the relationship between research, monitoring, and management, with research and monitoring activities focused at the data and analysis end of the process, and management focusing on engaging the community.

Common themes

Throughout the book certain themes are covered multiple times. These common themes have been intentionally included as they address some of the most important aspects to incorporate in a coastal assessment program to effectively integrate and apply science. Common themes include a balanced effort and strong communication, the use of conceptual diagrams, balancing complexity and explanatory power, and resolving spatial-temporal challenges.

Balanced effort and strong communication
A coastal assessment program or campaign, while made up of multiple organizations and individuals, needs to act as best as it can as a single unified entity. This can be achieved with a balanced role between research, monitoring, and management, and with open communication between these components.

Conceptual diagrams
A conceptual diagram is a picture used to depict essential attributes and processes of a system, and to capture increased understanding. Conceptual diagrams within this book are discussed as a tool for: (a) facilitating communication between people and organizations, whether to help design a monitoring program, select indicators, or scope-out environmental models, and (b) to communicate results or

information within a science communication product such as a newsletter or poster.

Balancing complexity and explanatory power
The research, monitoring, and data analysis conducted to understand ecosystem status and processes can be extremely complex. However, if the broader community is to be informed and engaged, the information needs to be understandable. Balancing complexity with explanatory power occurs at all stages of the program, from the types of statistical analysis and models applied, to the manner in which the information is communicated.

Spatial-temporal challenges
Questions related to spatial and/or temporal frequency arise at all stages of the program, from establishing monitoring methods and selecting appropriate instruments, to deciding the most relevant scales to presenting information in communication products. Appropriate spatial-temporal scales, as discussed in various chapters of the book, depend on factors such as the natural variability of the system, objectives of the program, and funding.

Delving into this book

The style and content of this book aims to be both a quick reference guide for the casual user who

Four types of coastal environments (clockwise from top left): mountainous coastline, tropical coastline, rocky coastline, and sandy coastline.

can flip to a topic for specific guidance and a more in-depth resource for those users that have little experience with coastal management principles. As espoused in the book, we do this using a range of science communication techniques such as providing a mixture of visual elements and text, conceptual figures, and iconic symbols. We have used text boxes to provide easy reference to salient points, such as 'recipes for success' or 'pitfalls to avoid'—the recipes and pitfalls are short statements that are based on personal experience. Finally, we have included case studies to illustrate and support the concepts presented. We have also provided personal perspectives to illustrate the influence an individual has had on the subject and to show how important it is to have champions of a cause. If you are a small program starting up or a coalition of forces with a large budget, you can use this book to optimize your coastal assessment program.

References

1. UNEP (2005) Global Environment Outlook (GEO) Year Book 2004/5 An overview of our changing environment. United Nations Environment Programme

Further reading

Liz Creel (2003) Ripple effects: Populations and coastal regions. Population Reference Bureau. http://www.prb.org/pdf/RippleEffects_Eng.pdf

COMMUNITY ENGAGEMENT

APPLYING KNOWLEDGE TO SOLVE ENVIRONMENTAL CHALLENGES

The first section of this book addresses what is arguably the most important aspect of a coastal assessment program—using the knowledge and information generated by the program to inform and engage the community. If the community as a whole is not informed, the full potential of the program's efforts is not being harnessed. Understandably then, engaging the community should not be an afterthought or add-on, but a primary purpose toward which all other stages are working. Subsequent sections of the book discuss the types of products and analyses needed to facilitate this communication and community engagement process. As will be evident in this section, engaging the community requires many scales of effort (from single individuals who may champion a cause to the all-encompassing act of running an environmental campaign) and many skill sets (from media relations to desktop publishing).

Environmental campaigns: A campaign needs to engage society in a unified effort to solve an environmental challenge. This is by no means an easy task, requiring leadership, commitment, and resources spanning across diverse sectors of society and the environmental community. This chapter discusses the philosophy behind running an environmental campaign: ensuring a shared vision, balancing research, monitoring, and management; and staging an approach in which there are measurable successes along the way.

Environmental leadership: An environmental campaign needs leaders or champions who will step up to the challenges and roadblocks that inevitably occur. This chapter discusses champions of science over the past 500 years, traits of champions (i.e., solving, not just studying, problems), and lessons learned from recent successful campaigns around the world.

Communication products: Within an environmental campaign, it is important to have a constant flow of communication products that provide new and interesting information to the target audiences. A rigorous timetable of product development also benefits the program itself, as new insights are gained during the production stage. In this chapter, a workshop-based approach to developing science communication products and a range of tips for improving the visual appearance and content of products is discussed.

Communication strategy: Integral to the success of an environmental campaign is ensuring that the message to be communicated is packaged and delivered in a manner that has maximum impact. This chapter discusses developing a communication strategy, defining the target audience, crafting the message, and working with the media.

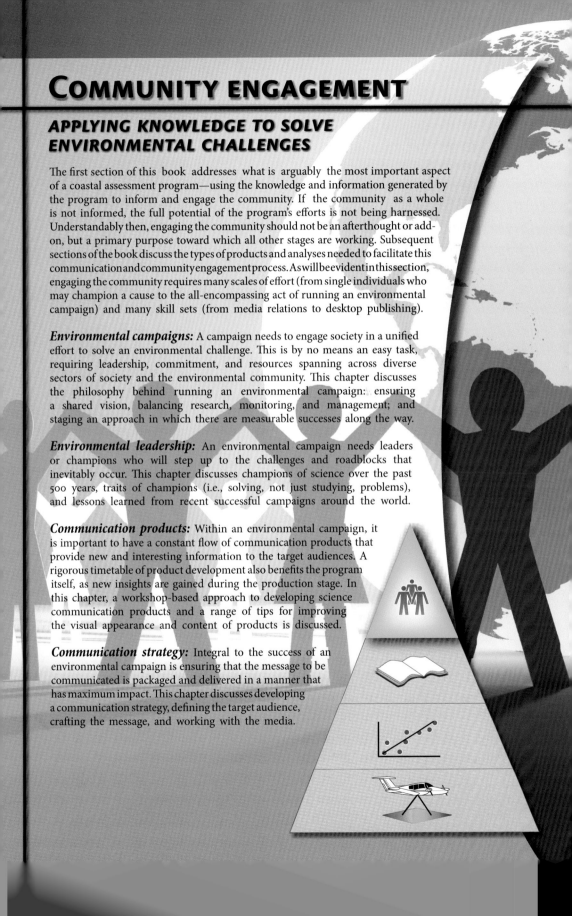

Chapter 1: Environmental campaigns

Achieving a shared vision using research, monitoring, and management

William C. Dennison and E. Caroline Wicks

First study the science. Then practice the art which is born of that science.

—Leonardo da Vinci

A coastal assessment program cannot simply draw from a few individuals; it takes contributions from an entire community and the creation of a shared vision. Keeping a balance among research, monitoring, and management is especially important and includes the dynamics of human interactions and strong communication between stakeholders and the broader community. In this chapter, we define an environmental campaign, which is part of a coastal assessment program, and describe some of the most important components for success.

Environmental campaigns

Campaigns generally are thought of in military or political terms and engage a broad swath of society, include a desired outcome, and require funding and staffing to carry out the strategies and tactics. Environmental campaigns also need to engage society and have both the resources and the strategic vision for implementation.[1]

Developing a shared vision

The development of a shared vision for the environmental campaign is a key initial step because it is the core of a coastal assessment program.[2] This vision needs to be developed by all key stakeholders (Figure 1.1). A vision conceived in isolation will not achieve the desired results, as the broader community needs to have ownership of the vision to be willing to effect changes.

Vision statements can be crafted, such as "Healthy Waterways" or "Save the Bay," to reflect the community values and aspirations. Developing a vision can involve some advocacy on the part of environmental groups, community leaders, and even scientists, but the process of developing a shared vision needs to be inclusive rather than exclusive. Marketing and branding are powerful tools that agencies and corporations often use to project an image or affect behavioral changes. These tools can be used to disseminate a vision, but there is a danger of losing the 'grassroots' champions, and having the vision associated with a particular individual, agency, or organization may restrict its overall acceptance.

Figure 1.1. A group of stakeholders meet to discuss a shared vision for conceptual ecological models for coastal Louisiana.

Engaging the community

Conceptual Ecological Model Focus Group

7

Well-defined objectives

In the absence of clearly defined goals, we become strangely loyal to performing daily trivia until ultimately we become enslaved by it.
—Robert Heinlein

Having a set of goals ensures that stakeholders agree about what the assessment is, how the program is going to accomplish its goals, and what time frame these goals are accomplished. Without these clear objectives, programs can lose their momentum, become mired in arguments, and fall apart altogether. Alternatively, it is important to be flexible about evaluating the objectives and changing them if needed.

Collaboration among partners

Collaboration among individuals, agencies, and institutions is a key mechanism to enhance overall achievements, tap individual and organizational strengths, foster effective communication, and build alliances that transcend personnel or organizational changes (Figure 1.2). To foster collaborations, incentives can be created that

reward partnerships through funding and personnel evaluation criteria. In addition, events can be scheduled (e.g., site visits, launches, symposia) that bring people together in different settings to foster interactions. The leadership of different agencies and institutions can set an example for collaborative activities by holding regular meetings, discouraging 'us vs. them' mentality, and actively seeking partnership opportunities.

It is important in developing collaborations to recognize various strengths and weaknesses of different people and to work to enhance the strengths and avoid certain weaknesses. In an attempt to compare different strengths and weaknesses of types of individuals who often are involved in coastal assessment programs, some sweeping generalizations about personal attributes were created (Figure 1.3), recognizing that many individuals do not conform to these generalizations.

Community leaders include elected or appointed officials, community organizers, and media personalities, and they are often impatient with the lack of clarity or certainty that many scientists convey. Their strength is that they can garner

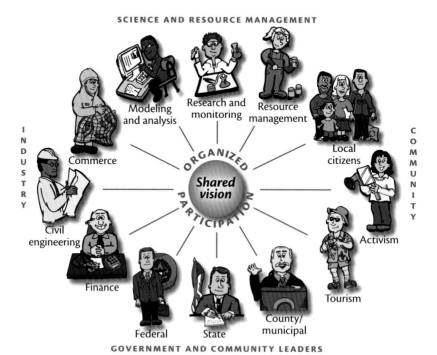

Figure 1.2. Each stakeholder plays a part in the shared vision of the environmental campaign. The collaboration among these stakeholders is key to a successful campaign.

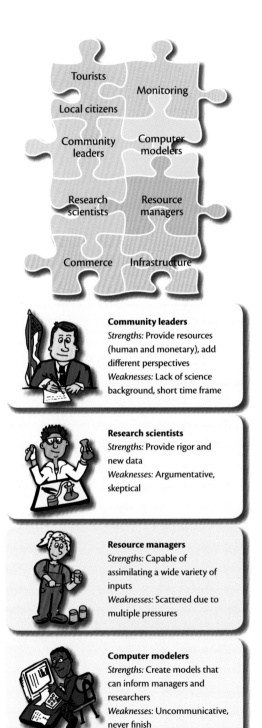

Community leaders
Strengths: Provide resources (human and monetary), add different perspectives
Weaknesses: Lack of science background, short time frame

Research scientists
Strengths: Provide rigor and new data
Weaknesses: Argumentative, skeptical

Resource managers
Strengths: Capable of assimilating a wide variety of inputs
Weaknesses: Scattered due to multiple pressures

Computer modelers
Strengths: Create models that can inform managers and researchers
Weaknesses: Uncommunicative, never finish

Figure 1.3. The attributes of different partners fit together like pieces of a puzzle, forming a stronger, more effective program.

resources (both human and monetary resources) and their ongoing relationship with constituents provides a reality check on how the public perceives the environmental campaign.

Researchers include academic scientists, agency scientists, students, and teachers, and are often trained to be argumentative and skeptical, which can distract from building collaborative teams. They can become highly specialized, which can lead to narrow perspectives. The strengths that researchers bring to an environmental campaign are the scientific rigor of hypothesis testing, data analysis, and peer review; the production of new data that can lead to new insights; and access to an international network of other researchers in their peer group.

Resource managers include managers of public lands and waters, government agency personnel, and rangers and are often pulled in many directions, becoming scattered as a result of multitasking. Their strength is their ability to assimilate data and observations from a wide variety of sources, often developing a deep knowledge of a particular ecosystem. Resource managers often spend more time in the field and can act as sentinels for change. They also play a decision-maker role in protection and restoration efforts.

Computer modelers include research scientists and engineers who create models that simulate the coastal ecosystem. These models inform management and help in decision-making processes. Modelers like to focus on model development rather than application, sometimes leading to a mismatch between what the model can say about an ecosystem and the questions that resource managers need answered.

Balanced research, monitoring, and management

A key element in a coastal assessment program is the balance among research, monitoring, and management (Figure 1.4). Attempts have been made to define the key parameters that need to be incorporated into a program in which science and management are combined to effect desired environmental outcomes. These attempts often result in lists of essential elements (e.g., common vision, scientific rigor, regional scale, diversified funding, stakeholder involvement, etc.). Although these lists are helpful, they do not necessarily distinguish the elements that actually cause a program to be successful from the elements upon which successful programs converge.

Engaging the community

Figure 1.4. Coastal assessment programs need a balance among research, monitoring, and management.

Some programs with all of the 'essential' elements seem to work, yet some programs with all of the same elements seem not to work. What is truly essential for success often remains elusive, and attempts to copy the formula that works in one location typically fail in an application elsewhere. The difficulties of extrapolating a model of science and management developed in a specific location to other locations stem from a lack of understanding of the driving forces. It is proposed here that the central driving force for developing an effective program is not the absolute amount of research or monitoring or management activity; rather, it is the balance among them. With balance, management is performed with an informed and rational basis.

Monitoring is essential

Effective monitoring is crucial to an overall campaign. Just the act of monitoring is an expression of caring. You can change perceptions about the system by measuring environmental parameters in that system. The act of monitoring is often a very visible expression to a variety of people. It provides an early diagnosis before irreversible environmental degradation can occur. If indicators are chosen carefully, they can be used to help you determine what is going on before it becomes very difficult to reverse (see Chapter 5).

Monitoring guides restoration activity to maximize the effectiveness of actions, which provides important feedback.[3] Long-term trends can be determined that are not evident in short-term data. For example, it took at least a half a decade of monitoring to see seasonal cycles of atmospheric carbon dioxide concentrations and distinguish between the seasonal cycle and an overall upward trend.

Coupled with an effective science communication strategy, monitoring also helps to inform, engage, and empower the broader community. Information based on monitoring data, such as ecosystem health indicators and report cards (discussed in more detail in Section 2), informs the community of current conditions and provides accountability of the action or inaction of resource managers and community leaders. In turn, this knowledge can motivate the public to take action to reduce their ecological footprint by participating in citizen activities, such as tree planting and petitioning community leaders.

Resource management is essential

Resource managers are those people actively involved in the environmental management of the region addressed in the program. This management can include maintaining protected areas (e.g., parks, reserves, wildlife refuges), restoring degraded areas (e.g., clean-up programs, enforcing regulations), or supporting community groups through education and coordination. The role of monitoring and assessment typically falls to resource managers. Resource managers are usually housed within a governmental agency, but ideally, monitoring and assessment also involve the community and research scientists. Resource managers provide the important reality check on the efficacy of various management actions and the applicability of various scientific research. Resource managers can both constrain the magnitude of environmental problems and help researchers to define the problem for the wider community.

Recipe for success

Whether a large governmental cooperative effort or a small non-profit, certain fundamental principles apply to your program:

- Have a shared vision
- Use well-defined objectives
- Collaborate
- Work with partners
- Balance management, research, and monitoring
- Use a staged approach
- Have a communication strategy

Research contributions are essential

Scientists are involved in the discovery of new knowledge that affects the coastal assessment program. Scientists with local experience contribute to this discovery, and very often, scientists without local experience will be involved because of their particular expertise that is relevant to the program. The researchers actively investigating the issues associated with the coastal assessment program serve as representatives of the wider scientific community. Ideally, the dissemination of knowledge through peer-reviewed scientific publications and presentations provides this link between the local researchers and the wider scientific community.

Researchers are responsible for providing information that helps to define and understand the problems and challenges in environmental assessment and management. Although they often view their role as simply information providers, in a coastal assessment program researchers often are asked to extend this role to enter the public debate about feasibility and importance of particular actions. While many government agencies and private consultants employ active researchers, researchers typically work in academic institutions.

Community contributions are essential

The community comprises the people living within the coastal assessment program boundaries. The program boundaries typically are regional in scale and attempt to encompass a functional unit relevant to the issue (e.g., watershed boundary vs. coastal management). Although the 'community' is inclusive of all sectors of society, only a small subset is actively involved or interested in any specific issue addressed by a coastal assessment program. Most programs will involve representation from appropriate indigenous peoples, resource extractors, environmental groups, and government agencies. The community is ultimately represented by the elected or appointed public officials in the different levels of government, and in a coastal assessment program, these officials provide policy directions and leadership for the societal responses to environmental challenges and enact appropriate legislation.

Spurring activism through writing

Rachel Carson, biologist and nature writer

U.S. Fish and Wildlife Service

Rachel Carson combined her scientific knowledge with eloquent writing to bring a scientifically complicated environmental problem to the public. She was already a well-known nature writer by the time she wrote *Silent Spring* in 1962. *The Sea Around Us* and *The Edge of the Sea* were bestsellers. However, she had been concerned with synthetic pesticides since the 1940s and believed that she needed to bring attention to the indiscriminate use of pesticide spraying. Moreover, she believed that humans were willfully destroying the environment that they relied on for survival.[4]

With the success of *Silent Spring*, Carson was in the public eye. President John F. Kennedy asked federal and state agencies to look into the validity of her claims, and communities organized into grassroots campaigns to fight local pollution. Carson did not stop at writing; she also attended federal hearings and eventually testified in front of the president's Science Advisory Committee.

Due to her commitment to bringing scientific information to the public through her writing and activism, Carson helped to spur the modern environmental movement—a campaign that has continued to this day.

The Manhattan Rare Book Company

The cover of the original edition, published in 1962.

Engaging the community

Resource managers, scientists, and community have different roles

The division of society into resource managers, scientists, and community is somewhat arbitrary. Membership in a particular group is not mutually exclusive. For example, scientists and resource managers are also members of the wider community, and many resource managers are scientists. Identification of the various roles that an individual plays is needed to avoid confusion. For example, scientists involved in research or monitoring strive for an objective assessment of data (Figure 1.5). However, as members of a particular community group, an advocacy role can be developed. Individuals can operate in both objective assessment and advocacy roles but only if these roles are distinguished and not used to confuse the public debate. All three major groups of people involved in research, monitoring, and management have an important role in the overall program. Each group has a particular expertise and brings to the overall program both a suite of skills and an important perspective. It is important that mutual respect for each of the other groups' perspectives and skills is fostered. With some working experience, this respect can grow into mutual trust. Greater outcomes can be achieved when these groups have this trust and learn to rely on one another's support (see Maintaining good relationships sidebar).

A coastal assessment program with simultaneous research, monitoring, and management can be somewhat messy. A more traditional linear model of conducting research, making management recommendations, developing management strategies, and establishing a monitoring program is often used. This linear model is cleaner but

Figure 1.5. A group of scientists and resource managers discuss monitoring data used to determine the health of coastal river systems in Maryland.

Maintaining good relationships

Several ground rules are important to maintain constructive interactions among the community, scientists, and resource managers.

First, vigorous debate is encouraged and fostered in workshops within each of the groups. Then a unified message is agreed on, with the issues that remain contentious highlighted for further investigation. This unified message then is presented in the public discussion about trade-offs and cost–benefits of various actions to achieve the desired ecological outcomes.

Second, the internal debate is not brought into the public realm, as scientists or resource managers can quickly confuse the issues and create uncertainty that leads to paralysis.

Finally, the merits of each of the different perspectives brought into the overall public discussion are explored. When a particular viewpoint is not adequately addressed, polarization of different factions leads to an acrimonious public debate that generally results in inertia in the program and less focus on the desired ecological outcomes.

ultimately much less effective. The time scales involved in the linear model can become prohibitive because each successive step depends on completion of the previous step.

The simultaneous model provides for more rapid feedback and increases the likelihood that the research findings are applicable and the recommendations are embedded into the community (Figure 1.6). A more rapid feedback system provides advantages to individuals within the research, monitoring, and management groups. Scientists obtain research funding or publish results based on the peer-reviewed quality of their work. Resource managers obtain funding for their programs based on the perceived value and effectiveness of monitoring. The rapid feedback provides more regular tangible evidence of progress; hence, the incentives to individuals are greater. This feeds into the community through public officials who get elected or reelected in part due to the success or failure in achieving the desired ecological outcomes.

An imbalance in the research, monitoring, and management cycle prevents the desired ecological

MANAGEMENT provides environmental values and resource management objectives to research and monitoring.

MONITORING provides feedback to researchers in the form of prioritized research based on patterns observed during the assessment of the ecosystem. Monitoring also provides management with feedback on various actions invoked.

RESEARCH provides the scientific linkages that support and create the various indicators used by resource managers that monitor the system. They also identify and communicate environmental issues so that the community is better informed.

Figure 1.6. The interactions among research, monitoring, and management all involve a two-way flow of information.

outcomes from being achieved (Figure 1.7). An imbalance toward too much management to the exclusion of research and monitoring means that decisions are too often not based on solid footing—knee-jerk reactions result. An imbalance toward too much research to the exclusion of management and monitoring leads to an academic exercise in which research priorities are entirely curiosity driven. Although curiosity-driven research plays a crucial role in science, it is the targeted research that addresses issues relevant to the assessment program. An imbalance toward too much monitoring to the exclusion of management and research results in a well-documented and sometimes inexplicable environmental decline (e.g., the last plant or animal is dutifully counted). Unfortunately, the world is rife with examples of unbalanced assessment programs. Balancing research, monitoring, and management requires continual adjustment and is rather difficult to sustain over time.

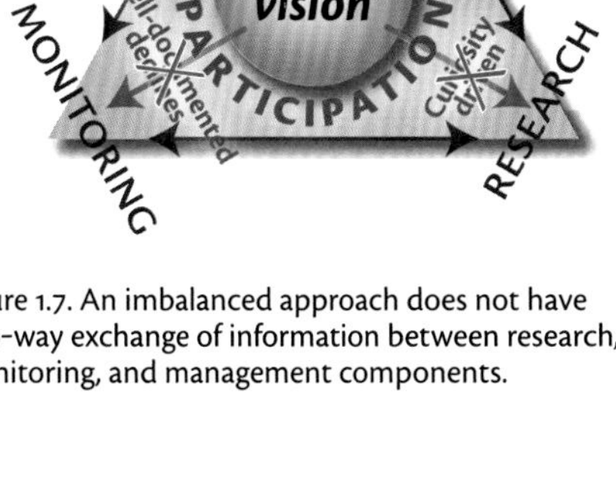

Using a staged approach

Once the objectives and partners in the program have been established, the focus can shift to implementing the program. By using a staged approach, you can break down your overall goal into manageable tasks (Staged approach sidebar and Figure 1.8). It also means that you will learn ways to accomplish your goals as you move through the approach, which, in turn, usually means easier and more efficient stages. A staged approach also ensures that you will see some immediate progress.

The first and second stages usually involve scoping out the project, determining an action plan, and setting goals for each stage. These stages also help with short-term goals that can be resolved more easily than long-term planning. For example, you may already know that wastewater treatment plants need to be upgraded, and based on the set of actions to get this accomplished, you will see reduced loads to a system within the first and second stages. In these stages, you also want to concentrate on a specific body of water rather than on a diffuse area with many parts. Therefore, focusing on a bay or ending point of a system can help to focus your goals.

Stage 3 is more long-term, with loftier goals for more complex processes. This stage also can expand the geographic area of the study. For example, urban planning and non-point source nutrients can fall under this stage. This would require moving away from the bay or body of water to the surrounding land and watershed (Figure 1.8).

Figure 1.7. An imbalanced approach does not have two-way exchange of information between research, monitoring, and management components.

Engaging the community

Staged approach

Initial stages
- Scoping
- Determining an action plan
- Setting goals for next stages
- Resolving short-term goals
- Focusing on specific water body

Intermediate stages
- Setting long-term goals
- Building more complex processes
- Expanding geographic extent of study

Final stages
- Sustaining the program
- Continuing successes in coastal management
- Expanding stakeholders

The final stages usually are focused on sustaining the success the program has had in the first three stages and incorporating more stakeholders into the program.

Creating momentum

A strategy to create initial momentum in an environmental campaign is to initially target easy challenges ('low-hanging fruit') to boost confidence and build skills. For example, an effective strategy could be focusing nutrient reductions on sewage treatment plant upgrades that are technologically possible and tractable initially and then tackling diffuse sources that are much more difficult both practically and socially.

Providing feedback on an investment, or, the adaptive management cycle

Monitoring is one part of the research, monitoring, and management triad. It should be conducted in a feedback loop with management and research known as the adaptive management cycle.[5] It takes a scientific approach to solving environmental problems. Monitoring and research are used to evaluate the health of an ecosystem, leading to improved understanding and policy planning and efficient implementation of actions that will restore and conserve a resource (Figure 1.9). This cycle is unique in that it must adapt to changing scientific paradigms and changing needs.[6]

The adaptive management cycle, and therefore an environmental campaign, requires a significant investment of resources, including people, equipment (instruments, boats, etc.), and money. Additionally, data analysis is very time intensive: Once the samples are collected, they need to be analyzed, databases developed and maintained, and statistical analyses performed. At the end of this process, the data have to be turned into meaningful, understandable information for stakeholders. Furthermore, the entire process must repeat itself (monitor, assess, communicate) over time to determine change in the system. The Chesapeake Bay Program, for example, spends $4.5 million annually on just this part of the process. Part of the adaptive management cycle is showing that money is being used effectively and without waste. Additionally, those dollars need to be converted into implemented, useful actions.

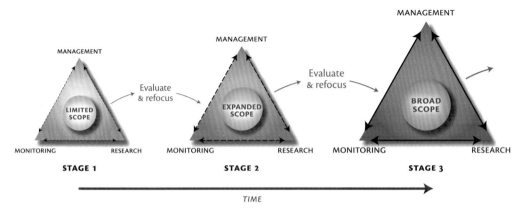

Figure 1.8. A staged approach can begin with shorter, limited scope stages and progress to a larger, broader scale approach.

Justifying your expenditures

First, there will never be enough funding for all the things you could do with a coastal assessment program. To justify expenditures, a proposal needs to be equitable, stable, and affordable. A realistic cost breakdown of what can get done and alternative ways to accomplish this while saving money (i.e., combining several monitoring trips into one) are good ways to justify spending.

One way to justify expenses is to show a direct link between the money you are spending and an improvement in the health of an ecosystem. For example, in the United States, local governments are spending large amounts of money on sewage treatment plant upgrades, and these actions need some kind of justification for those large expenditures. To do this, you could measure the amount of nitrogen in the effluent before and after the upgrades. Furthermore, the resulting health of the system ideally would improve due to the decrease in nitrogen pollution. Another example of

Pitfalls to avoid

While there are many right ways to do coastal assessment, some problems that commonly occur are:

- Undefined objectives
- Difficult partners
- Imbalance between research, monitoring, and management
- Lack of community involvement
- Expensive program with no resulting improvement in ecosystem health
- Poor communication strategy

justifying your expenses is a cost–benefit analysis of the specific actions you want to take and then prioritizing those actions based on funding and the return (improved ecosystem health) from that action. Additionally, calculating the effectiveness of actions and how much they will cost is important.

Measuring the effectiveness of actions

I have always thought the actions of men the best interpreters of their thoughts.
—John Locke

Once you have justified the need for funding and the program is underway, you will need to measure the effectiveness of the program and individual actions for continued funding. This is a real challenge to the overall campaign—organizing your program to be effective and cost-saving at the same time. If you can show effectiveness, you not only have justified your expenses, but also have turned the project into a successful environmental campaign.

Engaging the community

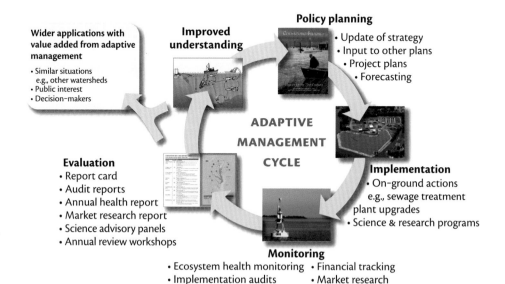

Wider applications with value added from adaptive management
- Similar situations e.g., other watersheds
- Public interest
- Decision-makers

Improved understanding

Policy planning
- Update of strategy
- Input to other plans
- Project plans
- Forecasting

ADAPTIVE MANAGEMENT CYCLE

Evaluation
- Report card
- Audit reports
- Annual health report
- Market research report
- Science advisory panels
- Annual review workshops

Implementation
- On-ground actions e.g., sewage treatment plant upgrades
- Science & research programs

Monitoring
- Ecosystem health monitoring
- Implementation audits
- Financial tracking
- Market research

Figure 1.9. The adaptive management cycle incorporates the science, management, and policy of coastal waterbodies. Each part of the cycle is affected by the coastal assessment program. Photo credits: Chesapeake Bay Program, Jane Thomas, Adrian Jones.

Strong communication linkages

The desired ecological outcome that results from the combined efforts of research, monitoring, and management needs to be explicit and shared by the community, resource managers, and scientists. Examples of a shared ecological outcome are being able to catch fish in a river, swim safely in a waterway, irrigate crops without degrading the soil, or watch natural habitat grow (Figure 1.10). The shared outcome forms the central core of the cycle linking research, monitoring, and management; the feedback interactions in that cycle; and the internal and external communication to maintain the cycle (Figure 1.9). Every coastal assessment program should have a strategy or plan for communicating the shared outcome, including program goals, projects, and results. This plan should include both internal (between partners) and external (to the public, managers, and stakeholders) communication. A timeline of updated content, such as monthly newsletters or a website, can help to focus the communication strategy and feedback into the program.

Communication involves information flow both within the research, monitoring, and management cycle and beyond the cycle to a more global context. Communication within the cycle is facilitated with meetings, newsletters, mailing lists, websites, workshops, and personal interactions. A structured system of committees and regular information exchanges is generally developed to facilitate this communication. Communication from the cycle to larger community is facilitated by peer group feedback. For example, the community has peer groups of other communities that address similar environmental problems. In an increasingly global economy and more rapid information exchanges, the incentives for best environmental management practices are being developed, and communities achieving the desired outcomes will be sought after for tourism and lifestyle amenity

External review

Conducting regular external reviews allows for corrections and feedback opportunities. The timing of these reviews needs to be chosen to maximize usefulness and minimize disruption to the program. The process of internally preparing for an external review often is of equal value to the review itself, as the process of summarizing progress and self-analysis of the program can be transformative.

External reviews should be conducted on all aspects of an environmental campaign, monitoring program, environmental reporting, and leadership effectiveness. A variety of mechanisms can be used for external review, including convening review panels of experts and other practitioners, conducting surveys of various sectors of society as to their level of understanding and their relevant actions, using focus groups and key stakeholders to probe the perception of the campaign, and tracking various implementation activities to test their relative effectiveness.

values. The scientific community has a well-developed peer group that uses scientific journals, societies, and conferences for communication. Resource managers also have peer groups through journals, societies, and conferences for communication, albeit not as highly developed as research scientists.

Science communication

Part of a successful environmental campaign is the evolution of new skill sets and the evolution of 'science communicators'. These science communicators have the ability and willingness

Environmental Concern, Inc.

Figure 1.10. Living shorelines provide natural habitat and are a visual sign of environmental action.

to communicate at a variety of levels such as peer scientists, key stakeholders, and the community (Figure 1.11). Communicating to non-peer groups requires synthesis, context, and visualization—all of which must be on the terms, in the setting, and within the time constraints of the audience (see Chapter 3).[7]

Regular science communication to stakeholders needs to provide 'news'—the recent findings. A large part of the communication is listening to the stakeholders to understand their concerns and their interpretation of the scientific results presented. The stakeholders with whom the science communicators interact should be broad and diverse. A common trap is to become aligned only with the environmental advocates, and not finding a middle ground that engages the spectrum of stakeholders needed to effect environmental solutions. Science communicators need to interact with community leaders and scientists in resource agencies while maintaining credibility within their scientific discipline. Scientific leadership skills are needed to solicit diverse opinions, have constructive debates, and resolve the issues into agreed actions and future research.

The challenge for academic institutions is to provide training for science communicators, combining the development of a scientific expertise with skills in using that expertise within a problem-solving team. A variety of approaches can foster this training, for example, interdisciplinary programs, experiential education, teaching by both scholars and practitioners, development of analytical and communication skills, and group projects that foster teamwork. The challenge for resource agencies and government institutions is to create positions for science communicators and foster long-term ties with academic institutions and other organizations in which science communicators can help to develop sustainable solutions to pressing environmental problems.

This chapter provided an overview of the elements needed for a successful environmental campaign. Subsequent chapters in this section discuss additional parts of an effective coastal assessment program, including fostering environmental leadership, producing science communication products, and developing a communication strategy.

References

1. Margoluis RA, Salafsky N (1998) Measures of success: Designing, managing, and monitoring conservation and development projects. Island Press, Washington, District of Columbia
2. Dennison WC (2008) Environmental problem solving in coastal ecosystems: A paradigm shift to sustainability. Est Coast Shelf Sci 77:185-196
3. Pantus FJ, Dennison WC (2005) Quantifying and evaluating ecosystem health: A case study from Moreton Bay, Australia. Enviro Manage 36:757-771
4. Lear, Linda (2009) The life and legacy of Rachel Carson. Accessed 28 Jul. www.rachelcarson.org
5. Lee KN (1994) Compass and gyroscope: Integrating science and politics for the environment. Island Press, Washington, District of Columbia
6. Boesch DF (2006) Scientific requirements for ecosystem-based management in the restoration of Chesapeake Bay and coastal Louisiana. Ecol Engineer 26:6-26
7. Thomas JE, Saxby TA, Jones AB, Carruthers TJB, Abal EG, Dennsion WC (2006) Communicating science effectively: A practical handbook for integrating visual elements. IWA Publishing, London, England

Further reading

Carson RL (1951) The sea around us. Oxford Press, New York
Carson RL (1955) The edge of the sea. Houghton Mifflin Co, Boston, Massachusetts
Carson RL (2002) Silent spring. Houghton Mifflin Co, Boston, Massachusetts

Integration & Application Network

Figure 1.11. A science communicator discusses challenges with a participant during a course on science communication.

Engaging the community

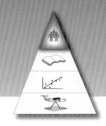

Never doubt that a small group of thoughtful, committed citizens can change the world. Indeed, it is the only thing that ever has.
—Margaret Mead

For every environmental campaign, a strong leader is needed for guidance and motivation. There have been a series of leaders or "champions" in the history of the world who have changed life on this planet. All of these leaders, no matter what area their specialty, have contained the following traits: knowledge of their field; passion for what they do; and an ability to successfully communicate their messages not only to their colleagues, but also to the broader community. This chapter discusses past champions and why they were so effective as well as discusses in detail the traits that are needed to become a successful champion and how to guide a successful coastal assessment program.

Fostering champions

A scientific champion is a person who infuses energy and provides leadership for an idea or an issue. A scientific champion effectively communicates the essence of the idea to peer scientists as well as to a broader, more public audience. There are often many champions of any idea, and as scientific ideas are not created in a vacuum, multiple scientists are involved in conceiving, testing, and communicating them. However, throughout the history of science, big ideas generally became associated with individuals (e.g., the Copernican revolution). In constructing a history of cultural paradigm shifts, individual scientific champions are singled out. The choice of the iconic scientists for each paradigm shift was informed by a rigorous assessment of the impact factor of various scientists.[1] The resulting list is biased toward European men, and this lack of gender or cultural diversity reflects the history of scientific impact. The reason for developing this

history is to better forecast the future paradigm shift(s) and to analyze the attributes of scientific champions.

As mentioned, a compelling common feature among past scientific champions is the effectiveness of the champion to communicate an idea to colleagues as well as to the broader public. Examples of the key publications for each scientific champion are presented as examples of effective communication. Other features of scientific champions are discussed as well—their ability to transfer individual knowledge to community knowledge; their ability to exert motivational power to others; and their passion for the subject, which is contagiously passed on to others.

Scientific champions were and are great communicators

The farther backward you can look, the farther forward you are likely to see.
—Winston Churchill

Science has progressed over time with a series of paradigm shifts. These paradigm shifts occur when *scientific understanding is effectively communicated to society.* In an attempt to predict the next major shift, an analysis of the history of scientific paradigms was conducted. Over the past 500 years, a series of major paradigm shifts has occurred. Dividing the historical timeline into 50-year periods, 10 paradigm shifts have occurred since the year 1500.

Astronomy: 1500–1550

The first paradigm shift was led by the astronomer Nicolaus Copernicus who postulated that the earth was not at the center of the solar system; rather, the earth revolved around the sun (Figure 2.1).[2] His book *De Revolutionibus Orbium Coelestium*

(*On the Revolutions of the Heavenly Spheres*) precipitated the "Copernican Revolution," which although controversial and considered heretical by the church, set the stage for modern astronomy. The book was written for a broad audience and used diagrams to convey Copernicus' theories. Copernicus died before his theory was debated by society, but his work was supported by the observations and writings of Galileo Galilei.[3] Both Copernicus and Galileo were responding to the impetus of a need to understand where the earth was placed in the broader spectrum of the universe.

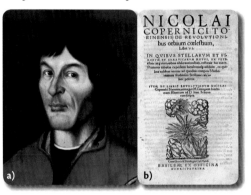

Figure 2.1. a) Portrait of Nicolaus Copernicus from Toruń, Poland, beginning of the 16th century. b) Title page of his 1543 book *De Revolutionibus Orbium Coelestium* (*On the Revolutions of the Heavenly Spheres*).

Physics: 1550–1600

The paradigm shift precipitated by Galileo (Figure 2.2) in the next half century was that heavenly bodies consist of physical matter, not ethereal substances.[3] Galileo integrated written words with his hand-drawn diagrams of the phases of the moon to convey his ideas.

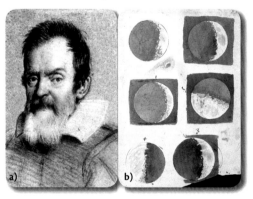

Figure 2.2. a) Portrait of Galileo Galilei by Ottavio Leoni. b) Phases of the moon by Galileo.

Astronomy: 1600–1650

Kepler's paradigm shift (1600–1650) was supported by three laws of planetary motion, now known as Kepler's laws, that stated that planets moved in elliptical, not circular, orbits (Figure 2.3).[4,5,6] Building on Galileo's presentation techniques, Kepler used diagrams and text effectively.

Figure 2.3. a) A 1610 portrait of Johannes Kepler. b) Title page of Kepler's 1609 book *Astronomia Nova* (*New Astronomy*).

Physics: 1650–1700

Sir Isaac Newton precipitated a paradigm shift with his book on the principles of mathematics in which he demonstrated that there were universal physical laws (e.g., gravity) that supplanted the belief that the forces of nature were only affected through physical contact (Figure 2.4).[7] He used a common, everyday object—an apple—to illustrate his point.

Figure 2.4. a) 1689 portrait of Isaac Newton by Godfrey Kneller. b) Title page of Newton's 1687 book *Philosophiae Naturalis Principia Mathematica* (*Mathematical Principles of Natural Philosophy*).

Biology: 1700–1750

As more of the earth was explored, the diversity of life and a need to categorize living things were evident. Carolus Linneaus and his students developed a uniform method of naming organisms, that is still in use today, replacing the multiple names for the same organism that previously existed (Figure 2.5).[8] Linneaus brought specimens back to his lab and made accurate drawings of key features of these organisms.

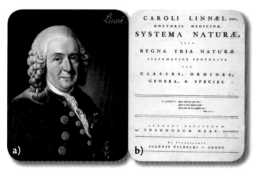

Figure 2.5. a) Portrait of Carolus Linneaus by Alexander Roslin in 1775. b) Title page of Linneaus's 1687 book *Systema Naturae* (*System of Nature*).

Chemistry: 1750–1800

In the period 1750–1800, the French nobleman and chemist Antoine Lavoisier disproved the phlogiston theory of combustion.[9] This earlier theory stated that all flammable materials contain *phlogiston*, a substance without color, odor, taste, or weight that is released during burning. Instead, Lavoisier used a visual demonstration (a candle and bell jar) to show that combustion requires oxygen, setting the stage for a new theory of what happens when objects burn and identifying and naming oxygen in the process (Figure 2.6).

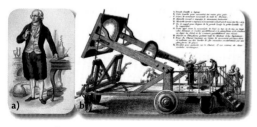

Figure 2.6. a) Line engraving of Antoine Lavoisier by Louis Jean Desire Delaistre after a design by Julien Leopold Boilly. b) Lavoisier conducting an experiment of combustion generated by amplified sunlight. Source: Chemical Heritage Foundation.

Geology: 1800–1850

Charles Lyell postulated that the earth was shaped by gradual processes, or "uniformitarianism," rather than by catastrophic events (Figure 2.7).[10] His cross-sectional diagrams of geologic rock were accurate and detailed. This followed James Hutton's (1795) theory that the age of the earth was much greater than the accepted 6,000 years.[11]

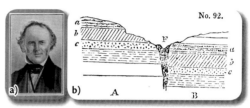

Figure 2.7. a) Daguerreotype of Charles Lyell by J.E. Mayal. b) Diagram depicting a geological fault that appeared in Lyell's 1873 book *Principles of Geology*.

Evolution: 1850–1900

The evolution period revolutionized the way people thought about the origin of the human species. Charles Darwin was an excellent writer; his books on evolution were bestsellers and sparked considerable debate throughout society (Figure 2.8).[12] A key aspect of Darwin's contribution was his ability to communicate the ideas of natural selection and evolution to society through his writings and diagrams.

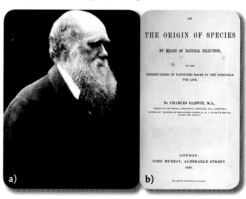

Figure 2.8. a) 1868 portrait of Charles Darwin by Julia Margaret Cameron. b) Title page of Darwin's 1859 book *On the Origin of Species*.

Physics: 1900–1950

This physics period was the era of substantial discoveries in the nature of matter. Albert Einstein's theory of relativity provided a paradigm shift in the view of matter and energy, postulating that matter and energy are interchangeable (Figure 2.9).[13] This improved understanding of matter provided the basis for nuclear physics and eventually led to atomic power and atomic bombs. Einstein was a prolific writer, producing over 100 papers and 15 books.

a)

b)

LIGHTS ALL ASKEW IN THE HEAVENS

Men of Science More or Less Agog Over Results of Eclipse Observations.

EINSTEIN THEORY TRIUMPHS

Stars Not Where They Seemed or Were Calculated to be, but Nobody Need Worry.

A BOOK FOR 12 WISE MEN

No More in All the World Could Comprehend It, Said Einstein When His Daring Publishers Accepted It.

Figure 2.9. a) 1947 photograph of Albert Einstein by Oren Jack Turner. b) Newspaper headline in the *New York Times*, November 10, 1919, about the discovery of gravitational deflection of starlight by the Sun—one of the predictions of Einstein's general theory of relativity.

Biology: 1950–2000

This biology period was stimulated by the elucidation of the structure of DNA (deoxyribonucleic acid) by James Watson and Francis Crick along with Rosalind Franklin (Figure 2.10).[14] They used a physical model of DNA and its structure, and published in a high profile journal (*Nature*). The ensuing advances in molecular biology led to biotechnology, the human genome project, and new insights into the evolutionary relationships of living things.

a)   b)   c)

Figure 2.10. a) James Watson (National Library of Medicine) and b) Francis Crick (Marc Lieberman) elucidated the c) double helix structure of DNA, sparking the biotechnological revolution.

Sustainability: 2000–2050

Previous paradigm shifts were stimulated by a societal need to understand our place in the universe, the physical laws governing life, or how our species evolved. Additionally, these shifts were stimulated by technological advances that allowed for new insights into the natural world.[15] Galileo's telescope and sailing ships that brought people to new lands are examples of technological advances that helped to shape new paradigms. The x-ray diffraction technological advances that Rosalind Franklin adopted and shared with Watson and Crick to directly view DNA was a key determinant in their collective ability to develop a model of the structure of DNA.

The next scientific paradigm shift that is critically needed by society is one of environmental sustainability. The societal need facing us now is to understand how to sustain human life on our planet with expanding populations, diminishing resources, and global change. The sustainability paradigm shift is facilitated by our ability to view the earth whole through spacecraft images (Figure 2.11). The indelible first images of the earth from early astronauts have been transformative in a public expression of 'spaceship earth.' This sustainability period is forecast as a revolution in the way humans perceive their interactions with their environment.

NASA Goddard Space Flight Center.

Figure 2.11. The global sustainability challenge will be the new paradigm of the 21st century.

Champions exhibit knowledge, power, and passion

Environmental campaigns often focus too heavily on developing or adhering to a formula which often ignores the human element. Attempts to emulate successful programs often fail, even when the organizational structure and the processes are faithfully replicated. The inability to replicate these successes has led to limited global progress in stemming environmental degradation. Programs need to embrace certain key elements of human behavior—knowledge, power, and passion.

Knowledge refers to the scientific understanding of the ecosystem that individuals can bring to bear in environmental assessment and management. *Power* refers to the ability of individuals to motivate change in human activities or behavior. This power can be manifested within government, non-government organizations, academia, or community groups. *Passion* refers to the expression of caring about the environmental issue or ecosystem.

Champions communicate knowledge

All men by nature desire knowledge.
—Aristotle

Knowledge refers to the scientific understanding of the ecosystem that individuals can bring to bear in environmental assessment and management. Knowledge that is acquired by an individual that is not transferred to others does not help because knowledge that is retained only by select individuals does not inform decision making, provides little political support, and does not empower people. Rather, individual knowledge needs to be transferred into community knowledge, which does inform decision making, provides political support, and empowers people. The measure of how successful an environmental campaign has been in terms of knowledge needs to be in the community knowledge that has been acquired rather than just what the scientists have learned.

Scientific knowledge of ecosystems is gained through data collection and information generation, the methods of which are discussed elsewhere in this book. The integration of scientific information to build knowledge requires synthesis, context, and visualization. Synthesis of information from different sources and typically different scientific disciplines can develop a

Pasteur's quadrant

Louis Pasteur, French microbiologist and chemist

Research may be divided into understanding-driven and use-inspired research, equating to basic research and applied research. Research driven by neither use nor understanding is rarely done.[16]

Niels Bohr, a Danish physicist, was a pure research scientist who developed a basic understanding of electrons and atoms. Thomas Edison, an American inventor and businessman, did pure applied research that had functional results, which led to technological innovations. He invented the phonograph and light bulb filaments still in use today. However, research that develops a better understanding of nature as well as provides useful technology is ideal. Louis Pasteur performed use-driven and understanding-driven research breakthroughs in germ theory of disease, rabies vaccine, and development of the pasteurization sterilization technique. Research to solve environmental problems needs to occur in Pasteur's quadrant—the intersection of basic and applied research.[16] Or in the words of Pasteur himself, "There are no such things as applied sciences, only applications of science."

synthetic understanding—an understanding comprising component pieces of information. Knowledge building also requires context—the setting into which the synthesized information is placed.

Having the proper background information to frame a scientific question is needed as well as the context into which the results are placed. For example, the measured rates of a given process need to be compared with measured rates elsewhere to determine whether they are high, low, or average. Finally, knowledge building involves visualization. The production of graphs, tables, maps, photographs, and diagrams that feature the data is an important aspect of knowledge building. "Word pictures," the stringing together of a narrative that allows the reader to build a visual image of the story, are also useful, with metaphors and analogies aiding the process. With proper synthesis, context, and visualization, the ensuing knowledge can be communicated to both specialists and non-specialists alike.

Champions exert motivational power

Power consists in one's capacity to link his will with the purpose of others, to lead by reason and a gift of cooperation.
—Woodrow Wilson

Power refers to the ability of individuals to motivate change in human activities or behavior. This personal power is akin to the ability of a coach who can motivate athletes to work together as a team, even though the coach is not actually playing the game. This power is achieved by persuasion and interpersonal skills that various people use within the context of a coastal assessment program. In some ways, this is the "magic" that occurs in a successful program—the personal power exerted by key individuals is often difficult to assess and emulate (Figure 2.12). Power can be manifested within government, non-government organizations, academia, or community groups.

In reviewing various environmental campaigns, it is evident that there is generally more than one charismatic individual involved in the

Recipe for success

- Creating an environment where science applications are rewarded
- Fostering an open and active dialogue among scientists, resource managers, and community leaders
- Giving champions proper media training and science communication support
- Allowing the most knowledgeable people to be heard, regardless of their rank
- Allowing less-than-perfect knowledge to be expressed

successful programs. If power is restricted to a single individual, there are several dangers for the program: Various sectors of society will not be particularly affected either due to access or bias; programs with only one individual exerting power are too sensitive to the fate of a single individual; and different kinds of power need to be exerted at different times during the maturation of a program.

Champions create passion

Only passions, great passions, can elevate the soul to great things.
—Denis Diderot

Passion refers to the expression of caring about an environmental issue or ecosystem. Environmental passion is important because it provides

Figure 2.12. The International Commission for the Protection of the Danube River, winners of the 2007 International River*prize*.

motivation and aids in learning. Environmental passion motives people who are making the extraordinary efforts needed to effect social change. Passion aids in learning—the 'student' (public) is compelled to learn when the 'teacher' (science integrator or science communicator) is excited about subject matter.

Passion needs to have a public expression and to be focused. The public expression of passion can be fostered with media events, slogans, fieldtrips, photography, poetry, and music. The focus on a particular place or issue needs to be maintained by consistent messages repeated and emulated in different venues.

Science practitioners need to be willing to stand up in public and say unequivocally "I care about this particular environment (or issue)."

Knowledge, power, and passion combined

Knowledge is power.
—Sir Francis Bacon

The relative importance of knowledge, power, and passion vary during environmental campaigns. Knowledge, power, and passion together are a potent combination. *Enthusiasm* for issues is necessary and contagious. *Quality time* is needed to keep the goals in mind and to work toward them, obtaining feedback and revision along the way. *Consistent effort* is essential.

Combining knowledge, power, and passion can lead to societal paradigm shifts. Figure 2.13 illustrates how passionate communication of knowledge by scientists, combined with a passionate desire to act on the knowledge by politicians, can lead to an informed and empowered public. An informed and empowered public will be able to leave behind dogmas of the past and act their new perception and beliefs.

Because individuals rarely possess all of these characteristics, collaborations are necessary to achieve the combination of knowledge, power, and passion needed in environmental campaigns. When scientists can effectively communicate ecosystem-level knowledge and community leaders can effectively empower people to action, then societal change is possible. Developing a passion about an issue or ecosystem requires personal experiences and motivates both knowledge and power brokers. Finding and fostering individuals with knowledge, power, and passion are essential elements of the program, as these individuals can overcome the challenges of environmental assessment and management.

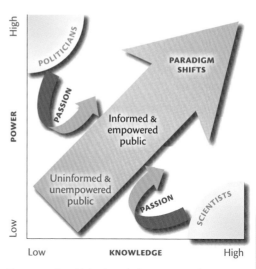

Figure 2.13. Combining knowledge, power, and passion leads to societal paradigms shifts.

Studying and solving environmental problems

A desk is a dangerous place from which to watch the world.
—John Le Carré

Environmental assessment needs to include both the studying and solving of environmental problems. Studying without solving will result in very little improvement, whereas solving without studying will lead to less-effective solutions. Here we review some of the personal attributes needed to study and solve environmental challenges.

Studying environmental problems

Most of the training that scientists receive is for studying problems, and being able to elucidate a new, previously undescribed problem is one of the greatest achievements that a scientist can obtain. Several personal attributes are necessary in order to STUDY environmental problems (Figure 2.14):

- Scientific rigor is required, usually manifested as scientific peer review for funding, publications, and promotion.
- Total commitment is also required, and a prerequisite for research includes advanced academic degrees that require years of study. In addition, a substantial commitment is required to obtain funding, develop specialized skills, and use various research tools.
- Researchers must Understand and embrace

Engaging the community

25

the complexity of scientific issues, using conceptual models and other methods to interpret the prodigious amounts of data generated in experiments or generated by measuring the natural world.

- Developing new methodologies and tools is a requirement of research. Asking new questions usually involves inventing a new tool or adapting an existing tool. In fact, many of the scientific breakthroughs come as a result of methodological advancements.

- Finally, a Yearning for truth is a key aspect of the scientific method. Developing a testable hypothesis, conducting experiments to test the hypothesis, reevaluating the hypothesis in light of new data, devising new experiments, and so forth, result in a never-ending series of research questions and activity. This produces a cycle of new and different questions generated with each set of data. The quest is always for the elusive "truth," which remains the researcher's goal.

Pitfalls to avoid

- Not matching personal skill sets with tasks
- Insufficient preparation and training
- A focus on the messenger and not the message
- Allowing too much "spin" and bureaucracy to interfere with the essential message
- Allowing the self-interest of organizations or individuals to influence the message

problems. It is in this step that objective and dispassionate results by scientists are thrown into the political milieu of society in which science is only one voice in the cacophony. The science practitioners involved in this process need to have a grasp of both the scientific issues and the political realm in which they are operating. Environmental problem solving involves combining power in the form of political will—and knowledge—in the form of scientific understanding. The public needs both power and knowledge so that it can go from uninterested and uninformed about an issue to being interested and informed sufficiently to develop approaches to solving the problem.

The balance among research, monitoring, and management becomes a key issue (Figure 2.15). Managers need the scientific foundation for policy decisions so that they are not reduced to making uninformed decisions (i.e., knee-jerk reactions). Researchers need to focus on the relevant questions and results and not be distracted by curiosity-driven research questions that are intriguing but not relevant to the issue at hand. Monitoring scientists need to develop effective feedback for the various management actions rather than focus on documenting, with ever greater precision, the decline of the resource.

To SOLVE environmental problems, the attributes required involve interactions outside the field of science:

- Developing a Shared vision, one that scientists and stakeholders can agree on, is essential. An example of a shared vision could be "Healthy Waterways," "Save the Bay," "Restore the Forest," and so forth, in which the scientific efforts support the stakeholder activities in achieving the common goal (Figure 2.16).

- Organized participation is crucial for solving environmental problems. A critical aspect of the organization of the various efforts is to achieve a dynamic balance among the various key components. Research, monitoring, and management activities need to occur simultaneously and require roughly equal effort, which translates into roughly equal resources available for each component.

- Leadership is a crucial feature of solving environmental problems, including political,

Solving environmental problems

Studying environmental problems fits within a larger framework of solving environmental

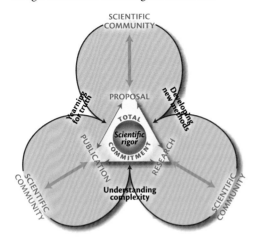

Figure 2.14. Studying environmental problems involves a cycle of proposals, research, and publications, each with feedback and review from peer scientists.

community, and scientific leadership. Political leadership needs to be exerted to enact legislation, empower agencies. and communicate the shared vision to the public. Community leadership is required for the various sectors of society to contribute to problem-solving activities. Scientific leadership is required to avoid scientific conflicts that paralyze people into inactivity. Scientific leaders need to facilitate constructive debate in which scientists can a) agree on what they agree on, thus making recommendations for action, and b) agree on what they disagree on, thus leading to further research.

- Varied communication is a key to solving problems, with communication directed at both peer audiences and non-peer audiences (e.g., public dissemination). Direct communication through workshops, meetings, and training sessions is important to inform and link the scientists in the research, monitoring, and management communities. Within each sector, there are a series of peer publication or presentation outlets, often through professional societies. But various other forms of science communication are required to reach the stakeholders and general public. Gains in scientific understanding need to be translated into community learning through print, spoken words, and experiential learning. These science communication tools can include newsletters, books, websites, phone

Figure 2.16. Workshop participants use the attributes of solving environmental problems (shared vision, organized participation, leadership, communication) to determine research, monitoring, and management recommendations for Palau's ecosystem.

hotlines, newspaper articles, electronic media segments, and so forth.

- Finally, Effective actions are required for problem solving. Many of the actions that are perceived as helpful are not actually achieving the desired environmental result. Discerning those actions that will be most helpful in achieving the shared vision, developing the tools and means for enacting them, and creating a method of assessing the effectiveness of the actions is crucial for achieving the desired environmental result.

Similarities and differences between studying and solving

Studying problems requires a dispassionate and objective perspective, yet solving problems requires a passionate attitude (e.g., "I really care about this issue!"). To study problems, embracing complexity to better understand the issue is crucial, but to solve problems, synthesis and ultimately simplifying the problem need to occur. To study problems, communication is directed toward peers, and funding is obtained through peer review. However, to solve problems, communication is directed toward stakeholders, and funding is obtained through stakeholder acceptance and approval.

Finally, the difference between studying and solving problems can be summarized as the bottom line for researchers, which is "getting it right," vs. the bottom line for practitioners, which is "getting it done." This different emphasis refers to the constant quest of researchers for

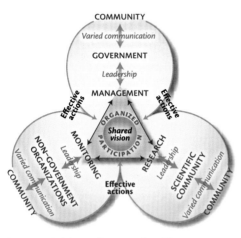

Figure 2.15. Solving environmental problems requires feedback among research, monitoring, and management as well as communication to the wider community.

27

the "truth," with publication and review focused on obtaining the most accurate version of the data and their interpretation as possible. The practitioners attempting to solve problems deal with time frames that are often dictated by events and external forces beyond their control, and performing the best research or analysis within the allotted time becomes paramount for effecting change. Thus, "getting it done," with the caveat of using the best possible science for the task at hand, becomes the paramount issue.

In spite of the various differences emphasized in the above treatment, there are various attributes required for both studying and solving environmental problems (Table 2.1). In the right brain–left brain analogy, these attributes represent the *corpus callosum*, the neural connection between the two hemispheres.

Credibility is an absolute requirement for both scientists and practitioners to withstand peer review and develop stakeholder trust. Scientists obtain credibility through their academic "pedigree" collaborations, publications, activity in professional societies, and production of reproducible results. A scientist's career is threatened or terminated when the he or she loses credibility by accusations of plagiarism, data fabrication, or irreproducible results. Practitioners obtain credibility through their record of environmental problem solving, through stakeholder dialogue, and by being consistent and knowledgeable. Practitioners lose credibility by being perceived as self-serving, biased, uninformed, or unresponsive to stakeholder needs.

Tenacity is another required attribute for both studying and solving problems. The great achievements in both science and resource management have come through consistent and prolonged efforts over long time frames. The ability to keep focused on an issue or a problem through the various high points and inevitable low points separates the successful from the unsuccessful.

Ben Longstaff

Intergration & Application Network

Figure 2.17. a) A river strategy team member participates in an annual wade-in to determine water clarity of a local creek. b) A science communicator helps kids and their parents to understand Chesapeake Bay health issues. These activities promote public awareness and involvement while gathering scientific data.

Table 2.1. The personal attributes needed to study and solve environmental problems.

Personal attribute	To study environmental problems	To solve environmental problems
Credibility	Undertaking periodic rigorous scientific peer review	Undertaking external program review to build stakeholder trust
Tenacity	Maintaining scientific inquiry through funding gaps and other setbacks	Maintaining environmental campaign through political and staff turnover
Creativity	Developing new understandings of nature	Developing new ways of solving problems
Virtue	Tackling important but difficult scientific questions	Tackling important, but difficult environmental problems

Creativity is often associated with artists, poets, and authors but not necessarily with scientists and certainly not with practitioners. Yet, creativity is at the heart of good science and resource management in order to develop new understandings of nature and new ways of communicating this understanding (Figure 2.17). Scientists must think creatively about problems, use creative inventions to study them, and explore creative ways to interpret and communicate their findings. Practitioners must think creatively to solve environmental problems, use creative means to engage stakeholders, and develop creative means of communicating to the public.

Finally, *virtue* is an attribute that is perhaps the most essential element of both studying and solving problems, and it is needed to develop ethical standards within a program of constant experimentation. Although virtuosity is usually associated with moral values and societal interactions, it is actually an attribute that combines the wisdom of knowing what needs to be done with the courage to tackle the most difficult and seemingly intractable problems. In the words of the naturalist and scientist David Starr Jordan, "Wisdom is knowing what to do next, virtue is doing it." (Jordan, 1902).

Environmental champions lead paradigm shifts

Several existing paradigms reduce the effectiveness of environmental restoration and protection, but these paradigms are shifting. In Australia, the establishment of the International River*prize* at the River*symposium* supports outstanding achievement in river management across the world (Figure 2.18). The recipients of the International River*prize* show how existing paradigms can be changed.

Figure 2.18. Lake Simcoe Region Conservation Authority is the 2009 winner of the River*prize*, and was chosen for their integrated watershed management approach.

The first recipient of the International River*prize* in 1999 was the Mersey Basin Campaign in

Existing paradigm: Environmental restoration will cost too much.

PARADIGM   SHIFT

New paradigm: Investment in protection and restoration will only get more expensive and can stimulate local economies.

northwest England. More than 5 million people live in the river basin, which includes the world's first industrial cities of Liverpool and Manchester. At the time of the inception of the 25-year Mersey Basin Campaign in 1985, the river was the most polluted estuary in the United Kingdom. Historically, raw sewage and industrial waste were discharged directly into the river. After the collapse of industrial England, the waterfront was littered with derelict land and abandoned ruins. Since then, the river has enjoyed a renaissance (Figure 2.19). There is now an annual triathlon, which involves a swimming leg in Mersey River waters.[17,18]

Figure 2.19. While industry still thrives on the Mersey River in England, restoration and preservation are also key components of the economy and culture.

The Mersey Basin Campaign started because then Secretary of State Michael Heseltine championed the idea of cleaning up the river while at the same time re-vitalizing the waterfront economy. He knew that the health and ecology of the river was linked to the economic welfare of the area. He also suggested innovative partnerships between politicians, scientists, resource managers, industry, and local stakeholders, with local action coordinators overseeing restoration activities. The Mersey Basin Campaign officially ends in 2010, with local authorities, industry, and stakeholders continuing the preservation of the river.

Farmers, government agencies, and citizens can be seen as having conflicting and potentially

Engaging the community

Existing paradigm: There are too many jurisdictions and stakeholders with divergent views.

New paradigm: A participatory and engaging process can create a shared vision among a variety of stakeholders.

Existing paradigm: Cultural differences preclude collaboration.

New paradigm: Sharing environmental goals can bring people together.

unresolvable priorities, especially when they come from many different countries. The case study debunking this paradigm is the International Commission for the Protection of the Danube River—based in Vienna, Austria—which won the International River*prize* in 2007. The second-longest river in Europe, the Danube has its origins in the Black Forest of Germany and winds its way through 19 countries before flowing into the Black Sea via its delta in Romania and Ukraine.

The Danube River basin is home to 81 million people with a wide range of cultures, languages, and historical backgrounds. The increasing human impacts, pressure, and serious pollution from agriculture, industry, and municipalities affect the water supply for communities, irrigation, hydropower generation, and industry as well as affect opportunities for transportation, tourism, and fishing.

In 1991, Hungary organized a meeting with other countries in the Danube watershed. Following the signing of the River Protection Convention in 1994, the International Commission for the Protection of the Danube River was established in 1998. Contracting parties include Austria, Bosnia and Herzegovina, Bulgaria, Croatia, Czech Republic, Germany, Hungary, Moldova, Romania, Slovakia, Slovenia, Serbia, Ukraine, and the European Union. Italy, Switzerland, Poland, Albania, and the Former Yugoslav Republic of Macedonia also cooperate with the Commission. The Commission consists of a Standing Working Group that coordinates and guides the Commission's activities, Expert Groups divided by topic, and a Secretariat that works with and supports the Expert Groups.[18,19] Each level of the Commission is populated by the contracting parties, dividing up the duties and control between the participating countries. The Commission has outlined a legal framework in which each country is fully engaged in protection of the Danube River.

The third case study involves the Alexander River Restoration Project, winner of the 2003 International River*prize*. The Alexander River

has its source in the Palestinian territories before flowing through Israel into the Mediterranean Sea. The Alexander River Restoration Project started when the Israeli Mayor of the Emek Hefer Regional Council contacted the Palestinian Governor of the District of Tul Karem to collaborate with him on the cleanup and restoration of the river. The project faces unique challenges. During a conflict outbreak in 2000, workers constructing a wastewater treatment plant on the river had to be shielded from gunfire by building a protective wall. The Israelis and Palestinians have transcended these geopolitical issues to achieve something greater than either could have done alone (Figure 2.20).

The success of the project can in large part be attributed to the leadership of Amos Brandeis, who's company "specializes in conducting planning that involves public participation, including capacity building and bringing people from different backgrounds together around one consent plan."[18,20]

Figure 2.20. Local volunteers helping to restore the Alexander River.

Restoration of the river has led to the concept of building a peace park, celebrating the Israeli and Palestinian cooperation. The park will be situated along the stream on both sides of the dividing wall between Israel and the Palestinian territories and will have diverse components, including sewage and trash removal, stream bank rehabilitation, visitors' centers, educational and publicity activities, and joint sporting events. The continuation of the excellent cooperation between Israelis and Palestinians on the local level will facilitate establishment of the park and serve as a model of peaceful coexistence in the Middle East.

In conclusion, after analyzing the history of a variety of science fields, it has been found that a "paradigm shift," or a revolutionary breakthrough, has occurred in these fields due to the actions of leaders. These leaders are knowledgeable, motivational, and excellent communicators. These champions are those that transform groups of people into collaborative teams and turn ideas into reality. Following the example of these unique individuals and their skills is essential for a successful coastal assessment program.

References

1. Murray C (2003) Human accomplishments: The pursuit of excellence in the arts and sciences, 800 B.C. to 1950. HarperCollins Publishers, New York, New York
2. Copernicus N (1543) De revolutionibus orbium cCoelestium (On the revolutions of the heavenly spheres). Nuremberg, Germany
3. Galilei G (1632) Dialogo sopra i due massimi sistemi del mondo (Dialogue concerning the two chief world systems)
4. Kepler J (1609) Astronomia nova (New astronomy)
5. Kepler J (1618–1621) Epitome astronomiae copernicanae (Epitome of copernican astronomy)
6. Kepler J (1619) Harmonice mundi (Harmony of the worlds)
7. Newton I (1687) Philosophiae naturalis principia mathematica (Mathematical principles of natural philosophy). Royal Society
8. Linneaus C (1735) Systema naturae (System of nature)
9. Lavoisier A (1789) Traité élémentaire de chimie, présenté dans un ordre nouveau et d'après les découvertes modernes (Elementary treatise of chemistry, presented in a new order and according to the recent discoveries), 2 vols. Chez Cuchet, Paris, 1789. Reprinted Cultures et Civilisations, Bruxelles, 1965
10. Lyell C (1873) Principles of geology, vol 1,2. D. Appleton Company, New York, New York
11. Hutton J (1795) Theory of the Earth, Project Gutenberg
12. Darwin C (1859) On the origin of species by means of natural selection, or the preservation of favoured races in the struggle for life. J. Murray, London, United Kingdom
13. Einstein A (1916) Die grundlage der allgemeinen relativitätstheorie (The foundation of the general theory of relativity). Annalen der Physik 49:769-822
14. Watson JD, Crick FHC (1953) Molecular structure of nucleic acids: structure for deoxyribulose nucleic acid. Nature 171:737–738
15. Kuhn T (1962) The structure of scientific revolutions. University of Chicago Press, Chicago, Illinois
16. Stokes DE (1997) Pasteur's quadrant: Basic science and technological innovation. The Brookings Institution Press, Washington, District of Columbia
17. Mersey Basin Campaign (2009) Mersey Basin Campaign. Accessed 1 Oct. www.merseybasin.org.uk/
18. Scheibenbogen S (2008) River Journeys. International Riverfoundation, Brisbane, Australia
19. International Commission for the Protection of the Danube River (2009) Legal documents. Accessed 1 Oct. www.icpdr.org/icpdr-pages/legal.htm
20. Restoration Planning (2009) Restoration Planning-Amos Brandeis. Accessed 1 Oct. www.restorationplanning.com/alex.html

Further reading

Abal EG, Bunn SE, Dennison WC (2005) Healthy waterways, healthy catchments: Making the connection in Southeast Queensland, Australia. Moreton Bay Waterways and Catchments Partnership, Brisbane, Queensland, Australia

Boyer EL (1997) Scholarship reconsidered: Priorities of the professoriate. Jossey-Bass, San Francisco, California

Dennison WC, Abal EG (1999) Moreton Bay Study: A scientific basis for the Healthy Waterways campaign. South East Queensland Regional Water Quality Management Strategy, Brisbane, Queensland, Australia

Dennison WC (2008) Environmental problem solving in coastal ecosystems: A paradigm shift to sustainability. Est Coast Shelf Sci 77:185–196

Dowie M (1996) Losing ground: American environmentalism at the close of the twentieth century. The MIT Press, Boston, Massachusetts

Healthy Waterways (2009) www.healthywaterways.org

Lane H, Woerner JL, Dennison WC, Neill C, Wilson C, Elliott M, Shively M, Graine J, Jeavons R (2007) Defending our national treasure: Department of Defense Chesapeake Bay Restoration Partnership 1998–2004. Integration and Application Network, University of Maryland Center for Environmental Science, Cambridge, Maryland

Margoluis R, Salafsky N (1998) Measures of success. Island Press, Washington, District of Columbia

Murray C (2004) Human accomplishment: The pursuit of excellence in the arts and sciences, 800 B.C. to 1950. Harper Perennial, New York, New York

South East Queensland Regional Water Quality Management Strategy Team (2001) Discover the waterways of Southeast Queensland. South East Queensland Regional Water Quality Management Strategy, Brisbane, Queensland, Australia

Engaging the community

CHAPTER 3: COMMUNICATION PRODUCTS

CREATING A PROCESS FOR GENERATING SCIENCE COMMUNICATION PRODUCTS

Jane E. Thomas, Jane M. Hawkey, Adrian B. Jones,
E. Caroline Wicks, and Joanna L. Woerner

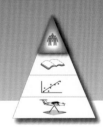

There is the link between science and policy. If that link is not understood, if the technical implications for good and ill are not made clear, democracy is at risk because the leadership can be caught up in fantasies ... and the citizenry cannot participate in the basic decisions that have technical components.
—Gerald Holton

This chapter discusses how to create the physical communication products needed to broadcast the messages within a communication strategy (see Chapter 4). To determine the kind of product needed, several different elements should be considered, including the background of the audience, the size of the audience, and the amount of time available to produce the product. The products discussed are conceptual diagrams, newsletters, presentations, websites, posters, and books.

Generating communication products

Effective communication has the power to influence opinion, change behavior, and build consensus. Thus, selecting appropriate communication products and distributing them to targeted audiences helps to engage the community and educate it about issues facing coastal ecosystems. When generating communication products, it is important to determine the suite of products, hold a workshop on the content and layout of the products, create or solicit text and visual elements, use conceptual diagrams, and format the visual elements. The authors of this book have previously published another book, *Communicating Science Effectively*, which delves into these topics in more detail.[1]

Determining a suite of products and timeline

Often, the suite of products and timeline are determined at the proposal stage, so make sure that sufficient time and resources are allotted to complete the products to which the proposal will commit. Each communication product engages a different audience and requires different time commitments (Figure 3.1).

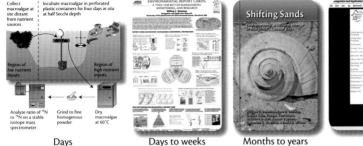
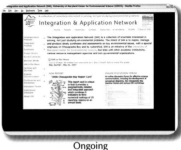

| Days | Days to weeks | Months to years | Ongoing |

Figure 3.1. Examples of effective science communication products and their approximate time commitments. From left: conceptual diagram, poster, book, and website.

Conceptual diagrams vary in complexity

Conceptual diagrams are useful tools for synthesizing information in an attractive and informative manner, and can be designed with readily available computer software. Conceptual diagrams are 'thought drawings' that provide representations of ecosystems or other complex natural processes. One reason why conceptual diagrams are so useful is that they can be used in products intended for audiences ranging from the general public to subject experts.

Depending on complexity, it will take at least a day or two to create a first draft of a conceptual diagram on a computer. Most of this time will be spent creating the base of the diagram—the representation of the system being depicted. Once this is done, the base can be populated with symbols relatively quickly, although editing of existing symbols and creation of new ones is usually required. Conceptual diagrams typically require five to 10 iterations before a final draft is approved by all the stakeholders involved. Incorporating conceptual diagrams into other aspects of coastal assessment programs is covered in more detail later in this chapter.

Newsletters and posters reach a large audience

Newsletters are effective at reaching a broad audience. They are easy to distribute so they have the potential to educate many people of various backgrounds. Depending on their content, posters can be appropriate products for technical or general audiences.

Three to four weeks is a rough guide to produce a newsletter or poster from start to finish, including creating and writing or sourcing all graphics and text. The more authors involved,

Recipe for success

- Create diverse products—posters, newsletters, presentations, books, websites, and peer-reviewed papers—to reach the widest possible audience
- Ensure inclusive and expanding authorship through consensus-building workshops to create a shared vision among authors (Figure 3.2)
- Use a variety of visual elements
- Format visual elements effectively
- Solicit extensive feedback and review, both internally and externally
- Remember to continually update materials with new data and new analyses
- Select the topics most important to the audience and only include information that supports these topics
- Create a group learning network by sharing skills and techniques and providing constructive feedback

the longer the process will take, which is true for all products, not just newsletters and posters. Obtaining text, graphics, and—most importantly—consensus from many authors is time consuming.

Books convey more information, but can be time consuming

Frequently, a topic will require more discussion than a newsletter or poster can accommodate. A book should contain only the topics required to convey the main message to the targeted audience. For more information on determining the target audience, see Chapter 4.

Timelines for producing books vary widely and will depend on the number and responsiveness of the contributing authors and the other commitments of the person responsible for producing the book. A rough timeline for production of a book would be one to three years.

Figure 3.2. Editing communication products at a workshop allows for consensus building.

Websites need planning, scoping, and maintenance

Detailed planning and scoping at the initiation phase of a website will reduce the work required for future expansion. In addition to the time-intensive initial planning and development stages, it is equally important to allot sufficient resources for the long-term commitment of maintaining, updating, and enhancing the website.

Workshopping the content and layout

Science communication products are usually the result of a consensus among the participating authors. The content and layout of these products will therefore require input and feedback from the authors. For newsletters, posters, conceptual diagrams, and websites, the content and layout can usually be determined during a single workshop, with subsequent drafts, edits, and corrections done through e-mail. As the content develops, it is important to think about both the text and the graphics together. Developing the text and graphics simultaneously helps to focus the topics being discussed and results in a more cohesive, integrated, and organized product.

For books, usually multiple workshops will be required—one workshop per chapter is appropriate. As this workshop series progresses, it is very useful to be able to have one chapter almost finished, instead of working on all chapters equally. Providing workshop participants with a finished, polished chapter—printed in full color and trimmed to size—is a psychological "great leap forward" because instead of just looking at pages of text, the participants can easily visualize the finished product and are more likely to become engaged in the project.

An effective technique used at these workshops is to mock up the general layout and content on large pads of self-stick paper. These sheets of paper can be peeled off and placed on the walls to give a rough first cut of the layout. This method is particularly useful for book layouts, as one double-page spread can be represented easily (Figure 3.3), and it will give an approximate page count.

Also during workshops, authors can construct a list of active titles that tell the story. An active title makes an active statement about the contents, e.g., instead of the passive title *Results*, an active title could be *Potential seagrass habitat depends on water quality and sediment composition*. The active title provides enough information for the audience to gain an understanding of the material and

Using visual displays to illustrate data

Edward Tufte, Professor

Edward Tufte is trained as a political scientist and statistician, but moved into analytic design (i.e., information design) and visual literacy in the 1980s. He is a pioneer in the field of visually displaying scientific data. He believes that each part of a graphic should display only pertinent information and convey it to the reader. His first book, *The Visual Display of Quantitative Information*, is still used today to help scientists to convey their data to peer and non-peer groups.

Tufte studies designs that help to describe the reasoning behind the data and how the data can be used. "At their best, graphics are instruments for reasoning."[2] Some of Tufte's more well-known ideas include the coining of the terms *chartjunk* and *sparklines*. He also is known for his criticism of PowerPoint and how it forces the information into useless bullet points and distracts the audience with needless "extras."[3]

Tufte continues to write and lecture on the communication of scientific data, bringing clarity to a field that can be confusing and overwhelming.

The front cover of Tufte's PowerPoint essay.

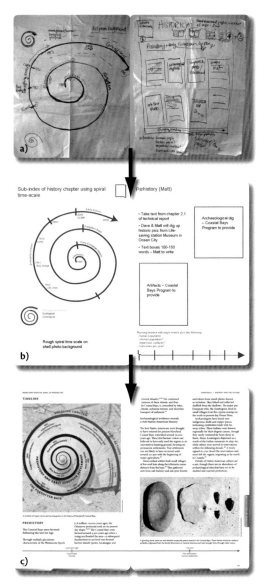

These workshops are a good opportunity to obtain commitments from the people present to provide text or visual elements, including data figures. Writing people's names on the self-stick paper layouts is a good way to get these commitments and to ensure that everybody has the same understanding of their commitments (i.e., literally getting everybody on the same page). During these workshops, a useful technique is to use placeholder text and graphics to represent the layout so that the workshop participants get nearly instant visual feedback on the layout and can comment (Figure 3.5).

After the workshop, send an e-mail to all the participants and attach the draft layout with placeholder text (with approximate word counts) and graphics and include the names of people responsible for providing the various content.

Creating or soliciting text and visual elements

Based on the assignments agreed on at the content and layout workshop, solicit text and visual elements from the appropriate contributors. Given

Figure 3.3. a) This figure shows the progression of a double-page spread of a book from the paper-drawn outline of the layout and contents, including people's names for contributions, to the b) mocked-up electronic layout emailed to authors immediately after the workshop, to the c) final layout produced using Adobe InDesign.[2]

sets the scene for the presentation of supporting material. Create a slide, chapter, or section based on each of these active titles. When the active titles are put together, such as in a table of contents, they provide an effective summary of the entire story (Figure 3.4).

CHAPTER 14 • HABITATS OF THE COASTAL BAYS AND WATERSHED

Forests

- The Coastal Bays watershed harbors diverse forests.
- Forests are the bedrock of the mainland ecosystem.
- Forests face many threats.
- Invasive plants are reducing species diversity.

Wetlands

- Wetland diversity abounds in the watershed.
- Wetlands provide flooding, water quality, and habitat protection.
- Human impacts on wetlands have been substantial.
- The future viability of tidal wetlands is uncertain.
- Unique wetlands dot the Coastal Bays watershed.

Figure 3.4. This example of a table of contents from a book shows how using active titles can provide an at-a-glance summary of the contents.

PROTECTING PALAU'S NATURAL HERITAGE

Lorem ipsum dolor sit amet, consectetuer adipiscing elit. Donec in enim et erat pharetra accumsan. It eget arcu ut ante semper volutpat. Cras libero sem, tristique sed, dignissim non, eleifend in, diam. Curabitur dui. Proin risus neque, congue et, iaculis sed, sagittis vitae, tortor. Praesent ultrices, turpis ut sodales. Lorem ipsum dolor sit amet, consectetuer adipiscing elit. Donec in enim et erat pharetra accumsan. Ut eget arcu ut ante semper volutpat. Cras libero sem, tristique sed, dignissim non, eleifend in, diam. Curabitur dui. Proin risus neque, congue et, iaculis sed, sagittis vitae, tortor. Praesent ultrices, turpis ut sodales.

PALAU HAS UNIQUE AND INTACT MANGROVE, SEAGRASS, AND CORAL ECOSYSTEMS

Nullam sollicitudin leo id quam. Sed vel risus. Phasellus ac ipsum. Donec sapien nisi, auctor scelerisque, lobortis a, suscipit sed, elit. Ut lobortis orci a elit. Quisque mauris. Aliquam erat volutpat. Vestibulum mattis aliquet velil.

Figure 3.5. This figure shows how placeholder (Latin) text can give a realistic look and feel to a document—a newsletter in this case—as well as provide an approximate word count to contributing authors.

people's often-overloaded work commitments, this phase will entail reminder e-mails and phone calls to chase down all the required elements. Many people are more comfortable with editing than creating and writing, so it is useful to provide draft conceptual diagrams, graphs, and other figures for authors to comment on instead of having them create these elements from scratch. Draft text can also be written for recalcitrant authors to edit.

Graphics and figures will need to be formatted consistently and effectively for the product being created (Figure 3.6). Creating graphics and figures using a vector drawing program such as Adobe Illustrator will give high-quality results that can be saved in a variety of ways for different products. If possible, for data figures such as graphs, obtain the

data from the author in a spreadsheet format so that the colors and formatting can be manipulated to keep the styles consistent.

When selecting and creating visuals, remember that they should do more than just look good. Visuals should provide information and support the message of the communication product.

Incorporating conceptual diagrams

Conceptual diagrams are effective communication tools because they facilitate communication and interaction and incorporate easy-to-recognize symbols. When used properly, they can provide context, visualization, and synthesis essential for effective science communication (Figure 3.7).

Conceptual diagrams facilitate communication and interaction

Conceptual diagrams are a communication tool that can be used to clarify thinking (words can be ambiguous, but a diagram commits to the message); facilitate one-way and two-way communication; identify gaps, priorities, and essential elements; and develop and present syntheses.

Conceptual diagrams are effective communication tools because they incorporate easy-to-recognize symbols, which are used as the basic language in these diagrams. Symbols are universal, language-independent, scalable, and information-rich. Good conceptual diagrams are visually interesting, and use the effective science communication principles of context, visualization, and synthesis.

Symbols are used in mathematics (π), music (♪), weather ( ), religion ( ), and organizations ( ). Symbols are universally understood, language independent, and an important feature of everyday life ( ). Scale can be important in the use of symbols, as size can represent relative importance (vs.). Color and shape of symbols are also important (5 and ▲).

The creation of conceptual diagrams provides an interface for engagement of various stakeholders, including scientists, managers, and wider public partners. The consensus-building process by which the processes and features in a conceptual diagram are agreed upon and represented is just as important as the final product itself. This way, all of the stakeholders feel engaged in the process, their opinions are valued and represented, and

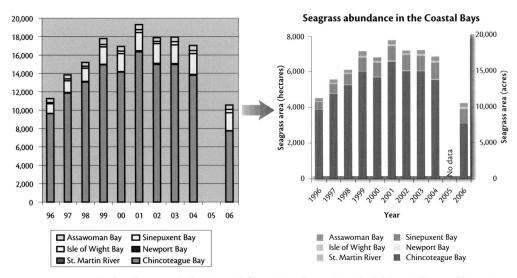

Figure 3.6. An example of ineffective and effective graph formatting. The graph on the left has gridlines and boxes in and around the plot and legend and an unnecessary grey box in the background. The axes have no units, and there is no title. The black outlines on the bars are thick and distracting. The well-formatted graph on the right shows the same data but with no extra gridlines, boxes, or backgrounds. The axes are labelled, the number of tick marks are minimized, and an explicit title is given. The colors used for the bars are complementary, with no outlines. In addition, both U.S. and metric units are represented, allowing understanding by people from all over the world. Data: Virginia Institute of Marine Science.

they feel ownership of the final product. The scientific community can ensure that their current understanding of a system is represented and lend their credibility and support to the processes communicated in the diagram, whereas the broader public community can ensure that their priorities, environmental values, and resources are represented in the diagram.

Formatting visual elements consistently and effectively

Consistent and effective formatting of visual elements facilitates the audience's interpretation and understanding of the information presented. Examples of consistent formatting include use of color and font style and size. Ideally, each visual

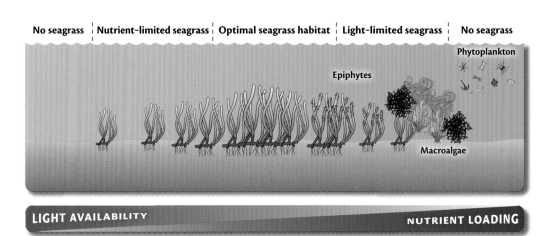

Figure 3.7. This conceptual diagram depicts the effects of nutrient loading on the dominant primary producer in aquatic ecosystems. In this case, the legend is included within the diagram, with labels alongside the relevant symbols.

element in a product will use a consistent font style and size for labels, captions, etc., and consistent colors for text, headings, and diagram elements. A useful way to achieve this is to use "master page" or "master slide" functions in software to ensure consistency.

Text and paragraph styles and color swatches can also be used to ensure a consistent look and feel within and between science communication products (Figure 3.8). These become especially important when dealing with multiple visual elements within a document, such as data graphs in a book chapter or diagrams in a newsletter (Figure 3.9).

To help ensure consistency, prepare a style sheet—which is a table that records the fonts, styles, sizes, colors, punctuation, and word choices used in a document. Style sheets are particularly important in collaborative works so that all authors can format their contributions appropriately.

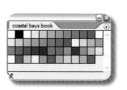

Figure 3.8. Defining colors and text and paragraph styles, such as these swatches and styles used in Adobe Illustrator and InDesign, will help to keep formatting consistent.

Producing posters and newsletters

Posters and newsletters are a common and effective way to communicate scientific results and information to a broad audience. Produced using effective science communication principles, posters and newsletters can be visually appealing, graphic rich, and easy to interpret (Figure 3.10).

Using appropriate software to create a poster or newsletter is the first step in producing an effective

Pitfalls to avoid

- Taking too long to edit and review and not focusing on getting the product finished
- Focusing on one kind of product
- Losing control of the product by always out-sourcing production to non-scientist graphic designers
- Not having an outside review, or not allowing enough time

product. Desktop publishing software, such as Adobe InDesign or QuarkXPress, will provide the most flexibility and minimize problems at the printing stage. Using alternative software, especially presentation software, will lead to file size problems, reduce the number of options for graphics handling and text formatting, and lead to printing problems due to the different color settings used for presentations vs. printed products.

As with other products, it is useful to draw mock-up layouts on a sheet of paper, using placeholder text and graphic boxes to plan flows and establish approximate locations of major elements. The layout will depend on the intended audience. A product intended for the general public will benefit from the inclusion of

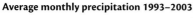
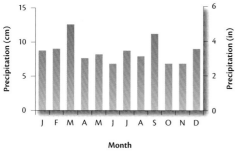
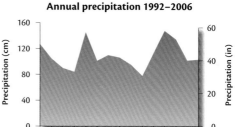

Figure 3.9. Using the same color palette and font choices to format all the visual elements so that they have a consistent look and feel increases the effectiveness of the message. The two graphs are obviously intended for the same product. Font sizes and styles (bold, italics, etc.), use of color and stroke width, and presentation of axes and units are just some of the elements that should be formatted consistently.

Engaging the community

more visually interesting elements, such as photos, and effectively synthesized information for easy comprehension. For more-informed or scientific audiences, more complex information can be included, although it should still be presented using visually attractive techniques, such as conceptual diagrams.

Posters and newsletters

- Use the right software
- Mock up layout on paper
- Make text clear and easy to read
- Use text to support graphics
- Avoid temptation to include too much information

Figure 3.10. a) This four-page newsletter contains a variety of visual elements to facilitate communication. b) These visual elements proved so effective that a two-foot by three-foot poster was prepared based on these elements. The poster can serve as a permanent record, whereas the newsletter can be distributed to many people.

The text in posters and newsletters, like any other product, should be clear and easy to read. Poster text should be used to support the graphics, not the other way around. At a conference poster session, there is a very small window of time to capture somebody's attention, so the title and subheadings should be active and communicate the main points of the story. A four-page newsletter can convey a lot of information using a variety of visual elements. A newsletter, or a small printout of a poster, can also serve as a "calling card" so ensure that all contact information is legible and easy to find.

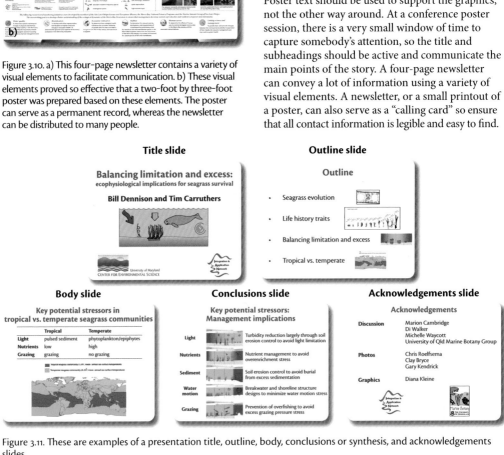

Figure 3.11. These are examples of a presentation title, outline, body, conclusions or synthesis, and acknowledgements slides.

Producing presentations

Giving presentations can be nerve-wracking, but with sufficient preparation and practice, they are an effective way to communicate scientific results and to elicit two-way communication with the audience. An effective scientific presentation should start with a title slide that includes the title, authors, and affiliations (Figure 3.11). An outline slide can be a guide to the presentation, explaining the organization of the talk and previewing the conclusions. Creating the outline slide first can help to determine the structure and story of the whole presentation. The body of the presentation should include the introduction to the topic, methodology, and results, using a variety of visual elements, such as conceptual diagrams, photos, maps, and data figures. The conclusions slide should contain the take-home messages and can be used to stimulate questions from the audience. An acknowledgements slide can be included at the beginning or end of the presentation, listing helpful or contributing individuals and institutions. Extra slides can be prepared in anticipation of questions from the audience.

Presentations

- Prepare and practice
- Structure the talk to tell a story
- Allow one minute per slide
- Explain key points only

A useful rule of thumb is to prepare one slide for every minute of the presentation, always allowing time for discussion after the talk. For example, a one-hour presentation should have 45–50 slides, to allow 10–15 minutes of discussion afterward. Providing appropriate background for the audience is essential, but it is a good idea to show the data or body of the presentation within five minutes to prevent the audience from becoming bored and disengaged.

Slide layouts should be clear and uncluttered, using bullet points only to jog memory and provide cues to the key points. Text should not replace the need for a live speaker or distract the audience. A well-designed presentation or component slides can be used multiple times, so it is worth the time to ensure that they are effective. Presentation slides can be considered as another building block in a resource library of effective visual elements.

Each slide needs to be explained to the audience. Visual elements, such as graphs and conceptual diagrams, should be described. Photographs are an especially effective element to use in presentations. An ongoing summary of the results or take-home messages is a useful technique to reinforce the story. Sufficient practice will help to alleviate nerves. Practice once to solicit feedback on the presentation structure and slide layout (have a colleague take notes of comments and edits) and practice again to rehearse timing.

Producing books

Producing books can be one of the most challenging science communication tasks. Coordinating and liaising with multiple authors and chapters while creating figures and keeping track of text edits and comments, usually with a fixed deadline, can seem a daunting assignment.

The editorial team overseeing the whole book should be a small group of people who are committed to the end product. A dynamic and productive collaboration is the goal—differing expectations and disagreements among editors can slow or even stall progress.

It is essential to assign tasks at the chapter workshop stage, including writing, data collection, and graphics contributions, as well as commitments for editing. In the case of a book with multiple chapters, it can be helpful to assign chapter coordinators—usually a member of the editorial team—who can solicit text, data, and graphics from the contributing authors for their chapter, edit the various text contributions into a coherent whole, and provide the chapter as a package to the science communicator.

Books

- Choose the editorial team carefully
- Assign tasks early and manage constantly
- Use science communication principles
- Focus on finishing a sample chapter first

A book produced using effective science communication principles should be full-color, synthetic (in that information is summarized and put into context effectively), and have an equal distribution of text and graphics (Figure 3.12). The process should be viewed as consensus building, with the final product communicating the outcomes so that all contributing authors and editors feel ownership and engagement.

Engaging the community

Focus on finishing a sample chapter first instead of on working on all chapters equally. Having a finished chapter (printed in color, trimmed, and stapled to mimic a real book) to bring to subsequent workshops will allow editors and authors to visualize the finished product and facilitate their support.

As with other science communication products, consistency is essential but can be more difficult to achieve in the multiple documents that make up book chapters. Using the same font styles and sizes in all figures, consistent color swatches, and text and paragraph styles will make this easier.

Producing a website

A website is now considered an essential science communication tool. It allows the widest possible audience to be reached in the mostly timely manner, without the normal delays of print media. The constant ability to edit and refine a website is one of the key features that make it effective for science communication. However, this can also be a trap because it is often too easy to publish something that is not well-designed, thinking that it can always be fixed later. The reality is often quite different, and as a result, the website can become a jumble of disjointed pages with a poorly designed structure and navigation system. Like other media, websites should follow the principles of effective science communication—they should be visually appealing and cleanly laid out with the right balance of meaningful graphics and informative text and a consistent look and feel. The key features of an effective website are a clear and consistent navigation system and obvious hyperlinks. Above

all, do not get too fancy—bells and whistles will not make up for poor content.

When planning out the information for inclusion in a website, think about what information would be most useful to have on there. By developing it to provide the publications, presentations, images, and other materials used by coworkers and colleagues, not only will it become an invaluable tool for your organization, but chances are these things will make it useful for others as well. A website should ideally include details of affiliation, research interests and projects, key findings, list of publications, PDFs of

Websites

- Plan the structure, navigation system, and layout
- Research other websites in your field for ideas
- Make website database driven so that it can be more easily updated
- Come up with novel ways to present data

non-copyrighted publications, and contact details. Copyrighted material should not be posted (if owned by someone else), nor should outdated material, coming-soon sections, or uninterpreted raw data.

The decision to hire someone to develop a website in-house (instead of contracting it out) will depend on the scope of the website and just how much future expansion is likely. There are pros and cons either way. In-house development and maintenance may not be financially viable if there is only a small site to set up with minimal

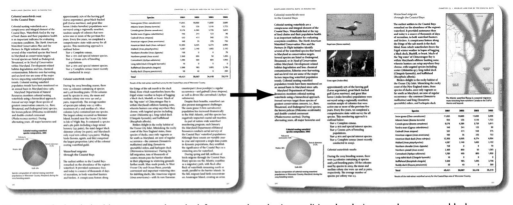

Figure 3.12. The book double-page spread on the left was produced using traditional techniques—the pages are black and white, are text heavy, and rely on data figures such as graphs and tables for their visual elements. The same pages on the right—produced using effective science communication techniques—are full color and have approximately equal distribution of text and graphics. These pages also use a variety of visual elements to reach as broad an audience as possible.[4]

Table 3.1. Advantages and disadvantages of different science communication products.

Product	Advantages	Disadvantages
Print media	• **Tangible, with contact details, logos, etc.**	• **Fixed in time** • **Unchangeable once done** • **Need financial and time resources for printing**
• Newsletters/fact sheets	• Fast to produce and fast to read • Allow for regular updates	• Limited space • Competition with marketing materials
• Posters	• Reach large audience • Long wall life	• Expensive • Limited mobility
• Books	• Synthetic • Long shelf-life	• Significant time investment to produce • Broad topics with lots of input that make management difficult
• Peer-review articles, book chapters	• Build credibility • Widely distributed to the libraries of the world	• Peer audience only • Time consuming • Graphic poor and color poor
Electronic media	• **Fluid** • **Updatable**	• **Less rigor** • **Often disseminated without permission or attribution**
• Presentations	• Tailorable to audience • Recyclable	• Good presenter needed • Limited audience
• Websites	• Unlimited space • Updatable • Broad audience	• Never finished • High maintenance • Build it and they do not come

future expansion. However, going for an external contractor may also cause problems if many small updates with a short turnover time are needed. This decision can be tough to make but always hire someone who has the right skills. It will save money in the end and will result in a much better product. Ideally, someone who has the web skills in addition to being knowledgeable in your area of science is ideal because they can be involved in creating and proofing the content rather than take up time having information fed to. The key is to find the right balance for your needs.

In conclusion, no matter what form of communication product you choose, it is important to remember the value a product has when it comes to influencing the general public (Table 3.1). Never underestimate the power of a logical, concise, and aesthetically pleasing product. With the right amount of time and training (Table 3.2), anyone can do it. Environmental

Table 3.2. Steps and recommendations associated with various science communication products.

Product	Steps and recommendations
Posters and newsletters	• Use the right software (Adobe or Quark) • Mock up layout on paper • Make text clear and easy to read • Use text to support graphics
Presentations	• Prepare and practice • Structure the talk to tell a story • Allow one minute per slide • Text should explain key points only
Books	• Choose editorial team carefully • Assign tasks early and manage constantly • Use science communication principles • Focus on finishing a sample chapter first
Websites	• Plan the structure, navigation system, and layout • Research other websites in your field for ideas • Make website database-driven so that it can be more easily updated • Come up with novel ways to present data

Engaging the community

campaigns and campaign leaders require science communication products to help explain and publicize the program's results and progress. The following chapter provides information on how these types of communication products fit within the overall campaign communication strategy.

References

1. Thomas JE, Saxby TA, Jones AB, Carruthers TJB, Abal EG, Dennison WC (2006) Communicating science effectively: practical handbook for integrating visual elements. IWA Publishing, London, England
2. Zachry M, Thralls C (2004) Cross-disciplinary exchange: An interview with Edward R. Tufte. Tech Comm Quarter 13(4): 444-462
3. Aston A (2009) Tufte's invisible yet ubiquitous influence. Business Week Jun 10 2009, http://www.businessweek.com/innovate/content/jun2009/id20090610_157761.htm
4. Dennison WC, Thomas JE, Cain CJ, Carruthers TJB, Hall MR, Jesien RV, Wazniak CE, Wilson DE (2009) Shifting sands: Environmental and cultural change in Maryland's Coastal Bays. IAN Press, Cambridge, Maryland

Further reading

Cribb J, Hartomo TS (2002) Sharing knowledge: A guide to effective science communication. CSIRO Publishing, Collingwood, Victoria, Australia

Montgomery SL (2003) The Chicago guide to communicating science. The University of Chicago Press, Chicago, Illinois

Penrose AM, Katz SB (2004) Writing in the sciences: Exploring conventions of scientific discourse. Pearson Longman, New York, New York

Tufte ER (1990) Envisioning information. Graphics Press, Cheshire, Connecticut

Tufte ER (1997) Visual explanations: Images and quantities, evidence and narrative. Graphics Press, Cheshire, Connecticut

Tufte ER (2001) The visual display of quantitative information. Graphics Press, Cheshire, Connecticut

Tufte ER (2006) Beautiful evidence. Graphics Press, Cheshire, Connecticut

Valiela I (2001) Doing science: Design, analysis, and communication of scientific research. Oxford University Press, New York, New York

Chapter 4: Communication strategy

PACKAGING AND DELIVERING THE MESSAGE FOR MAXIMUM IMPACT

Christopher S. Conner, William C. Dennison, and Jane E. Thomas

The difference between the right word and the almost right word is the difference between lightning and a lightning bug.
—Mark Twain

Drawing from the last chapter and its emphasis on the importance of communication, this chapter discusses ways to broadcast a message internally within a coastal assessment program and externally to the general public. Throughout the chapter, the steps involved in broadcasting the message (such as determining target audience, ways in which to relay the message, and how to create an appropriate timeline) will be explained in detail. Specifics such as how to choose a spokesperson and how to determine the look of the communication product will help create and project the most effective message to the audience. Additional tips on types of media that are available and the best way to prepare for interviews are also included.

Getting the message out

You are not doing anything if nobody knows what you are doing.
—Anonymous

An effective communications strategy allows everyone working on a coastal assessment program to share a common understanding of the purposes and goals of a program. By outlining what is going to be said and to whom it is being said, the communications strategy allows everyone involved in a program to sing from the same sheet of music.

A well-rounded communications strategy outlines key messages (what one wants to convey), identifies target audiences (with whom one wants to communicate), helps choose a spokesperson, and determines communication vehicles (the documents or techniques through which one communicates).

Determining the target audience

Clear communications rely upon knowing exactly to whom you are talking.
—Anonymous

Determining the target audience's identity is the first step in developing an effective communications strategy. By closely defining a target audience, correct terminology and communication techniques can be used that resonate with that specific group of people.

Often, we humans tend to group ourselves with others who share similar experiences and values. When this happens, groups can develop their own way of communicating with each other. They may prefer to use words that convey a very specific meaning to those in the group, or they may find a particular medium through which to communicate that they find works best. To effectively reach people in one of these groups, it is critical to find a way to present information in a tone and format the group easily understands.

> ### Communications strategy components
>
> - Key messages
> - Target audiences
> - The correct spokesperson
> - Communication vehicles

Those in the environmental and scientific communities can be guilty of using technical jargon and scientific terms—it is important to "translate" this style to make it digestible to the target audience.

These groups (or target audiences) can range from small (one person) to large (the general public) and can vary with regard to level of technical expertise, interest, and understanding of the issue (Figure 4.1). This combination of audience size and technical knowledge greatly influences what is said and how it is said.

As a communications strategy is built, the skills and needs of the target audience need to be taken into account. If information is presented in a way that is too complicated for the audience to quickly grasp, it becomes lost in translation, that is, it merely bounces off and is not retained. Similarly, information must be presented in a format that they can easily access, or person-to-person information transfer will not take place.

When answering the questions to determine the target audience, try to be as specific as possible. For example, avoid answers like "everyone" and focus on groups that can be lumped together by common interests. Good target audiences for coastal issues could be "legislators in the Magothy River watershed," "waterfront homeowners," or "boaters who use public boat ramps." By defining these audiences as narrowly as possible, the communications strategy will evolve into an action plan for informing them and motivating change.

Crafting the message

While each of us has something to say, it is important how we say it or we run the risk of others not hearing us.

—Anonymous

Crafting messages is as much an art form as it is a science. Clear messages resonate with the target audiences in ways that make ideas memorable and help them stand out from other messages (Figure 4.2).

Scientists often think of their work as data, research, projects, or reports. Although important to researchers, those words can be meaningless to target audiences. The message needs to be packaged in ways so that the audience will care about it. Remember that data and research are part of a larger picture that ties into larger societal issues. When research and information intersect with those larger ideals is when the best opportunities to communicate occur. Ask the question, "How does my information relate to the big picture?" and develop the message accordingly.

Although there are volumes of books detailing tips and tricks to creating messages, the old adage of "keep it simple, stupid" is the best advice ever given. For each project, work to develop one key message built upon a few (two to four) supporting points. This allows the team to focus its attention on what matters the most while still being able to provide the most salient information supporting that view.

The key message

The key message is the primary point the audience should understand. If the audience remembers nothing else than the key message, then the goal of communicating the most important information has been met.

Although creating key messages can be complex, one simple approach used by many communications professionals relies on making a claim, citing a supporting fact, and providing an example of this claim in action.

Determining the target audience

- Who needs to hear what I am saying?
- Who will find my information useful?
- Who can use my information to do their job better?
- Who can use my information to change things?

| Individual | Civic leaders | Community watershed group | Environmental group | General public |

Figure 4.1. Different target audiences have different sizes, knowledge, and consequently require different communication techniques. Effective communication methods include a personal letter or email for individuals, group letter or email for civic leaders, community flyer for homeowners associations, a website for environmental groups, and television or broadcasted news for the general public.

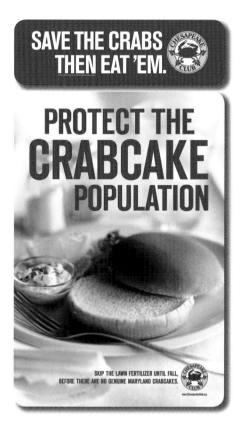

Figure 4.2. To combat the problem of urban fertilizer runoff in the Chesapeake Bay region, the Chesapeake Bay Program developed an innovative marketing campaign focusing on one key message: Skip the lawn fertilizer in the spring and wait until fall. By focusing on one simple message, the campaign was able to motivate residents to change their behavior. Campaign developers believed that previous efforts built upon providing residents with a complicated list of multiple actions needed to be simplified to elicit action. Products from the campaign are shown above.

The claim is the most important idea that should be heard. To be considered credible, however, several facts supporting this claim must be provided. By basing these facts on scientific research, a coherent argument can be made while highlighting the relevance of the work. Finally, the example ties the two together and shows how the claim and supporting facts are well-grounded and make sense.

Choosing a spokesperson

You only have one chance to make a first impression.
—Will Rogers

Like it or not, some people are more trusted than others. That is why it is so critical to select the right person to carry the message to the target audience.

The primary spokesperson should be selected based on several principles, including their knowledge of the issue, role in the project, organizational affiliation to the project, and their ability to communicate with others.

Knowledge
As the spokesperson, the person should have a thorough understanding of the project and be able to provide insight into how the project fits into the big picture.

Project role
Just as each team member filled a special expertise in the development of the project, each team member offers a unique understanding of the importance of the findings. When selecting a spokesperson, take into account these characteristics. If the key message centers on political recommendations, choose a person who understands the politics of the issue. If the key message ties to new scientific findings, a

respected scientist may be the best choice. If the message advocates a behavior change, consider a spokesperson affiliated with a civic or conservation organization.

Organizational affiliation

Studies undertaken over the past few decades indicate that people place a higher trust factor in people affiliated with certain groups.[1] When talking about the environment, people tend to trust local environmental organizations most and government representatives least. Keep this in mind as a spokesperson is selected.

Communication skills

As was stated earlier, the ability to communicate clearly is part art and part science. Take advantage of any team members who have media training or communications experience and of people who are naturally charismatic and good public speakers. Additionally, consider having the spokesperson take a course before releasing the information. A half- or full-day media training course can really help.

Packaging and delivering the message

The way a product or idea is presented can determine how well it is accepted by the recipient. When it comes to influencing the way another person feels or thinks about an issue, it is critical that it be dressed up in the appropriate way for the audience.

The "look and feel" or graphic design of a communication product can either add to or detract from the importance and believability of the key message. Good graphic design complements the key message and projects an image of the idea-generating group. Like a set of new clothes, the graphic design gives the audience its first impression of one's group.

Attributes of a good spokesperson

- Understands the issues and is credible
- Sees the big picture
- Is passionate about the work/ issue
- Is personable
- Tells stories well and uses metaphors that people can understand
- Knows how to use a period (i.e., say what they need to and then shut up)

The cocktail party test

Although people care about a lot of things, a few areas tend to rise above the rest. An effective way to figure these out is the "cocktail party test." Picture yourself at an evening cocktail party filled with a large number of guests, none of whom you have met previously. To be part of the crowd, you are forced to talk with others. But what do you talk about? More often than not, you bring up ideas that fall into one of three categories—life, home, or food—things that mean a lot to a large number of people. Use that to your advantage and try to craft your message in a way that affects the target audience's life, home, or food.

Graphic design can range from a slick, polished look to a bare-bones, black-and-white design at the far end of the spectrum (Figure 4.3). The trick to developing the right look and feel for the work is to first determine where along the spectrum the work lies.

The advent of desktop publishing and development of new printing technology that allows for smaller, more affordable, high-quality print runs has changed the game on the presentation of environmental ideas.[2] When combined with the greatest, free mass-distribution system ever developed—the Internet—there are fewer and fewer reasons to skimp on the presentation of an idea.

The corporate look

Many people associate the four-color, glossy look of a publication with large companies with vast sums of money to spend on producing a document that sells their product. Take a quick look at the annual reports from *Fortune 500* companies, and virtually all fall into this category.

At first thought, many conservationists may not want to go this route for their publication because it reminds them of a big corporation that cares only about the bottom line. But before immediately dismissing the idea, ask one question: "Why do they package their message that way?" It is not because they can, it is because it sells.

In today's society, we are bombarded with thousands of messages a day—buy this, eat that, wear those. Like it or not, the message about protecting and conserving coastal resources must compete with those messages for the audience's attention. Maybe dressing up the environment in a *Prada* bag is the best way to help it break through and become more important to the target audience.

The grassroots look

There is nothing more 'Mom and apple pie' than grassroots activism in the United States. As a nation, we love to root for the underdog. When that person or group has a good point, there is no limit to how they can change the world.

The choice of graphic designs can help to accentuate this grassroots feel by using simple fonts and basic graphics. Many people like to rely on this approach because it conveys their message as a simple, common-sense approach that does not need dressing up to resonate with their community.

On the downside, the grassroots look can also lead the target audience to believe that the opinions put forward are those of only a few people. Although this may score well with true believers in the cause, it may also scare away some people who do not stand behind a cause until it is more accepted by the mainstream.

Recipe for success

- Keep the message simple and clear
- Build a relationship with key media and community members
- Capitalize on opportunities
- Remember that time is of the essence
- Deliver memorable and pithy sound bites
- Remember that perfection is the enemy of the possible

The grassroots look generally conveys the sense that it was created using a basic word processing program like Microsoft Word and reproduced at a local copy shop. This type of approach generally works best when trying to highlight an issue that is important to a small community or group of people.

Shifting from mass to micro media

In the past few years, there has been a dramatic shift in the way people obtain news and information with the expansion of social media on the Internet. People are now turning to websites such as Facebook, Twitter, and YouTube to stay current on local and world events. With that shift, environmental communicators need to balance their communications strategies between mass media and "micro" media, being sure to consider the pros and cons of reaching hundreds of thousands of members of the general

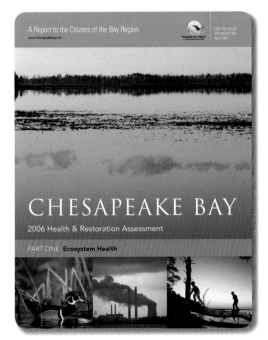

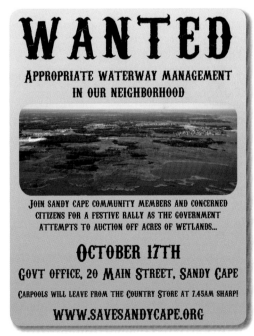

Figure 4.3. The "look and feel" of a publication is very important to determining how it is received by the public. Above are examples from both ends of the graphic design spectrum. On the left is an example of a corporate-style publication produced by the Chesapeake Bay Program.[3] The full-color, glossy nature of this publication gives it a polished look and feel. The example on the right is a grassroots-style flyer that resonates with local groups.

public through mass media or connecting with fewer (but far more targeted audiences) using social media.

By their nature, social media outlets are an effective way of targeting audiences already interested in an issue, as their visitors have already selected to receive information about certain topics.

Establishing a social media network should be part of any communications plan and should take place well before your information is ready to go to the public. Consider establishing a Facebook "fan page" if the work is affiliated with an organization, or setting up a YouTube channel for your organization. It is important to do this early, as social networking heavily relies on regularly disseminating information that target audiences find useful and interesting. By building an online community ahead of time, they will be ready to receive the information once it is ready to go out to the public.

Generating science communication products

Regardless of the graphic look decided on, it is critical that the information be presented in a way that people understand. The challenge of generating science-based materials lies within translating complicated science into common-sense principles that a lay audience

Case study: Engaging the community

When the Southern Maryland Oyster Cultivation Society (*www.smocs.org*) wanted to motivate the local community to support oyster gardening to improve water quality in local creeks, the organization's leader, Len Zuza, started talking to people in the greater Solomons area.

Selecting his target audience—waterfront residents and businesses— was simple because his ultimate goal was to get property owners to attach floating oyster cages under their docks. He then approached these individuals in two main ways: one-on-one visits and speaking at local community meetings. By carefully targeting his audience and engaging them in proactive ways, Len's group now boasts nearly 60 members in their first year and is steadily growing stronger with solid backing from the community.

can understand. This topic is covered in detail in the previous Chapter 3.

Engaging the community

To some, making a new scientific finding is the end goal of their work. But to those who seek to develop new information in order to improve their environment, it is only the first step. To initiate changes that will help to improve the quality of water, land, and air, it is critical to engage local communities and pass this information along to others who are better positioned to influence those changes.

Community engagement can take place on many levels, from local to national to even global. But regardless of level, it is critical to seek involvement with people outside of one's own field. Generally speaking, people do not suddenly become engaged in an issue but transition from the uninformed to the informed and then from informed to engaged. Only when people are engaged do they take the action needed to see tangible results in the health of coastal ecosystems (Figure 4.4).

Although there are a number of best practices for spreading ideas and information through various segments of society, we can look at past scholarly work about the "diffusion of innovation"

Figure 4.4. The overall purpose of the environmental campaign is to take the uninformed to the informed and the informed to the engaged, the premise being that only the engaged will really become sufficiently involved to take the necessary action.

by Everett Rogers[4] and slightly modify it to provide a blueprint for the "diffusion of information."

Rogers breaks down society into five groups: innovators, early adopters, early majority, late majority, and laggards. He theorizes that innovation will spread through society in a bell-shaped curve, beginning with innovators and then through each subsequent group until it is widespread and accepted.

Similarly, information about environmental issues can follow the same course. As environmental advocates, our goal is to get information into the hands of other innovators and early adopters and then foster relationships with them to further help spread the word throughout society.

Empower community groups

Whereas someone's expertise may be collecting and analyzing data, someone else may excel at making local political officials aware of social problems in their community. To maximize distribution of information, identify these people in the local community. Once relationships are developed with them, be proactive and regularly provide them with information about the work with the hope that they will pass it along to their contacts.

This type of information dispersion can be very effective when releasing information about a local watershed's health. While the socially connected friend carries the message directly to the people who can implement change, credibility and recognition for one's work are being built.

Speak to local organizations

Sometimes local residents need more than information—they need motivation. When releasing new environmental information, consider engaging local civic groups at their regularly scheduled meetings. They are always looking for speakers, and scientists interested in motivating environmental change are always looking for people to talk to. By taking the time to help them see the scientific point of view, they may become more interested in the work and want to play an active role in future endeavors.

Develop distribution networks

Disseminating information to a core group of messengers is imperative to widening one's sphere of influence. By compiling a list of targeted messengers, dissemination of information can be maximized. Concentrate on people and institutions that broadcast information to a large number of

Crafting the message for the average moviegoer

Al Gore, former Vice President and climate change activist

Brett Wilson

For the past 30 years, the environmental movement has done an impressive job motivating its followers to do the right thing for the Earth. Until recently, however, the movement has had a difficult time reaching beyond the 'choir' and making meaningful connections to the average person. This disconnect has caused many environmental initiatives to stall.

In 2006, former Vice President Al Gore was able to break this cycle and bring the issue of climate change to the forefront of many Americans' minds. For one of the first times in history, environmentalists began talking about environmental problems in terms regular people could understand and pointing out how regular people will be affected unless we change the way we treat our environment.[5]

Gore marketed his environmental arguments through the Academy Award-winning film *An Inconvenient Truth*, providing an easy and entertaining way for people to learn more about his issue. The film combines scientific data with documentary-style filmmaking. Additionally, Gore provides a charismatic and articulate front-man for the show, keeping the viewer interested throughout. This technique managed to persuade millions that the theory of climate change is indeed fact.

An iconic image of a smokestack is used as the cover of the movie poster and on the website.

Engaging the community

Final product only uses a small part of interview

A reporter will use only a small fraction of an interview. The following is a transcript from an interview with a reporter. Although most interviews can last anywhere from five to 30 minutes, it is not uncommon for a reporter to include only 10 to 15 seconds of the interview in the final piece. It is important to remember that even though one may not be extensively quoted in a piece, the ideas discussed with the reporter likely helped him or her to better understand the issue and, therefore, provide more accurate coverage of the topic.

The transcript below represents about 20% of an interview, from which only the highlighted text was quoted in the article:

Reporter: What's wrong with the health of the Chesapeake Bay?

Expert: Too much pollution is flowing into the bay from people and their everyday activities. Nutrient and sediment pollution comes from runoff from farm fields, pastures, urban roofs, and suburban backyards. When that pollution is combined with excess nutrients from sewage treatment plants and exhaust from cars and power plants, it spells disaster for the bay and its rivers.

Reporter: Where does most of the pollution come from?

Expert: About 40% of the nutrient pollution harming the bay comes from the agricultural sector. **In recent years, farmers have taken a more active role in being stewards of our waters as well as the land, but clearly more needs to be done if we are to see a** **healthier bay.**

Reporter: How do we reduce pollution?

Expert: Citizens need to hold their political leaders accountable for cleaning up our waters. If we do not convince them that the health of the bay's rockfish, crabs, and oysters are important enough to protect, they will continue to spend taxpayer dollars on other things than the bay cleanup. The Chesapeake Bay is important to the region's economy, environment, and cultural identity—political leaders throughout the state need to do more to help protect the bay for future generations.

Reporter: What steps can the average person take to reduce pollution?

Expert: There are three easy steps people can take to help bring the bay back into balance. First, we can all reduce the amount of things we use. By using less stuff, we are creating less pollution to harm the bay. Second, we can drive fewer miles. It is a simple equation—fewer miles equals less pollution escaping into the air. Finally, we can hold our elected leaders accountable by voting for public officials who share our views about the health of our local environment.

Even a front-page article is likely only to include a small portion of an interview and the message.

---

people, such as:

- environmental websites, blogs, and listservs;
- community civic groups and associations;
- non-profit environmental organizations;
- homeowners associations;
- members of the media who cover the environment;
- local political leaders; and
- county and state agency employees focusing on the environment.

Using the mass media

Like it or not, we live in a world dominated by a 24-hour news cycle. If it happens in the next 10 minutes, millions of people will know about it in 20 minutes. No matter the time of day, there are television stations and websites broadcasting news. But what exactly is "news"? More importantly, how do we package our environmental science, management, or restoration work in a way that makes it news?

What is news?

Today, news means something different to almost every single person. But there are some common attributes around which a large percentage of today's news stories tend to center: conflict, damage, fear, struggle, and threats. Although none of these ideas are pleasant, they have become an unfortunate reality of today's news cycle. On the positive side, these negative themes provide an entry for today's scientists to provide unbiased insight into their causes and effects. It is also an opportunity for those working on environmental issues to get the public to pay attention to the poor conditions they are seeing in their local ecosystems.

Although the term news is used to describe a very broad notion of current events, as communicators, we can drill down into the different media used to cover news and develop strategies to disseminate our messages through each one (Tables 4.1, 4.2).

Television

Television has the broadest reach of all media. With multiple national and local news operations, the airwaves are virtually full of programs that both entertain and inform millions on a daily basis.

Television news segments tend to be very short in duration, compared with other traditional media, such as newspapers and magazines. But what is lost due to the short duration, television makes up for by using images to help tell a story (Figure 4.5). This unique mix of video and audio makes television an effective choice when attempting to convey the context of emotional situations.

Ben Longstaff

Figure 4.5. This television interview took place on the shores of Chesapeake Bay—an appropriate choice for an interview about the Chesapeake Bay Report Card. The location of an interview can retain the audience's interest and also convey the dedication of the interviewee to the cause in question.

Table 4.1. Advantages and disadvantages of using the various media to disseminate a message.

Media	Advantages	Disadvantages
Traditional media:		
Print	• Reaches opinion-makers • Provides in-depth stories • Is generally more accurate • Has a long shelf-life	• Is difficult to get coverage • Thrives on contention and disagreement
Radio	• Has a broad reach • Reaches people when they have idle time (e.g., in the car)	• Is very brief and compact • Lacks visual supporting information
Television	• Conveys emotion • Includes visual elements • Has the broadest reach	• Provides the shallowest coverage (reporters cover many issues simultaneously)
All media	• **Informs the public about an important issue** • **Is part of the solution to societal problems**	• **Lacks control at final stage** • **Cites opposing perspectives** • **Is stressful**
Contemporary media:		
Speaking events	• Allows personal interactions • Is motivational • Is the foundation of building relationships	• Time-consuming • Is targeted to small audiences • Can be difficult to get on the agenda • Requires a lot of preparation
Internet	• Provides in-depth information • Is always on and always there • Increases control of the message	• Is an effective way to reach people but can be hard to reach outside the choir. • Has high maintenance costs

Table 4.2. Advantages and disadvantages of using local vs. national media to disseminate a message.

Media	Advantages	Disadvantages
Local media	• Improves stature in local community • Allows the story to bubble up into larger media • Is geographically targeted	• A smaller audience • May not bee seen by opinion leaders • Has a chance that reporters are not as skilled
National media	• Is seen by many people • Is seen by policy-makers • Provides validation as an expert	• Need to answer tough questions • Article likely to be shorter • Mistakes known by a large audience

For those who work on environmental issues, television is an effective venue because they can use the media to show viewers sick fish, polluted waters, or destroyed rainforests. Often, these visuals are more compelling than the scientifically supported statements being made about the same issue.

Print media
Print media, including newspapers and magazines, is another way to reach a large segment of the public. Although generally reaching fewer people, newspaper articles tend to go into more depth than television segments, allowing reporters to provide a more detailed look into the issue.

In general, newspapers tend to reach more people than television. This audience—comprising of elected officials, policy-makers, and civic leaders—can greatly help forward one's work to help improve the environmental health of an area.

Finally, the daily nature of the newspaper news cycle allows print reporters to take more time to ensure that they present the article in the most accurate way possible, telling the whole story and trying to cover all angles and provide fair and balanced reporting.

Radio
Radio is the most compact of all media, leaving a very short window in which to make a point and disseminate the message. With the average radio news segment lasting only about 30 to 45 seconds, it is imperative to condense the message as tight as possible so that a reporter can package it into a full news segment (see Soundbites on the next page).

However, in this age when so many of us spend a great deal of time trapped in our cars, it is an opportunity to reach the target audience when they are paying attention.

The give and take of the media
A positive working relationship between an environmental advocate and the media is a symbiotic relationship built on interest and trust. To keep the relationship going, the advocate must

Why do we want the media to cover us?

- Calls attention to the importance of our work
- Builds credibility in our organization
- Helps to teach a broader audience about what it can do to help the environment
- Validates us as an expert

Why does the media want to cover us?

- We possess information that others may find helpful.
- We influence choices that affect other people.
- We are the experts on environmental health.
- We do cool stuff.
- We provide input into important policy issues.

be able to provide the reporter with accurate, compelling information and the reporter, in turn, must provide accurate, compelling coverage to readers.

In a world where news generally is about negative things, why do we want the media to cover what we are doing? Media coverage of one's work provides a teaching opportunity with the public. The environment belongs to everyone, and the more the public understands it, the better the chance of protecting it. Media coverage also helps to bolster the credibility of individuals, their work, and their organization. As more people hear about one's work, new opportunities for collaboration and interactions with others will likely follow.

From the reporter's perspective, he or she is able to gain insight into an issue a segment of population cares about—the environment. Often, environmental issues include the conflict and struggles reporters like to write about, which, as was said earlier, makes good news. Many reporters also feel that environmentalists make telling characters for their stories. Most are passionate about their work (they certainly do not do it for the money), and that emotion comes across in their interviews.

Preparing for interviews

Although the average interview with a reporter can last anywhere between five and 20 minutes, preparing for that interview takes far longer—sometimes as much as four or five hours. One will find, however, that this additional time is well spent and often is the key to conducting a successful interview (Figure 4.6). To make the most of the preparation time, focus on three main activities—map out the key messages, construct a list of likely questions, and develop answers to those questions.

Develop key messages
The key message is the main point one wants to convey to the reporter. It should be stated in plain language (no jargon), and be less than 50 words in length. It should say what is important

Bad soundbites

- "We need to implement best management practices on suburban, agricultural, and maritime lands to improve dissolved oxygen levels in area waterways."
- "Forecasting water quality parameters requires significant scientific scholarship and is more complex than work taking place in other scientific fields."
- "Climate change will make Maryland warmer in both summer and winter months."

Good soundbites

- "We need to improve the way we manage every backyard, boatyard, and barnyard in the region if we are going to get this river cleaned up."
- "Forecasting water quality two months from now is not rocket science … it's harder."
- "The good news about climate change is Maryland will have winters like Charleston. The bad news is we'll have summers like Phoenix, but with humidity."

Figure 4.6. Being prepared for interviews with the media will ensure that the focus is on the message.

and then back up the statement with two to four supporting points. This approach allows one important message to be conveyed throughout the entire interview, allowing its importance to be emphasized and keeping the interview on track. As the adage goes, "Tell them what you're going to tell them, *tell them*, then tell them what you told them."

List likely questions

When scheduling an interview, be sure to ask the reporter to outline what he or she would like to talk about. Although the reporter should not be expected to send a list of questions beforehand, you should already have an idea about the general topic. Use this to your advantage and develop a list of the questions the reporter will likely ask. After the interview, review the list to see that it is likely that about 90% of the questions were anticipated.

Develop likely answers

After thinking about likely questions, take time to develop answers. Sit down at a computer and draft responses in a word-processing program, then read them aloud. If they sound clunky or inaccurate, edit them and try again. By the time the editing is finished, saying the answers out loud should feel comfortable, and indeed, you will sound like the educated expert that you are. A good target length to shoot for is about 20 words. Considering this should take about eight to 10 seconds to say, that is the first soundbite. However, care must be taken to not sound overrehearsed.

Another advantage of typing and editing answers on a computer is that it can form the basis of the FAQ (frequently asked questions) for the website.

For the release of the first Chesapeake Bay Health Report Card (Chapter 6), communicators brainstormed a list of questions that they thought reporters may ask them. Here are a few examples:

- Was the bay healthier or in worse shape than last year?
- How can the health of one river be compared to another?
- How is this report card different from those generated by other organizations?
- Who is to blame about the bay's poor health?
- What are government leaders doing to help the bay?
- What can citizens do to help the bay?

Working with reporters

It is not uncommon to be a little nervous before a media interview. After all, the reporter has the last word on an interview and can choose to include or omit any information provided. But as long as one is helpful and courteous, the reporter will hopefully write a fair and balanced account of the story.

It is also important to remember that reporters are people too. Like everybody, they have a job to do and want to do it the best that they can. But keeping a few things in mind will help to foster a solid working relationship.

Engaging the community

Be conscious of the reporter's time. Often, a reporter will only have a few hours to digest the information garnered in the interview and draft an article to meet the deadline. Do not rush the interview, but be sure to be ready at the agreed-on time. Additionally, when pitching a story to a reporter over the phone, contact him or her in the morning when there is more time to talk and he or she is not coming up on a tight deadline.

Prepare printed information for the interview. It is always helpful to assemble a folder that contains background information, including reports, background on your organization, contact information, and so forth, that will help fill out the story. This also allows the interview to focus on the most important part of the story.

Do not ask to review the article or television segment before it is published. Most media organizations have a policy that forbids reporters from doing this, so refrain from asking. In addition, do not expect a reporter to mail a copy of the segment or article. Make preparations to obtain the clip independently. However, it is reasonable to ask when the segment or article will run.

Provide the reporter with contact information for the remainder of the business day. If planning on being out of the office, be sure to leave a cell phone number should the reporter need to clarify some points.

Know the reporter and his or her media outlet. Knowing some information about the individual reporter and their newspaper, radio station, and so forth (e.g. such as their ideological position) will help in tailoring the message and how best to communicate it.

Keys to successful interviews
While preparation is the key to conducting a good interview, there are several other things you can do to help the message resonate with the reporter and the target audience.

The interview begins the second you meet the reporter. Although the camera or tape recorder may not be rolling,

Building bridges

A few phrases upon which to build bridges:
- "That's a good point, but the most important thing to remember is… [insert key message]."
- "Opinions may differ, but the science tells us that… ."
- "That's a little out of my expertise, but I do know that… ."
- "I would describe it differently… ."

Pitfalls to avoid

- Focusing on data and not on conclusions and recommendations
- Preaching only to the choir.
- Using jargon and acronyms with no explanation
- Failing to deliver the message due to fear of criticism
- Selecting the wrong messenger

your are already interacting with reporter. Be sure to dress appropriately, as your attire can either add or detract from your credibility (a solid-color top in a color other than white is usually advisable), be courteous, and remember, most importantly, everything is "on the record."

Develop soundbites. Soundbites are critical to communicating important information in short, memorable phrases that give the listener key insights into the issue being discussed. They can be used to summarize the big picture or compare the issue to a situation with which the target audience can easily relate. Although reporters may conduct 30 to 60-minute interviews for television and newspaper interviews, they regularly only report a few brief quotes in their coverage. They tend to home in on certain phrases, as a good soundbite manages to say a lot in a limited number of words. Good communicators take time to develop soundbites because they are one of the most effective tools in the spokesperson's box. More often than not, the only thing the audience may remember the next day is an eight-second quote about the issue.

Take advantage of off-camera time. Meeting and greeting the reporter and camera operator allows a rapport to be built with them and gives a chance to interview without being on camera. This also allows time to explain the news hook and steer them to the key messages.

Answer the first question with the key message. Whatever the first question, steer the answer to the key message. This is the best opportunity to make the primary point and convey that to the reporter.

Think through the response before speaking it. Listening, pausing, and thinking between each question allows time to deliver a well-reasoned and prepared response.

Each response should stand on its own. Make a conscious effort to answer questions so that the response does not refer back to an earlier part of the conversation. This allows the reporter to lift the quote directly for the story.

Stay in one's area of expertise. Only provide answers when qualified to do so. During an interview, it is easy to get drawn into an area outside one's comfort zone. When that happens, simply respond with, "That's a great question, but I'm more comfortable talking about ..." in order to keep out of trouble and on message.

Build bridges to the key messages. Ever noticed how politicians seem to evade tough questions when they are being interviewed on television? Although it is not a skill that many of us think about, it can be a powerful tool to use when working with the media. This technique, called "bridging," shifts the interview back to a topic one would prefer talking about—the key messages. The bridge starts by recognizing the reporter's question, then turning the remainder of the response back to the key message. Bridging takes a little practice, but is one of the best techniques for controlling an interview and sticking to the points to be made.

When it comes down to it, effectively summarizing and communicating ideas to others is the most important step to elevating public knowledge and concern about environmental issues. Not only does it draw more people to the cause, but also it helps to give them the ammunition they need to fight for it.

In conclusion, remember that an effective communication strategy includes key messages, target audiences, and communication vehicles. A key message should make a claim, support the claim, and provide a real-world example. Using a qualified spokesperson, as well as a clean presentation and design will also increase the effectiveness of the message. Overall, preparation and thorough audience analysis are the only way to successfully broadcast the desired message. The next chapter describes some approaches to consider when publicizing program efforts and the supporting science communication products.

References

1. Yale Center for Environmental Law & Policy (2007) Yale Center for Environmental Law & Policy survey on American attitudes on the environment. Accessed 30 Jun. www.loe.org/images/070316/yalepole.doc
2. Williams R (2005) The non-designer's type book, 2nd ed. Peachpit Press, Berkeley, California
3. Chesapeake Bay Program (2007) Chesapeake Bay 2006 health and restoration assessment. Part one: Ecosystem health. Chesapeake Bay Program, Annapolis, Maryland
4. Rogers EM (2003) Diffusion of innovations, 5th ed. Free Press, New York, New York
5. Al Gore (2009) Al Gore. Accessed 28 Jul. http://www.algore.com/index.html

Further reading

Bonk K, Griggs H, Tynes E (1999) Strategic communications for nonprofits. Jossey–Bass, San Francisco, California
Consortium for Ocean Leadership (2009) Science Communication and Marine Public Integration (SCAMPI). Accessed 28 Jul. www.coreocean.org/?anchor=scampi
Cribb J, Hartomo TS (2002) Sharing knowledge: A guide to effective science communication. CSIRO Publishing. Collingwood, Victoria, Australia
Eckl E (2009) Water words that work—environmental awareness, writing, and communication. Accessed 28 Jul. www.waterwordsthatwork.com
Hayes R, Grossman D (2006) A scientist's guide to talking with the media: Practical advice from the Union of Concerned Scientists. Rutgers University Press, Piscataway, New Jersey
WK Kellogg Foundation (2009) Overview: Communications toolkit. Accessed 28 Jul. http://www.wkkf.org/default.aspx?tabid=75&CID=385&NID=61&LanguageID=0

Engaging the community

COMMUNITY KNOWLEDGE

INTEGRATING INFORMATION TO BUILD PRACTICAL KNOWLEDGE

In the previous section, some of the theory and practice of applying community knowledge to solve the challenges of coastal ecosystem protection and restoration was discussed. To follow the processes and ideas laid out in the previous section, such as using the mass media and creating communication products, it is essential that an appropriate suite of products and analyses can be accessed or is provided. The products that should be generated are those that will provide knowledge not only to resource managers, but also to the research and monitoring community and the general public. This differs slightly from traditional approaches, such as producing technical reports (although the important role these more traditional products play are recognized), in that a larger audience is being targeted. In this next section, three different approaches to directing data synthesis and integration into products that can build community knowledge are covered.

Ecological indicators: Indicators represent parts of an ecosystem that, when synthesized, can educate the community about ecosystem health. This chapter describes the practical aspects of indicators, such as different indicator types, how to select appropriate indicators, and linking indicators to management and communication needs.

Ecological report cards: Report cards are not only an effective tool for communicating the health of an ecosystem, but also serve as a framework for a monitoring program and data analysis. In this chapter, the process of developing report cards from the indicator selection process through the communication of the report card to stakeholders is discussed.

Ecological forecasts: Forecasting is an emerging discipline that is likely to have an increasing role in management and communication. In this chapter, some of the reasons for forecasting, elements of a successful forecasting program, and linking forecasts to a communication strategy are discussed.

As mentioned above, it is recognized that these three approaches are targeted toward building community knowledge and as such, do not address the more traditional approach of focusing on management knowledge, such as producing technical reports and model outputs. However, these will be addressed in Section 3 of the book.

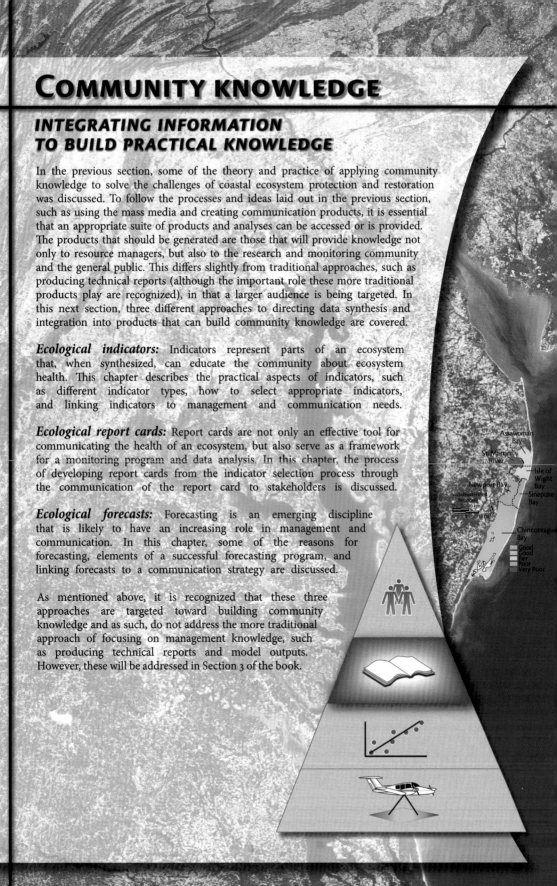

Chapter 5: Ecological indicators
Assessing ecosystem health using metrics

E. Caroline Wicks, Ben J. Longstaff, Ben Fertig, and William C. Dennison

To halt the decline of an ecosystem, it is necessary to think like an ecosystem.
—Douglas P. Wheeler

Chapter 4 discussed how selecting an appropriate communication product can affect an audience and persuade opinions. This chapter discusses how using another tool, an indicator (Figure 5.1), not only can persuade opinions, but also can be used to evaluate the health of an ecosystem. It starts by introducing what an ecological indicator is and why it is important and then describes different kinds of indicators, the process of selecting an indicator, how indicators are used to aid in management decisions, and how to structure indicators. Selecting, developing, and communicating ecological indicators are perhaps the most important, yet challenging aspects of a coastal assessment program and, therefore, should be given appropriate effort and resources.

Scientists and resource managers use ecological indicators to assess the health of an ecosystem and its resources. There is a large, varied, and growing array of indicators, ranging from simple measures, such as water temperature, to complex biological measures, such as indices of biotic integrity. Indicators are the mainstay of coastal assessment programs, dictating aspects such as the field program, data analysis, and communication.

For these reasons, the selected indicators have an overriding influence on program budget and resource allocation. Clearly, selecting appropriate indicators is a critical stage of an established or a developing monitoring program (see Chapter 11) because the process helps to turn simple measurements (data) into information about a system that scientists, managers, and the public can use.

What is an indicator?

An indicator is a sign or signal that relays a complex message, potentially from numerous sources, in a simplified and useful manner. The most recognized use of indicators is in the medical field where they are used to assess and diagnose human health and disease. For example, the body mass index (a measure of body weight relative to height; Figure 5.2) is a measure of body fat that indicates potential health problems, such as diabetes and heart disease. Similarly, ecosystem health indicators, such as dissolved oxygen, are used to assess and diagnose the health of the ecosystem.

An ecological indicator reflects biological, chemical, or physical attributes of an ecological condition. It is a measure, an index of measures, or a model that characterizes an ecosystem or one of

Figure 5.1. Examples of indicators: Secchi depth (water clarity), water quality (pH, dissolved oxygen), sediment type, seagrass coverage, and number and type of fish.
Photo credits left to right: Maryland Department of Natural Resources, LeHigh River Stocking Association, Paleoecological Environmental Assessment and Research Laboratory, National Oceanic and Atmospheric Administration, Maryland Department of Natural Resources.

its critical components (Figure 5.2).[1] The primary uses of ecological indicators are to characterize current status and track or predict significant change (i.e., trends).[2] Additionally, indicators are intended to convey more information than a simple measurement of some system component.[3] A health indicator can be directly or indirectly linked to human impacts on the ecosystem. For instance, the term *bioindicator* is defined by Oak Ridge National Laboratory[4] as "an anthropogenically induced response in biomolecular, biochemical, or physiological parameters that has been causally linked to biological effects at one or more of the organism, population, community, or ecosystem levels of organization." The Laboratory's Biological Indicators Program evaluates stream health based on a set of defined bioindicators that incorporate human impacts and stressors on stream organisms (e.g., fish).[5]

Several studies have attempted to define what an ecological indicator is in terms of its characteristics and function (Table 5.1). A review of these studies shows that there is no overall consensus, with some studies focusing on technical characteristics such as cost–benefit analysis and sensitivity to natural variation, and others approaching it from a communications viewpoint, arguing that the importance of an indicator is that it's easily understood and explained. Almost all the studies, however, agree that the indicators should address management questions and be based on reference conditions or threshold values. The take-home message from this survey is that the definition of an ecological indicator depends on its purpose or intended use, and this raises the question about the usefulness of the indicator toward the intended purpose.

Later in this chapter, we discuss the process of selecting appropriate indicators, which will, in effect, help to define what an ecological indicator is for your program. However, the basic elements for defining an indicator also can be used to evaluate the usefulness of any indicator. The basic elements are:

- the spatial and/or temporal scale of the issue being addressed;
- the specific questions to be answered, including a snapshot of current state, identification of causative factors, communication to the public, and evaluation of the effectiveness of management actions; and,
- context of the question (reference site).[6]

Furthermore, no matter what indicator definition or characteristics you choose, it is important to continually evaluate the usefulness of the indicator, which needs to be reviewed in terms of 1) accuracy at reflecting the underlying ecosystem response[9]

> ## Indicator terms
>
> *Environmental indicators* measure pressure (impacts on), state (health), and response (management actions) of an ecosystem.
>
> *Ecological indicators* measure the state (health) of an ecosystem. These indicators are the focus of this chapters
>
> *Ecosystem health indicators* is a descriptive term for ecological indicators.

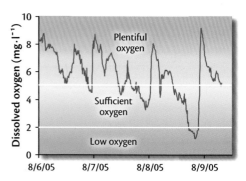

Figure 5.2. The Body Mass Index (BMI) is an indicator of human health. Dissolved oxygen is an indicator of ecosystem health. Source: Maryland Department of Natural Resources.

Table 5.1. Characteristics that indicators should include have been determined by a variety of studies.[1-3,6-8] Several studies have overlapping ideas, and almost all agree that indicators should be tied to management.

	Jackson et al. 2000	Gibson et al. 2000	Hershner et al. 2006	Wardrop et al. 2006	Pantus and Dennison 2005	Dale and Beyeler 2001
Management question/objective being addressed	X	X	X	X	X	
Reference value/ threshold	X		X	X	X	
Spatially and/or temporally explicit	X	X		X	X	
Easy to communicate				X	X	X
Predictive				X	X	X
Insensitive to natural variation/sensitive to stressors	X	X				X
Cost–benefit analysis	X	X				
Monitoring design	X	X				

and 2) appropriateness of the indicator to answer the management question or objective that the indicator was initially meant to answer.

Types of ecological indicators

Indicators used to assess ecosystem health fall under one of three categories: physical, chemical, or biological. Physical and chemical indicators are measures of the physical and chemical components of the ecosystem, whereas biological indicators (or bioindicators) refer to organisms, species, or communities whose characteristics show the presence of specific environmental conditions. A survey of national and international research and coastal assessment program websites and peer-reviewed literature showed that physical and chemical indicators are slightly more common than biological indicators, with those indicators of nutrient enrichment (e.g., dissolved oxygen and nutrient concentrations) and chemical contaminants being the most common (Figure 5.3, Table 5.2). One reason physical and chemical indicators are common is that they are relatively quick and easy to measure with water quality probes, test kits, or routine laboratory analysis. The relative simplicity of physicochemical indicators (not withstanding the effort required to obtain quality data) means that these indicators often become the mainstay of coastal assessment programs, particularly

community or small-scale programs that have small funding sources. Although the most frequently used biological indicator in the survey was chlorophyll *a* concentration, a relatively large proportion of the programs based their indicators on habitat, such as wetlands and submerged aquatic vegetation. Habitat indicators have the advantages of being easy for the broader audience to understand compared to more obscure physical and chemical indicators.

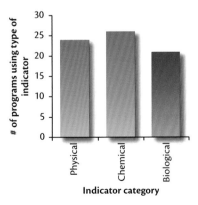

Figure 5.3. A survey of research and monitoring programs illustrates the diversity of indicators that are currently in use. Source: Web and peer-reviewed literature survey of 30 government agencies and non-profit organizations.

Building community knowledge

Selecting the right indicators is crucial

The hub of your program

Indicators are the most essential element of any coastal assessment program. Without indicators, the health of the system cannot be determined and tracked, effects of management actions cannot be assessed, and specific problems cannot be identified. The essential role of indicators highlights the importance of selecting the right indicators in the first place and periodically reviewing the effectiveness of the indicators and revising as necessary. Figure 5.4 illustrates how indicators are the hub of a coastal assessment program; influencing the field monitoring program; data storage and analysis protocols, communications; and, therefore, the overall allocation of program resources.

Choosing the right indicator is important as is choosing the right number of indicators for your program. Too few indicators can lead to data and knowledge gaps, whereas too many can be costly and ineffective. An analysis of indicators in

Recipe for success

Certain principles for choosing indicators apply to all types of monitoring and assessment programs.

- Be adaptable
- Use conceptual diagrams
- Apply the appropriate spatial and temporal scale
- Select criteria to determine indicators
- Link indicators to management actions
- Group indicators into reporting and diagnostic indicators

the National Park Service's Rock Creek Park Inventory and Monitoring Program showed that an optimal number of indicators for its objectives was six to 11. The standard error of the mean of a set of indicators was compared against the number of metrics.[10] This is just one way of determining the right number of indicators for your program and may be based on individual program needs.

Hypothesis-driven indicators

Although the following section discusses the process of selecting indicators, a crucial principle to always keep in mind is that the indicator is based on a hypothesis or theory, with a hypothesis being a suggested explanation or possible correlation between cause and effect. The hypothesis may not be tested at the onset but appropriate research needs to be undertaken to test underlying relationships. For example, the hypothesis that increased nutrient loading leads to increased algal growth, which can result in low dissolved oxygen levels, is the basis for many indicators, such as chlorophyll *a*

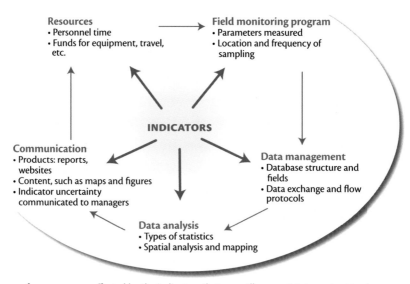

Figure 5.4. All areas of a program are affected by the indicators that you will use, so it is important to choose carefully.

concentration and dissolved oxygen levels. However, it was this hypothesis that was perhaps incorrectly applied to monitoring the health of the Great Barrier Reef (GBR) lagoon in Australia. A long-term chlorophyll *a* monitoring program was established to study the effects of nutrient loads on the GBR lagoon, and although chlorophyll *a* levels remained relatively stable, other aspects of the ecosystem such as corals and seagrasses, were independently found to have deteriorated.[11] Therefore, in this instance, chlorophyll *a* was not a good indicator of lagoon health. This example highlights the importance of ensuring that your monitoring is ultimately based on a tested hypothesis.

How to select appropriate indicators

Not everything that counts can be counted,
And not everything that can be counted, counts.
    —Sign hanging in Albert Einstein's office

Selecting appropriate indicators is perhaps one of the most important, yet challenging aspects of a coastal assessment program. Although in essence it can be simple to select and produce an indicator (Figure 5.5), the challenge is ensuring that indicator is providing information that will be used, be it for management purposes, educational purposes, or both.

Caroline Wicks

Figure 5.5. Health of local invertebrate populations can be an indicator of the overall health of a system.

There are two general approaches to the selection of indicators, with the indicators chosen often reflecting a combination of both processes. The first approach, in which indicators are selected based on the available data, is the simplest and often used by organizations with limited resources. In coastal ecosystems, this invariably results in indicators based on water quality that can be measured with

probes or simple test kits. The second approach is based on selection of indicators to meet specific management or policy needs and is the preferred approach because the results will be used to better manage the system rather than to just study it. Selecting indicators using the second approach (e.g., What are the management needs?) relies on a continual process that includes conceptualizing the ecosystem and the proposed indicators; selecting the indicators based on an agreed set of criteria; producing the indicator; and finally reviewing and, if necessary, revising the indicator. As entire books have been dedicated to the process of ecological indicators and their selection,[12] here we present an overview of the key steps in the indicator selection and development process (Figure 5.6).

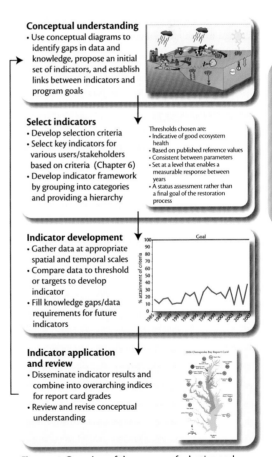

Conceptual understanding
• Use conceptual diagrams to identify gaps in data and knowledge, propose an initial set of indicators, and establish links between indicators and program goals

Select indicators
• Develop selection criteria
• Select key indicators for various users/stakeholders based on criteria (Chapter 6)
• Develop indicator framework by grouping into categories and providing a hierarchy

Thresholds chosen are:
• Indicative of good ecosystem health
• Based on published reference values
• Consistent between parameters
• Set at a level that enables a measurable response between years
• A status assessment rather than a final goal of the restoration process

Indicator development
• Gather data at appropriate spatial and temporal scales
• Compare data to threshold or targets to develop indicator
• Fill knowledge gaps/data requirements for future indicators

Indicator application and review
• Disseminate indicator results and combine into overarching indices for report card grades
• Review and revise conceptual understanding

Figure 5.6. Overview of the process of selecting and reviewing indicators.

Building community knowledge

A variety of indicators

A vast number of indicators exists for every type of ecosystem. One major problem with choosing indicators for your program is the large volume of measures that are available to use as indicators. Virtually anything in the ecosystem, from water temperature to the number of whale sightings, can be used as an indicator. An easy way to organize indicators is to put them into categories (Table 5.2). Categorizing indicators helps to clarify which part of the ecosystem the indicator is describing and whether the group of indicators you eventually decide on span the features—from water quality to habitat to fisheries—of the ecosystem.

Another way to start narrowing down indicators is to compare your program to other similar ones (i.e., do not reinvent the wheel). Table 5.2 shows what type of indicators research and monitoring programs around the world are using to describe and track their systems and that a large number of programs use physical and chemical indicators. Additionally, indicators from a variety of categories are used. As new environmental problems are clarified and accepted (e.g., climate change), new categories of indicators will be added.

Using conceptual diagrams to aid indicator selection

A useful exercise when selecting indicators is to create conceptual diagrams (see Chapter 3). These provide a diagrammatic representation of the ecosystem in which key features, processes, and impacts can be illustrated (Figure 5.7). There are many reasons why drawing conceptual diagrams is a useful exercise. First, the process of producing a diagram in a group or community setting facilitates communication between participants such as

Pitfalls to avoid

Some common problems when selecting indicators:
- Too many indicators
- No connection between indicators and response by managers
- Confusing messages to the public
- Using the wrong indicators for your region
- Costs associated with indicator—is it worth it?

Table 5.2. Summary of categories and types of indicators used in monitoring and research programs both nationally and internationally. Source: Web and peer-reviewed literature survey of 30 government agencies and non-profit organizations.

Category	Indicator	# of programs
Physical	Temperature	17
	pH	12
	Water clarity	9
	Salinity	14
	Turbidity	3
	Sediments	2
	Wave exposure	1
Chemical	Dissolved oxygen	20
	Nutrients	19
	Chemical contaminants	18
	Dissolved organic carbon	2
Biotic		
Algae	Chlorophyll a	12
	Phytoplankton Index of Biotic Integrity	3
	Harmful algal blooms	2
	Macroalgae	2
	$\delta^{15}N$ in macroalgae	1
Benthic	Wetlands	9
	Submerged aquatic vegetation	7
	Bottom habitat	6
	Macroinvertebrates	4
	Benthic algae	3
	Corals	2
Fisheries	Fish type and abundance	4
	Invertebrate type and abundance	3
	Reef fish endemnism	1
	# of larvae of key species	1
Other	Waterfowl	6
	Turtles	1
	Whales	3
Invasive species		~6

scientists and managers. Conceptual diagrams promote dialogue and interaction among people (often people with very different perspectives or levels of understanding) because they are visual, easy to understand, and can be rapidly viewed and assimilated. Most importantly, producing conceptual diagrams provides a format in which indicators can be evaluated, helping to guarantee that they will provide the type of information

Figure 5.7. Using conceptual diagrams within a group setting facilitates the indicator selection process.

Integration & Application Network

needed. Within the conceptual diagram, indicators can be identified and linked to the features such as impacts and management actions (Figure 5.8). Another benefit of producing conceptual diagrams is identifying gaps in knowledge that may be addressed by additional indicators or research programs.

Conceptual diagrams should not be set in stone, rather they should be updated periodically to represent the latest understanding of the system and monitoring program and the associated indicators. In addition to the process of producing conceptual diagrams, the product itself has many benefits, especially as a communication tool. That is, the diagram itself is a useful tool for helping to explain to a broader audience what is known about the system, what indicators are being used, and why.

Using selection criteria to determine indicators

Although conceptual diagrams provide a useful framework for identifying the role of indicators in an ecosystem context, there are many other considerations to take into account during the indicator selection process. The most systematic way of making a selection is to evaluate candidate indicators against predetermined criteria. No single set of criteria can be recommended because coastal environments are diverse and management actions and policies differ. Here, we present a few important criteria to consider, with a more in-depth array of selection criteria available in the broader indicator literature (Table 5.3).

Using selection criteria to determine indicators is a two-step process. The first step is to choose the criteria that will define your indicators. Some questions that help with choosing criteria are: Is the indicator cost-effective? Is the indicator relevant to management or policy decisions (Figure 5.9)? The second step is to evaluate potential indicators against the criteria. In some cases, this may be a simple exercise (e.g., Can the indicator be understood by the stakeholders?), whereas in other cases it can be complex (e.g., Is the indicator cost-effective? What is the indicator level of uncertainty?). Both steps in the process need to be conducted in a transparent and objective manner so that the reasons why an indicator was chosen can be justified and clearly articulated, which may become critical in the future when competing for resources or justifying expenditures.

Building community knowledge

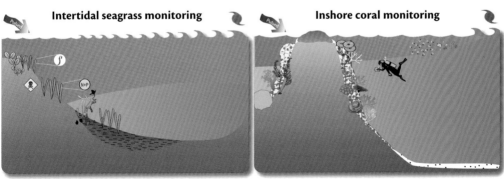

Intertidal seagrass indicators include percent cover of seagrass , epiphytes , tissue nutrients (N+P) , and reproductive potential .

Coral indicators include benthic cover , juvenile density , coral diversity , and forams .

Figure 5.8. Conceptual diagram developed for a workshop to help select indicators for monitoring the health of the inshore GBR. The conceptual diagram was updated based on the scientific understanding gained during the first three years of monitoring, was adopted within the program's monitoring framework, and used frequently as a communication tool.[13]

Table 5.3. Examples of criteria that are used for indicator selection.

Criteria		Explanation
Inform management		Will the indicator help measure the effectiveness of management actions and/or enable better management decisions to be made? • Indicators selected need to measure progress toward targets or goals.
Responsive		Will the indicator be responsive to ecosystem stressors, such as nutrients? • If assessing the effects of management actions, the indicator should be sensitive to anthropogenically derived stressors but insensitive to natural variation.
Cost-effective		Is the indicator affordable and cost-effective? • A cost–benefit analysis will help to determine whether there is a suitable return (usable information) in relation to the cost of producing the indicator. • Cost of producing an indicator can be reduced by seeking efficiencies (e.g., piggy-backing collection on other indicators) or replacing an expensive indicator with a comparable, cheaper alternative.
Integrative		Does the indicator integrate across multiple ecosystem components and/or over long timeframes? • Integrative indicators are usually of greater value than indicators that respond to a single aspect of the environment or snapshots in time. • Integrative indicators reduce the number of indicators needed. • Indicators that integrate over time reduce repetitive monitoring.
Transparent and understandable		Is the indicator easy to understand or explain, and can the audience relate to the indicator? • Ensuring that indicators (or at least a group of indicators) are simple, easy to present clearly, and intuitive will greatly enhance the chance of them being used.
Robust		Is the indicator underpinned by quality data and based on valid methods and principles? • An indicator should be based on quality-assured data and peer-reviewed methods. • The indicator must show changes in the ecosystem, not changes in methods and poor quality control.
Timely		Can the indicator be produced in a time frame that is useful for its intended purpose? • There is no use in producing an indicator that can only be compiled in a time frame that significantly reduces its application to communication or management needs.
Spatially explicit		Can the indicator be mapped and spatially interpolated? • Maps are very effective at illuminating ecosystem patterns and processes and impacts, such as floods. Can the sampling method be designed to help produce useful maps? Does the indicator vary spatially and temporally to be meaningful? • This could be within one system or comparing it to other systems.
Uncertainty		Can the level of uncertainty be determined and communicated effectively? • It is particularly important to communicate the uncertainty to managers who are basing their decisions on these indicators.
Climate change		Is the indicator responsive to climate change? In the face of climate change, will the indicator be able to discern between anthropogenic stressors and climate change?

Jane Thomas

Figure 5.9. Using seagrasses as an indicator can be time and effort intensive. Seagrasses would be used on a yearly temporal scale.

Selecting appropriate temporal and spatial scales

Indicators most frequently represent a change in condition over a period of time or geographic area and in some cases, a combination of the two. Indicators that compare conditions over time (e.g., trend analysis) are useful to illustrate factors such as extreme events, seasonal changes, and responses to management actions (Figure 5.10). It is perhaps for this last reason (responses to management actions) why most indicators are represented as a change over time, as the key question within most coastal assessment programs is, "Are management actions leading to improvements in the region's health?" Time series figures are one of the most appropriate ways of answering this question.

Comparing indicator values over time may not provide sufficient information on the spatial variability of the system or the ability of the indicator value to represent all possible values in the study region. To fill this need, it is necessary to incorporate indicators that are spatially explicit. Spatially explicit indicators enable regions at differing scales to be compared and contrasted and identify gaps in geographic coverage. Common to both types of indicators (spatial and temporal) is selecting the appropriate scale based on the intended audience and application. Here we present a few considerations in the decision process.

Spatial scale

An indicator needs to be represented at a spatial scale that suits the associated decision-making process (Figure 5.11). This is separate from determining the correct spatial representativeness of measurements (see Chapters 10 and 11). In most

Chlorophyll a *as an indicator of eutrophication*

John Ryther, aquatic biologist

www.johnryther.com

John Ryther was an aquatic biologist who spent 50 years studying coastal ecosystems. One of his most prestigious accomplishments was his ongoing investigation into the relationship between nutrients and phytoplankton. Along with colleagues at Woods Hole Oceanographic Institution, Ryther described the process by which duck farms along the tributaries of Great South and Moriches Bays, New York, led to increased nitrogen and phosphorus flowing into the system. Combined with the specific physical constraints of the system (shallow depth, low flushing rate), this increase in nutrients led to dense, low-diversity phytoplankton blooms of long duration. Ryther's work led him (and William Dunstan) to propose the theory of nutrient limitation of phytoplankton. A seminal paper in *Science* (1971) illustrated this theory with fertilization experiments (figure below).

The nutrient limitation paradigm continues to be a cornerstone of coastal assessment programs in high nutrient loading ecosystems 30 years after the theory was first proposed. Furthermore, chlorophyll *a* (as a proxy for phytoplankton) is a ubiquitous indicator throughout coastal assessment programs.

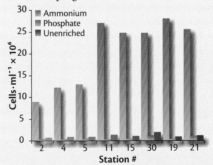

John Ryther and colleagues showed that a specific nutrient was the limiting factor to phytoplankton growth, a now-common biological paradigm.[15]

Building community knowledge

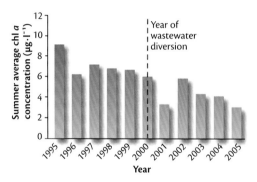

Figure 5.10. Changes in Boston Harbor chlorophyll *a* concentrations after wastewater diversion away from the harbor. The effectiveness of the management action was seen in the long–term data set.[14]

cases, selecting the right spatial scale depends on whether the program is primarily aimed at informing local, regional, or national decision-makers. Generally, the larger the spatial scale represented by the indicator, the less spatial detail portrayed and vice versa.

National-scale indicators enable large geographic regions or whole waterways, such as bays or estuaries, to be compared and contrasted (Figure 5.12). Because national- and even global-scale indicators tend to rely on a variety of data sources, the density and uncertainty of data used to generate the indicator values tend to be low and variable, respectively, between regions. Indicators at this scale tend to target high-level management decisions, where large overall spatial trends are required for national strategies and policy decisions. The indicators used in the National Estuarine Eutrophication Assessment (NEEA) report provide a good example of broad-scale indicators.[14] In this report, a single indicator score is provided for each major estuary and coastal region in the United States. One of the main aims of the NEEA report is to help develop a national strategy to address potentially worsening problems of estuarine eutrophication.

Regional-scale indicators enable areas of approximately 10 to 100 km to be compared and contrasted based on data from a single overarching assessment program or a combination of smaller programs. Spatial detail offered by regional indicators enables broad ecosystem gradients within the assessment region to be identified, such as gradients in water quality and habitat area, and the impacts of large events, such as floods. Indicators at this scale tend to target management decisions made by federal and state government.

Local-scale indicators enable relatively small areas of under 10 km to be compared and contrasted, usually based on data collected from a single assessment program (Figure 5.13). Local indicators are effective at identifying small-scale patterns and events, such as plumes from point sources and harmful algal blooms. Local-scale indicators tend to have high data density and detailed geographic coverage and, therefore, are most effective at informing local decision-makers and the community.

Temporal scale

Ecosystem processes and responses to management occur across a broad spectrum of time, from short-term events that change on an hourly-to-daily timescale to long-term events operating over years to decades. When selecting an indicator, it is critical to select a time frame that best suits the intended use of the indicator (Figure 5.14). For example, if you are interested in indicating the potential cause of fish kills, you may want to choose an indicator that shows short-term (hourly to daily) variability in dissolved oxygen levels. On the other hand, if you want to indicate the effects of land use changes on dissolved oxygen levels, a more appropriate time scale for the indicator would be years to decades.

When selecting the time scale of an indicator, the financial and logistical aspects of the associated monitoring program have to be considered. In some instances, such as using water quality sensors, it can be relatively cheap to collect high-frequency data, because of the simplicity of the measurement, logging capabilities of the instrument, and so forth. On the other hand, collecting large data sets increases the challenges of storing, analyzing, and

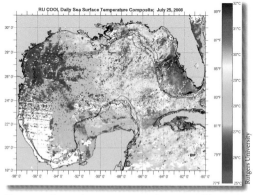

Figure 5.11. Sea surface temperature is measured from satellites. It provides a spatially large–scale view and can be used for decisions on the global or national scale.

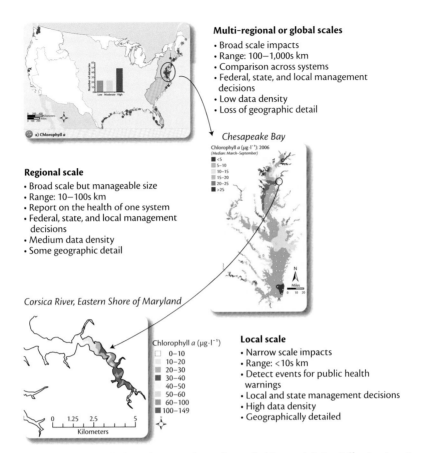

Multi-regional or global scales
- Broad scale impacts
- Range: 100–1,000s km
- Comparison across systems
- Federal, state, and local management decisions
- Low data density
- Loss of geographic detail

Chesapeake Bay

Regional scale
- Broad scale but manageable size
- Range: 10–100s km
- Report on the health of one system
- Federal, state, and local management decisions
- Medium data density
- Some geographic detail

Corsica River, Eastern Shore of Maryland

Local scale
- Narrow scale impacts
- Range: <10s km
- Detect events for public health warnings
- Local and state management decisions
- High data density
- Geographically detailed

Figure 5.12. The same indicator, chlorophyll *a* in this example, can be applied from a global scale[14] to local creek scale and provides different information based on the level of spatial detail. Management decisions are carried out on all levels based on this information. Source: EcoCheck, Maryland Department of Natural Resources.

synthesizing copious amounts of information (see Chapter 11). Additionally, staff changes and short funding cycles affect long-term data sets, and it becomes a challenge to defend collecting data over long time frames.

Another problem to consider is that the data needed for a proposed indicator may not be available at the temporal frequency required to make the indicator useful. For example, the indicator may be too costly to be collected within a useful time frame. In these cases, it may be more appropriate to choose another indicator or seek ways to increase the sampling frequency to the desired level.

Uncertainty surrounding the indicator values will depend on the frequency of the supporting data (see Chapter 8). Summarizing high temporal frequency data into single values (e.g., hourly data points calculated into a monthly average) will lead to less uncertainty of the indicator value compared

Figure 5.13. A researcher collects a vertical water sample as part of a stream survey in Maryland.

Building community knowledge

71

Interannual time frame (years to decades)
- Trends over time
- Management actions
- E.g., decline in water clarity

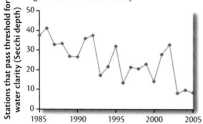

Seasonal time frame (months to years)
- Recent conditions
- Report on health of system
- E.g., seasonal variability of dissolved oxygen

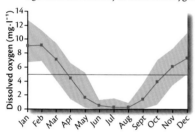

Intraseasonal (hours to days)
- Event detection and tracking
- E.g., fish kills due to low dissolved oxygen

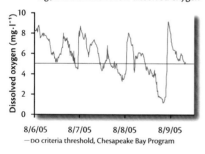

— DO criteria threshold, Chesapeake Bay Program

Figure 5.14. Different temporal scales can show varying patterns. Source: Maryland Department of Natural Resources.

to a single measurement in time. Higher temporal frequency data also improve the statistical power of any subsequent analysis, such as detecting trends. Again, when selecting an indicator, it is important to balance sample frequency (and the associated improvements in uncertainty and statistical power) with the associated costs of the monitoring program. One strategy to consider is to vary the sampling frequency based on the expected temporal variation of the indicator, for example, collecting more data during summer or wet seasons when conditions are more likely to be variable.

Indicators for different climates

One easy way to cross certain indicators off your list is to focus on the type of climate that you are trying to assess (Figure 5.15).[16] The polar regions, for example, have different drivers than the temperate regions or the tropical regions. In the polar regions, the issue is too much blue water (i.e., the ice is melting fast in the Arctic and Antarctic, leading to too much water compared to ice). There are similar pressures as well as known responses among temperate systems. In the temperate zone, the issue is too much green water (i.e., phytoplankton). The water quality is degrading as a function of agricultural and human nutrient inputs into the coastal zone. Eutrophication (excess chlorophyll *a* in the water column) is a common problem in temperate estuaries. Therefore, chlorophyll *a* may be an appropriate indicator. In tropical waters, the problem is brown water

Polar

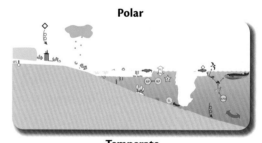

Temperate

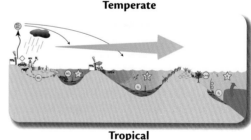

Tropical

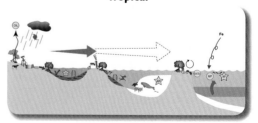

Figure 5.15. The type of indicator for coastal assessment may change based on climate type.

(i.e., turbidity, where the water is overwhelmed by sediments from the land). A suitable indicator for tropical systems may be corals, whether it be diversity of corals or area of bleaching. Therefore, indicators can be chosen that address the specific issue in your climate region.

A mix of physicochemical and biological indicators

As discussed above, indicators generally fall into one of two main categories—physicochemical and biological. There are intrinsic advantages and disadvantages in each of the two indicator types that need to be considered when selecting indicators (Table 5.4). The advantage of physicochemical indicators is that they tend to be relatively quick and easy to measure. However, although the relationship between the measured value and the implications to ecosystem health is often well-defined for single parameters, such as dissolved oxygen, the interactive effects between the physicochemical and biological aspects of the ecosystem are less well understood. Another disadvantage of physicochemical indicators is that they usually represent a snapshot in time (when the sample was collected), providing little

When selecting an indicator, make sure you can:

Measure—It must be a feature that can be reliably and consistently quantified.

Model—It must be a feature that can be conceptually modeled and linked to management.

Map—There needs to be enough data to create a map.

insight into conditions between sample collection times. Due to the limited information offered by many physicochemical indicators, they tend to be used to help diagnose the health of a system rather than as a key indicator for communication and management guidance.

The main advantages of using biological indicators are that they directly relate to the health of the ecosystem and integrate the effects of multiple environmental stressors over longer time periods than physicochemical indicators do. Biological indicators can be selected to indicate specific ecosystem stressors (e.g., depth range of seagrass as a long-term integrator of water clarity) or the interaction of multiple stressors (e.g., macroinvertebrate community composition as an indicator of overall stream health). One of the main reasons for limited use of biological indicators is the prohibitive cost associated with the labor-intensive nature of biological indicators. Unlike physicochemical indicators, there are very few quick-and-easy biological indicators. Biological indicators also have the added challenge of interpreting what the measured biological response means in terms of the health of the ecosystem.

Table 5.4. Advantages and disadavantages of different types of indicators. Source: Maryland Department of Natural Resources.

	Physicochemical indicators	Biological indicators
Advantages	• Simple and rapid measurements • Relatively low cost • Relatively well-established literature • High Quality Assurance/Quality Control	• Relate to publicly relevant aspect of ecosystem (biology) • Integrates over time • Integrates multiple stressors • High interpretive power
Disadvantages	• Snapshot in time • Basic information for a complex system • Need to interpret biological/ecosystem relevance	• Variable time frames • Can be difficult to interpret results relative to management • May need sophisticated analyses • Can be costly and time consuming
Example	pH, Otter Point Creek, Maryland	Menhaden biomass, Chesapeake Bay

Link indicators to management action

As discussed, one of the main criteria for selecting an indicator is its ability to aid in management decisions, usually in the form of measuring progress toward agreed targets or goals. In many coastal ecosystems, management goals include reducing nitrogen inputs. Unlike industrial toxicants that come from a particular type of source (industry), nitrogen enters aquatic ecosystems from both diffuse (e.g., agriculture, urban runoff) and point (e.g., sewage treatment plants, septic systems) sources. Therefore, to reduce nitrogen, managers have multiple, potential courses of actions from which to choose, but identifying the most important one for a particular ecosystem can be difficult. In such a scenario, managers may use an indicator that can discriminate between diffuse and point sources of nitrogen, such as stable nitrogen isotopes ($\delta^{15}N$, or the ratio of ^{15}N to ^{14}N of a sample compared to that of a standard). Measurements of $\delta^{15}N$ in various biological indicator organisms, such as oysters, discriminate between these types of

> ### The P–S–R Model divides indicators into three categories
>
> *Pressure*—factors that affect the health of a system
>
> *State*—condition or health of a system
>
> *Response*—effort taken to restore or preserve a system

sources because $\delta^{15}N$ is relatively enriched in biologically processed wastes (e.g., sewage or septic sources) compared to those of chemically synthesized fertilizers (e.g., diffuse agricultural runoff). Furthermore, deployments of biological indicators can help to identify spatial patterns of septic and fertilizer nitrogen sources.

An assessment of nutrient concentrations and their potential sources was made in Maryland's Coastal Bays (Figure 5.16). Both conventional water quality monitoring (providing a "snapshot" in time) and a biological indicator (providing a four-day average) were used to examine nitrogen concentrations and sources, respectively. High total nitrogen concentrations were found in St. Martin River, whereas low concentrations were found in Isle of Wight Bay and southern Chincoteague Bay (near the two inlets where oceanic exchange occurs). Conversely, isotope ratios from macroalgae deployed throughout these coastal lagoons were enriched in both St. Martin River and southern Chincoteague Bay (Figure 5.16).[17] By analyzing these two datasets in conjunction, it was concluded

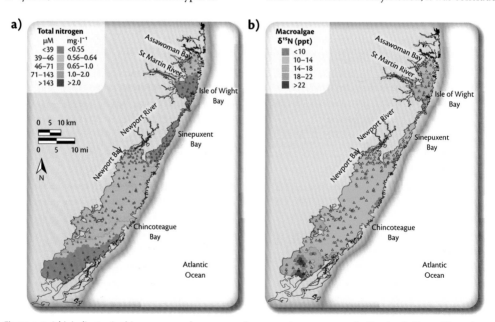

Figure 5.16. A bioindicator, in this case macroalgae, was used to trace nitrogen sources in Maryland's Coastal Bays. a) Routine monitoring of total nitrogen concentration in the water column. b) Bioindicators ($\delta^{15}N$ in macroalgae) shows concentrated nutrient enrichment from septic systems in southern Chincoteague Bay.[17]

that septic systems were an important source of nitrogen to this aquatic ecosystem at both St. Martin River and southern Chincoteague Bay, even though the overall pollutant load varied regionally. By using both conventional water quality monitoring and a biological indicator, resource managers can identify areas of concern and potential pollutant sources that contribute to degraded water quality. Based on the indicator data, transferring human population centers in this region from septic systems to wastewater treatment plants is a management action that will likely improve water quality.

Structuring indicators—grouping and hierarchy

Due to the trend of increasing data availability and pressure to provide performance measures for management actions, the number of indicators produced by coastal assessment programs can be quite large. Although this chapter has focused on ecosystem health indicators, these should not be confused with indicators aimed at assessing management efforts and stressors to the ecosystem. The most commonly adopted framework for distinguishing between these broad indicator types is the pressure–state–response (PSR) model (Figures 5.17, 5.18). The PSR model is essentially a horizontal process that links management effort to ecosystem health. However, there are other frameworks that organize indicators into different groups, and these also can be used.[18]

Pressures on a system include any factor that influences the condition of a system and are usually considered related to human activities

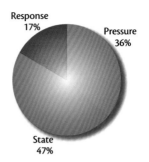

Figure 5.17. Most programs surveyed use state indicators, but pressure and response indicators are also common. Source: Web and peer-reviewed literature survey of 30 government agencies and non-profit organizations.

and impacts. Pressures can be any hydrologic and physical characteristics of a system as well as inputs and anthropogenic impacts in a system. Examples of indicators of pressure are nutrient inputs, residence time, and impervious surfaces.

The state of the system answers the questions, "How is the system doing?" and "What is the current health of the system?" An ecosystem should be in a state of homeostasis, or internal stability. Furthermore, the physical, chemical, and biological components of that system should be within their normal range and should help to maintain the equilibrium. For example, dissolved oxygen would be high enough to support healthy organisms, and predator–prey interactions would be stable. If these components have been pushed out of the normal range (by pressures on the system), then they would indicate whether a system is out of balance or unhealthy.

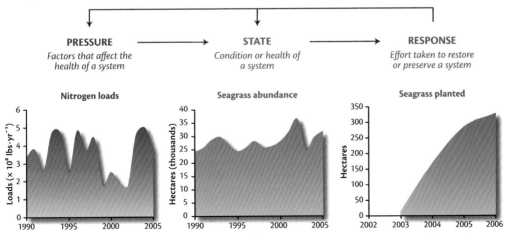

Figure 5.18. PSR indicators measure different aspects of an ecosystem. Source: U.S. Geological Survey, Chesapeake Bay Program.

The response of stakeholders, managers, and policy-makers to the state of the system is an important component in coastal assessment. Response indicators measure the effort of humans to restore or preserve a system. This response is determined by measuring such areas as pollution reduction efforts, habitat restoration, and decreasing anthropogenic impacts (e.g., development). Ideally, if the response of stakeholders, managers, and policy-makers is significant, the effect can be measured in the pressures and state of a system.

If the indicators are not divided into groups and ordered into a hierarchy, you run the risk of both confusing the audience and not being able to identify or communicate the most important issues or results. Therefore, within each PSR category, it is useful to develop an indicator hierarchy that separates overarching indices, reporting indicators (otherwise known as headline or key indicators), and diagnostic indicators (Figure 5.19). These indices represent an aggregation of individual indicators in order to provide a simple overall assessment of ecosystem health. The overarching indices are used to provide the most basic snapshot or synthesis of information that can be communicated to a very broad audience (see Chapter 6). Reporting indicators are those used to communicate important messages or issues, so they need to be relatively simple in nature and limited in number. Diagnostic indicators provide a more in-depth assessment, and as their name suggests they help to diagnose or explain reporting indicators. Diagnostic indicators can be relatively complex in nature and may be more useful to a technical audience than to managers or the interested public.

In summary, this chapter discussed what an indicator is, the kinds of indicators, how to select an indicator, how indicators are used to aid in management decisions, and how to structure indicators. An indicator is a sign or signal that relays a complex message in a simplified, useful manner. Indicators can reflect biological, chemical, or physical attributes of a condition. Indicator selection is a critical step because indicators affect all parts of your coastal assessment program. There are a variety of criteria to keep in mind when selecting indicators. Finally, indicators should ideally be organized in order to have the most impact, which can include hierachies and groupings.

OVERARCHING INDICES

- Simple score/grade
- Aggregates multiple indicator scores
- Useful for broad-scale communication

- E.g., Chesapeake Bay report card

REPORTING INDICATORS

- Simple
- Used to tell the key story/message
- Limited in number
- Can be used to diagnose problems
- E.g., change in seagrass habitat area

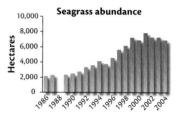

DIAGNOSTIC INDICATORS

- Can be more complex
- Used to help explain reporting indicator or other complex condition
- Larger in number
- E.g., turbidity

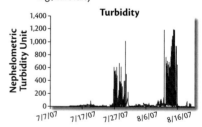

Figure 5.19. Indicators can either be divided into diagnostic or reporting indicators or can be combined into indices. Some indicators can be both diagnostic and reporting. Source: EcoCheck, VA Institute of Marine Science, MD Department of Natural Resources.

References

1. Jackson JE, Kurtz JC, Fisher WS (2000) Evaluation guidelines for ecological indicators. U.S. Environ Protect Agency Office of Res Dev EPA-620-R-99-005, Research Triangle Park, NC

2. Gibson GR, Bowman ML, Gerritsen J, Snyder BD (2000) Estuarine and coastal marine waters: Bioassessment and biocriteria technical guidance. U.S. Environ Protect Agency Office Water EPA-822-B-00-024, Washington, D.C.

3. Hershner C, Havens K, Bilkovic DM, Wardrop D (2007) Assessment of Chesapeake Bay Program selection and use of indicators. EcoHealth 4:187-193

4. McCarty LS, Munkittrick KR (1996) Environmental biomarkers in aquatic toxicology: fiction, fantasy or functional. Human Ecol Risk Assess 2:268-274

5. Oak Ridge National Laboratory (2002) Bioindicators of aquatic ecosystem stress. Accessed 21 Jul. www.esd.ornl.gov/programs/bioindicators

6. Wardrop DH, Hershner C, Havens K, Thornton K, Bilkovic D (2007) Developing and communicating a taxonomy of ecological indicators: A case study from the mid-Atlantic. EcoHealth 4:179-186

7. Pantus FJ, Dennison WC (2005) Quantifying and evaluating ecosystem health: A case study from Moreton Bay, Australia. Enviro Manage 36:757-771

8. Dale VH, Beyeler SC (2001) Challenges in the development and use of ecological indicators. Ecol Indicators 1:3-10

9. Murtaugh PA (1996) The statistical evaluation of ecological indicators. Ecol App 6:132-139

10. Florkowski LN (2009) Development of a recommended analytical framework for environmental report cards: an example from Rock Creek Park, Washington, D.C. and its watershed. MS Thesis, University of Maryland, College Park

11. Furnas M (2003) Catchments and corals: terrestrial runoff to the Great Barrier Reef. Australian Institute of Marine Science, Townsville, Queensland, Australia

12. Jorgensen SE, Costanza R, Xu F-L (2006) Handbook of ecological indicators for assessment of ecosystem health. CRC Press, Danvers, MA

13. Integration & Application Network, Great Barrier Reef Marine Park Authority (2008) Reef plan monitoring: Marine water quality impacts. www.ian.umces.edu/pdfs/gbr_reefplan_newsletter.pdf

14. Bricker S, Longstaff B, Dennison W, Jones A, Boicourt K, Wicks C, Woerner J (2007) Effects of nutrient enrichment in the nation's estuaries: A decade of change. NOAA National Centers for Coastal Ocean Science Coastal Ocean Program Decision Analysis Series No. 26, Silver Spring, Maryland

15. Ryther JH, Dunstan WM (1971) Nitrogen, phosphorus, and eutrophication in the coastal marine environment. Science 171: 1008-1013

16. Dennison WC (2008) Environmental problem solving in coastal ecosystems: A paradigm shift to sustainability. Est Coast Shelf Sci 77:185-196

17. Fertig BM, Carruthers TJB, Dennison WC, Jones AB, Pantus F, Longstaff B (2009) Oyster and macroalgae bioindicators detect elevated $\delta^{15}N$ in Maryland's Coastal Bays. Estuaries Coasts 32:773-786

18. Collaborative Assessment Network (2003) Strategy paper on environmental indicators. United Nations Environment Programme, Klongluang, Thailand. rrcap.unep.org/projects/envIndicator.cfm

Further reading

Burgan B, Carpenter D, Gould D, Keeler B, McGovern C, Miller S (2007) Indicator development for estuaries. U.S. Environ Protect Agency Office of Water EPA-842-B-07-004, Washington, D.C.

McKenzie DH, Hyatt DE, McDonald VJ (1992) Ecological Indicators: Volumes 1 and 2. Proceedings of the International symposium on ecological indicators. Elsevier Science Publishers, Ltd, Essex, England

Building community knowledge

CHAPTER 6: ECOLOGICAL REPORT CARDS
INTEGRATING INDICATORS INTO REPORT CARDS

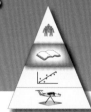

Michael R. Williams, Ben J. Longstaff, E. Caroline Wicks,
Tim J.B. Carruthers, and Lisa N. Florkowski

*Think like a wise man but communicate in the
language of the people.*
                                    –William Butler Yeats

This chapter continues the discussion of ecological
indicators but with the specific application of
producing ecological report cards. It explains the
reasons for producing report cards, the steps to
produce indicators based on ecological thresholds,
and the process of combining indicators into
overarching indices. Ecological report cards, like
the indicators that they are based on, are one of
the most important products for directing data
collection and analysis.

Reasons to produce a report card

Ecological report cards, much like school report
cards, provide performance-driven numeric grades
or letters that represent the relative ecological
health of a geographic region or component of
the ecosystem. They are an important tool for
integrating diverse data types into simple scores
that can be communicated to decision-makers and
the general public. In other words, large and often
complex amounts of information can be made
understandable to a broad audience.

Ecological report cards enhance research,
monitoring, and management in several ways.
For the research community, they can lead to new
insights through integration schemes that reveal
patterns not immediately apparent, help to design
a conceptual framework to integrate scientific
understanding and environmental values, and
help to develop scaling approaches that allow
for comparison in time and space (Figure 6.1).
Within monitoring realms, report cards justify
continued monitoring by providing timely and
relevant feedback to managers and can have the
added benefit of accelerating data analyses. For
management, they provide accountability by
measuring the success of restoration efforts and
identifying impaired regions or issues of ecological
concern. This catalyzes improvements in ecosystem
health through the development of peer pressure
among local communities. Report cards also can

Building community knowledge

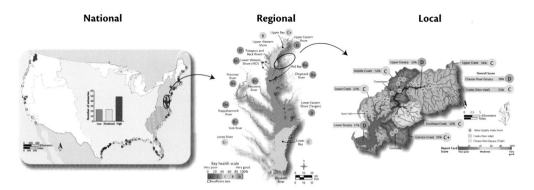

Figure 6.1. Report cards can be produced at any geographic scale from National to local. The scale of a report card
depends on factors such as the purpose and data availability. The three assessments shown (left to right) were
conducted for the entire United States,[1] the Chesapeake Bay watershed,[2] and a small tributary of the Chesapeake Bay.[3]

guide restoration efforts by creating a targeting scheme for resource allocation.

Due to the ability of report cards to reach and be understood by a broad audience, they have become a popular and effective tool for promoting numerous issues, ranging from the bacteria levels at California beaches to the ecosystem health of freshwater streams. Typically, after a report card has been released, awareness and responsiveness to a particular issue increases substantially, leading to a change in community and political knowledge and will.

Ecosystem health assessments have become more common in recent years, and report cards are being produced by a variety of groups from small, community-based organizations to large partnerships. Although methods, presentation, and content of report cards vary, the underlying premise is the same: to build community awareness and raise the profile of health impairment issues and restoration efforts. A few examples of places where report cards have become an integral component of monitoring and assessment programs (several of which are discussed in more detail in this chapter) include Gippsland and Moreton Bay in Australia, the San Francisco Bay and Chesapeake Bay in the United States, and Lake

Producing a report card

- Enhances research, monitoring, and management
- Enables large amounts of complex information to be communicated to a broad audience
- Can provide accountability, measuring the success of a particular effort
- Identifies regions or issues of concern

Simcoe in Canada (Figure 6.2).

Ideally, a report card should be based on recent data that summarize ecological conditions from the previous year. Audiences commonly relate better to information presented on an annual time frame, and annual reporting is particularly important if trying to explain conditions caused by weather events or management actions. When possible, it is useful to put the previous year's results into context by relating these to historical results calculated using the same methods.

How to develop a report card

There are essentially four major steps to developing a report card (Figure 6.3):

1) Selection of indicators and approach—This step involves reviewing currently available indicators to determine whether they accurately represent ecosystem health and whether new indicators should be developed. Boundaries for reporting regions must also be carefully defined in order to accurately represent the spatial variability of the indicators.

2) Developing indicators—This step is required if it is determined in step one that additional

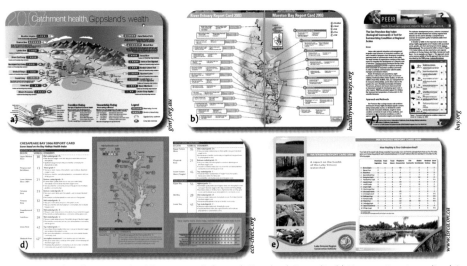

Figure 6.2. Examples of ecosystem health report cards from a) Gippsland, Australia; b) Moreton Bay, Australia; c) San Francisco Bay, California, United States; d) Chesapeake Bay, United States; and e) Lake Simcoe, Canada.

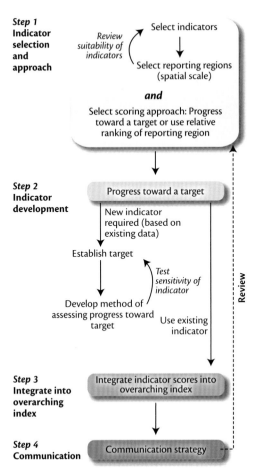

Figure 6.3. The four major steps needed to produce a report card.

Step 1 Indicator selection and approach

Select indicators

Review suitability of indicators

Select reporting regions (spatial scale)

and

Select scoring approach: Progress toward a target or use relative ranking of reporting region

Step 2 Indicator development

Progress toward a target

New indicator required (based on existing data)

Establish target

Test sensitivity of indicator

Develop method of assessing progress toward target

Use existing indicator

Review

Step 3 Integrate into overarching index

Integrate indicator scores into overarching index

Step 4 Communication

Communication strategy

the development stage, especially if new indicators are required. However, once the methods have been developed, reproducing report card grades from year-to-year should become much easier.

Report cards are based on indicators and indices

The most appropriate approach to ensure a meaningful and defendable product is to base the grades that represent the level of ecosystem health on peer-reviewed indicators and indices. The data and methods underlying report cards need to be scientifically defendable and transparent, especially if the results are to influence management and policy decisions. Although a report card that is not based on defendable science can be a useful tool to increase public awareness, this comes at a risk of losing credibility if the grades do not match reality.

Selecting indicators

The process of selecting indicators for your monitoring and assessment program is covered in detail in Chapter 5. Other factors to consider when selecting indicators for a report card include the following:

- Is there an appropriate suite of indicators to include in the report card? Do the indicators available provide an adequate representation of ecosystem health, and are they relevant to the management of the system of interest? If some of the indicators have overlapping representation as a health metric, then one or more of these indicators may need to be omitted.
- Do the data supporting the indicators have an appropriate spatial density for each of the reporting regions? This is discussed in more detail later in this chapter.
- Are the data supporting the indicator available on a time frame that allows for proper analysis, and does their availability coincide with the scheduled release date of the report card? For example, sample processing for some indicators can take months, and such indicators may only be available after the scheduled release date.
- What is the appropriate number of indicators to include in an overarching index? This is important because too many indicators may be difficult to communicate and will confuse the intended audience, whereas too few may not give an accurate health assessment.

It is important to recognize that the audience

indicators need to be developed. Targets (e.g., management goals or ecological thresholds) and the most appropriate methods of assessing progress toward the targets need to be developed and evaluated for each indicator.

3) Integrating indicators into an overarching index—This step requires developing a method for integrating all the individual indicators used in the report card into a single index value.

4) Maximizing the effectiveness of a report card—This step ensures that the report card is available to all stakeholders and, therefore, that the appropriate products and materials are provided for this purpose. This is done through a communication strategy (see Chapter 4).

As with any new product, there can be a considerable investment of time and effort during

Building community knowledge

will seek varying levels of detail from the report card. Most of the audience will only seek the report card grades but others (e.g., scientists, managers) may want to evaluate the supporting indicators and data that allow them to identify causality or an effective remedial action. To satisfy this requirement, a hierarchy of indicators and data that readily enable the user to access the level of information needed should be produced. For example, a hierarchical approach has been used for the Chesapeake Bay and is being developed for the Great Barrier Reef (GBR) report card (Figure 6.4).

After determining the most appropriate suite of indicators for the report card, it is quite feasible that developing and sustaining the desired indicators will not match the current resources and time frames. When this occurs, the pros and cons of using what is immediately available versus the consequences of

Recipe for success

- Ensure that managers and scientists are aware of the benefits of producing a report card and keep repeating the message if necessary
- Use a geographically detailed approach
- Use targets that are appropriate for measuring progress this is time-consuming but critical
- Keep methods as simple as possible
- Use peer-reviewed and scientifically defendable methods
- Make improvements each year
- Release report card in a timely fashion
- Maintain a unified message with relevant agencies during media release
- Use various communication products to target different audiences

not releasing a report card until the desired indicators are available need to be evaluated.

Selecting reporting regions

One of the first tasks in developing a report card is defining the geographic boundaries (i.e., reporting regions) for the report card scores. Defining the reporting regions at the start of the process is necessary because it will help you to determine what indicators can be included. For example, you must ensure that there are a sufficient number of sampling sites in a reporting region to provide a representative and accurate score for that region (Figure 6.5). Although there are no specific rules to follow when defining the boundaries, here we present a few recommendations that you may want to consider.

First, it is important to decide on an appropriate number of reporting regions.

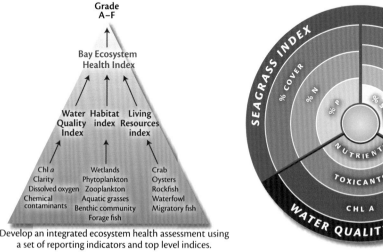

Develop an integrated ecosystem health assessment using a set of reporting indicators and top level indices.

Figure 6.4. Examples of how indicators and index frameworks are presented for the Chesapeake Bay report card (left) and a report card under development for the GBR, Australia (right). The framework shows how indicators and indices are grouped and ordered into a heirachy based on level of integration. For more details, see Chapter 5. Source: Chesapeake Bay Program, Great Barrier Reef Marine Park Authority

Water quality parameters (chlorophyll *a*, dissolved oxygen, and Secchi depth)   Benthic Index of Biotic Integrity (BIBI)   Phytoplankton Index of Biotic Integrity (PIBI)

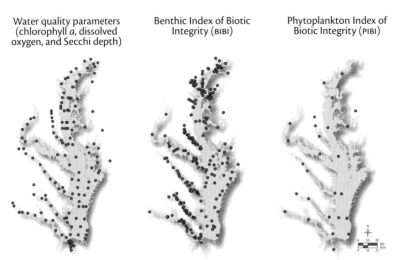

Figure 6.5. Spatial densities of sampling sites will inevitably differ among indicators. In this example from Chesapeake Bay, there were relatively few sample stations for the Phytoplankton Index of Biotic Integrity, but because of the high temporal sampling frequency (12 times during the summer and fall) and the fact that most reporting regions had at least one site, it was considered suitable for inclusion in the report card. Source: Chesapeake Bay Program.

Too many regions may overload the audience with a level of detail that they cannot easily assimilate, whereas too few may not provide the geographic detail needed to best inform the audience. The audience of a geographically detailed (i.e., spatially explicit) report card wants to know what is happening locally (i.e., What's in my own backyard?) and how this compares to other locations (i.e., How does my backyard compare to others?). Therefore, the regions should be detailed enough to allow people to make such comparisons.

Second, you may consider aligning the reporting regions with existing management or political boundaries. For example, if restoration efforts are managed in defined regions, it would be best to align the regions so that the report card can be a means of tracking and reporting on the effectiveness of the restoration efforts.

Finally, the reporting regions may be aligned with geographic features such as watersheds or the extent of an estuary or bay (Figure 6.6), and it would be advantageous if these correspond with the boundaries for restoration efforts. If divisions within the broader features are required, they may be based on features such as salinity, water depth, or residence time.

Combining indicators with different spatial scales and temporal frequencies

It is increasingly recognized that monitoring data collected for specific purposes, such as assessing the implementation of environmental regulations, often does not allow for regional assessments of ecosystem condition.[4,5] The main reason for this is the challenge of integrating data with different spatial and temporal scales into a unified reporting framework.[6] There are two aspects to

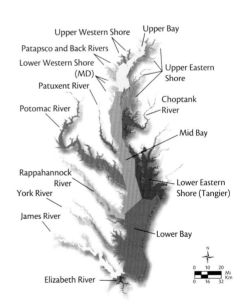

Figure 6.6. Areas being assessed with a report card should be divided into smaller reporting regions if possible. For example, Chesapeake Bay is subdivided into 15 regions, allowing major tributaries and sections of the bay to be compared.[2]

Building community knowledge

this challenge, one is the inherent scale associated with our understanding of the relevant ecological processes, and the second is the spatial and temporal density of collected data (Figure 6.7a).[7]

The National Park Service's Inventory and Monitoring Program has developed an indicator framework that is instructive in considering inherent spatial and temporal scales of monitoring indicators (Figure 6.7a).[6] For example, air quality indicators such as ozone have patterns at watershed or regional scales (km^2 to 1,000s of km^2), and depending on concentration, ozone can have ecosystem impacts on mammals and plants within weeks, days, or even hours.[8,9] Water quality patterns are relevant from the stream scale (meters) to the watershed scale (100s of km) and can vary daily due to point source inputs of nutrients, seasonally with winter addition of road salt, and decadally with watershed urbanization.[10] The challenge is to find ways to synthesize data at different spatial scales and temporal frequencies that provide information at these vastly different scales and to produce an integrated assessment of ecosystem condition.

When data are available for either very small or very large spatial scales, integration requires either aggregation of data or use of synthetic metrics, respectively (Figure 6.7b). Water quality measures often provide highly localized information and are relatively easy (and cheap) to collect. In this case, an aggregated index of overall water quality is often an appropriate way to simplify these data and allow for broader comparison (either over time or between different locations).[2,11] In contrast,

measures such as impervious surface are most meaningfully calculated at a large scale and can be costly and time consuming to collect. However, such indicators provide important information about multiple potential changes to an ecosystem[12] and so can be used directly in an integrated assessment of ecosystem condition. Slightly different solutions are required to allow integration of indicators collected at different temporal scales (Figure 6.7b).

Some indicators change very quickly, and data are collected at very high frequency (sometimes every minute or even every second), whereas others change very slowly and are generally only measured every year or every decade. Integrating these different types of data requires consideration of both the mean and the variance of the data (Figure 6.7b). Interpreting data measured at high frequency can be challenging, requiring careful assessment to determine long-term trends. For example, the three-year mean of the fourth-highest daily maximum, eight-hour mean concentration has been determined to be a reliable measure for ozone.[13] For indicators related to long-term trends, measures of central tendency are often suitable; long-term monitoring of land cover changes often relies on key spatial pattern indices.[14]

By recognizing what information is provided by different indicators and, specifically, the relevant spatial and temporal scales to interpret individual measurements, straightforward approaches can be used to successfully integrate them into an overall assessment of natural resource condition.

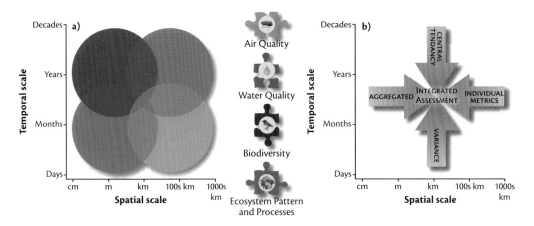

Figure 6.7. Diagram of the multiple spatial and temporal scales relevant to a) interpreting different data metrics and b) synthesizing these different data types.

Developing indicators

Once you have established what indicators the assessment program will use and resolved spatial and temporal issues, you will need to establish targets, develop thresholds, and assess progress toward the target.

Establishing targets

Establishing targets for each indicator can be done by developing thresholds or using management goals as well as other methods. A threshold ideally indicates a tipping point where current knowledge predicts an abrupt change in an aspect or some aspects of ecosystem condition (Figure 6.9). Thus, from the perspective of choosing meaningful, health-related thresholds, this must be the point beyond which prolonged exposure to unhealthful conditions actually elicits a negative response. For example, prolonged exposure to dissolved oxygen concentrations below criteria thresholds elicits a negative response in aquatic systems by either compromising the biotic functions of an organism (e.g., as reducing reproductive efficiency) or causing death.

More generally, however, thresholds represent an agreed-on value or range indicating that an ecosystem is moving away from a desired state and toward an undesirable ecosystem endpoint.[15] Recognizing that many managed ecosystems have multiple and broad-scale stressors, another perspective is to define a threshold as representing the level of impairment that an environment can sustain before resulting in significant (or perhaps irreversible) damage.[16]

When selecting thresholds, it is important to recognize that there are many already available, and more than likely, there are thresholds available for the indicator you choose. A good place to start looking for existing thresholds and goals is in other report card methods or scientific reports and publications. The main point is to avoid spending a great deal of time creating meaningful thresholds when they may already exist in a manner where they could be adapted to your particular indicator and ecosystem.

One way to develop threshold values is to relate them to management goals, and these goals can be used to guide the selection of appropriate indicators. Even with the definition of agreed-on thresholds, there is still the question of how best to use these threshold values in a management

Measuring and evaluating efforts to restore Chesapeake Bay

Martin O'Malley, Maryland governor

www.gov.state.md.us

In 2007, the O'Malley administration created a program called BayStat to help restore the health of Chesapeake Bay.[17] BayStat, a new initiative based on the CitiStat program O'Malley implemented as Mayor of Baltimore City, gathers information from an array of performance indicators on the health of the bay, sources of the problems, and restoration solutions. As an overall measure of success, BayStat adopted the Chesapeake Bay report card to provide a timely, transparent, and geographically detailed annual assessment of ecosystem health.[17]

The BayStat process requires agency (e.g., Department of Natural Resources) and university representatives to attend BayStat meetings every two to four weeks with Governor O'Malley. Each agency is required to provide an analysis of key indicators two weeks before each meeting. Analysis is conducted using standard data software (e.g., Microsoft and Excel) to facilitate compatibility among individuals and agencies. During the meetings, strategies are developed, managers are held accountable, and results are measured. In O'Malley's words, BayStat "puts a face on the problem."

www.baystat.maryland.gov

Main page of BayStat website.[17]

a) **Direct measurement of biological impacts**
(e.g., dose–response curves)

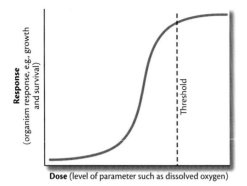

Threshold values based on direct impacts of an environmental parameter on a target organism.

b) **Comparison to reference conditions**
(e.g., least impaired or historic conditions)

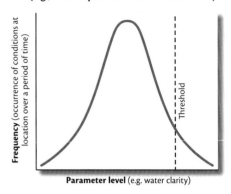

Based on the premise that some small departure from a reference or least-impaired condition is acceptable. Requires a good knowledge of reference conditions and implications of the extent of an acceptable departure.

Figure 6.9. There are multiple approaches to establishing ecological thresholds. Two common examples are a) measuring the biological response to given conditions, whereby the threshold is set at a level where conditions below the threshold will lead to a negative response and b) comparison to reference conditions whereby the target is set based on a knowledge of either historical conditions or conditions at a less affected area.

context.[18] Recognizing this challenge, thresholds can still be effectively used to track ecosystem change and define achievable management goals.[19] As long as threshold values are clearly defined and justified, they can be updated in the light of new research or management goals and, therefore, can provide an important focus for the discussion and implementation of ecosystem management.[20,21] Alternatively, if stressors are correctly identified and habitats appropriately classified, there should be multiple attributes (indicators) of the biological community that discriminate in predictable and significant ways between the least and most impaired habitat conditions. Reference communities can then be characterized using these data, which in turn can be used to develop threshold values.

Various approaches to developing thresholds

When thresholds are chosen that have a basis in the concept of ecosystem health, then combining the indicators into subindices and ultimately an overarching index will be possible. Otherwise, the

Goals and thresholds

Goals—Stakeholder (e.g., management, community, industry)-derived definition of ecosystem function or service that the restoration program is trying to achieve.

Thresholds—A point that must be exceeded to begin producing a given effect or elicit a response. In ecosystem health terms, this must be the point beyond which conditions elicit a negative, or unhealthy, response.

concept of ecosystem health is compromised by inappropriate thresholds and indices that incorporate unwanted bias.

Various methods of creating multimetric indices are available to scientists, and here we give an example of a health index recently created for Chesapeake Bay.[2] The approach used to create a meaningful Bay Health Index (BHI) was based on the premise that certain thresholds represent conditions that are healthy in the aquatic environment and that exceeding these thresholds means that the system is less able to support living resources. Hence, particular attention was given to the thresholds used for each metric and how the thresholds were derived. Some standardization of the thresholds used for subindices was done so that the overarching index would be most representative of healthy conditions in the bay.

The three indicators used to create a Water Quality Index (WQI) for the BHI were chlorophyll *a*, dissolved oxygen, and water clarity (i.e., Secchi depth). The thresholds for chlorophyll *a*, dissolved oxygen concentrations, and Secchi depth were derived from the reference community, threshold criteria, and relative status values, respectively, all of which are available in scientific reports and publications. A reference community method was used to determine chlorophyll *a* thresholds for Chesapeake Bay in various salinity zones using a calibration data set.[22] Reference conditions were represented by growth-limiting, or near growth-limiting, concentrations of both dissolved inorganic nitrogen and phosphate and relatively deep Secchi depths. A slightly different approach, the relative status method, was used to determine water clarity characteristics of the least impaired areas of Chesapeake Bay. In this case, scoring criteria were derived from the distribution of Secchi depths from monitoring sites that consistently demonstrated the most desirable depths in each salinity zone (tidal fresh, oligohaline, mesohaline, and polyhaline) by season (March–May used for spring and July–September for summer). All data from these sites were then used to determine quartiles and establish threshold criteria.[23]

As an alternative to developing thresholds using either reference or relative status methods, criteria based on biological impairment thresholds are sometimes available. For instance, dissolved oxygen criteria were developed for various designated uses and seasons in Chesapeake Bay.[24] Designated uses in Chesapeake Bay include open water (above the highest pycnocline), deep water (within the upper and lower boundaries of the pycnocline), and deep channel (below the lowest pycnocline). The dissolved oxygen criteria for these designated uses are meant to protect the living resources that inhabit them over the period from June to September when anoxic and hypoxic conditions in the bay are most severe.

Thresholds may vary both spatially and temporally
As indicated in the previous section, in large systems such as Chesapeake Bay (surface area = 11,470 km²), different thresholds may be necessary to accommodate different salinity regimes, water column depths (i.e., above or below the pycnocline), and seasons (spring vs. summer)

Pitfalls to avoid

- Methods of producing the report card grades are not scientifically defendable or explicit
- Grades driven by politics, not data and science
- Abruptly releasing report card grades to the organizations and people that will most likely be affected
- Waiting too long to release report card as the information can become outdated

(Figure 6.10). Accordingly, how these thresholds are selected will depend on the system and the available research that can be used to define possible thresholds that are meaningful within the context of that particular ecosystem.

Sensitivity analysis
Additional tests can be used to determine whether a particular threshold will yield meaningful differences among sampling stations and reporting regions, which is desirable for a spatially explicit report card. For instance, the sensitivity or responsiveness of all of the metrics and indices used in the Bay Health Index (BHI) was tested to ensure that there was significant discrimination among the results, which in a system such as Chesapeake Bay varies a great deal from year to year because of variations in nutrient loads. In other words, water clarity (i.e., Secchi depth), dissolved oxygen, chlorophyll *a*, and the Phytoplankton Index of Biotic Integrity (PIBI), and to a lesser degree aquatic grasses and the Benthic Index of Biotic Index (BIBI), are very

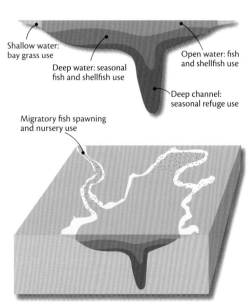

Shallow water: bay grass use

Deep water: seasonal fish and shellfish use

Open water: fish and shellfish use

Deep channel: seasonal refuge use

Migratory fish spawning and nursery use

Figure 6.10. Designated use areas in Chesapeake Bay help to determine the threshold values needed for different indicators.[24]

responsive to interannual changes in nutrient and sediment loading. Accordingly, the sensitivity of the indicators and subindices (i.e., combined indicators) used in the BHI was tested using a snapshot of data from the years representing the extremes in flow to Chesapeake Bay. In this analysis, it was determined that over the period of recorded total annual discharge to Chesapeake Bay (i.e., 1938–present), extreme years representing low and high discharge end members include the years of 2002 and 2003, respectively (Figure 6.11). Nutrient loads in 2002 (dry year) approximated the 175 million- and 12.8 million-pound restoration loading goals (determined by the U.S. Environmental Protection Agency watershed model) of nitrogen and phosphorus, respectively, and, consequently, 2002 was a year of relatively good water quality conditions. In contrast, water quality conditions were generally much worse in 2003 (wet year) because Nitrogen and Phosphorus loads were roughly three and eight times the restoration loading goals, respectively.

Data from the 2002–2003 water years (October–September) were used in the sensitivity analysis in order to help select the thresholds to be used for each parameter of the Water Quality Index (WQI) and thereby improve its sensitivity to different flow and nutrient regimes. Thresholds were chosen if they showed distinct differences between 2002 and 2003, with most of the bay above (dissolved oxygen concentrations and Secchi depths) or below (chlorophyll *a* concentrations) the thresholds over much of the growing season in 2002 (i.e., all metrics had higher frequencies of attainment and therefore better water quality in 2002, as indicated by the WQI in Figure 6.11).

Nevertheless, although this type of sensitivity analysis is useful, it is important to recognize that the threshold values used must be based on the concept of ecological health derived from approaches such as dose-response and reference conditions (Figure 6.9). Indeed, this is the most important criterion for threshold selection (as opposed to thresholds that appear to yield the correct result, best sensitivity, and discriminating power among reporting regions).

Assessing progress toward targets

Multiple approaches can be used to assess compliance of a metric to a chosen threshold. These include simple ones, such as grading on a curve, spatial compliance, and temporal compliance, or more complex approaches, such

as a cumulative frequency distribution that combines temporal and spatial compliances (Figure 6.12). Each approach has specific strengths and weaknesses that have to be considered. For instance, selecting which assessment approach to use will depend on the metrics being used and the extent of spatial and temporal coverage. Multiple approaches can be used for the subindices or metrics within an overarching index but should be standardized as much as possible within a particular subindex. For instance, in the BHI, a frequency analysis (i.e., the number of times a sample value was in a healthy category relative to the threshold represented as a percentage of the total number of samples) was used for the WQI, PIBI, and BIBI. The analysis for aquatic grasses was simply a ratio of total area coverage to its restoration goal coverage (Table 6.1).

Different approaches and analytical techniques can make large differences in the index values and must be evaluated in order to understand these differences and select the most representative analysis.[25] Therefore, when making an overarching index, every attempt to provide consistency and to standardize metrics used will result in a better and more accurate product. For example, during the development of the BHI, the original threshold used for the PIBI was a value of 4.0. Because values for both the PIBI and the BIBI range from 1.0 to 5.0 (the higher the number, the more rigorous the threshold), the PIBI threshold was in obvious contrast to the threshold used for the BIBI (3.0), and subsequent analyses were conducted with the

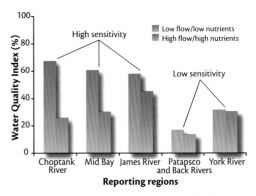

Figure 6.11. Sensitivity of indices can be checked using historical data. In this example, 2002 was a low flow/low nutrients year, and 2003 was a high flow/high nutrients year, allowing for comparisons between extremes. Higher index values indicate better water quality conditions than lower values.

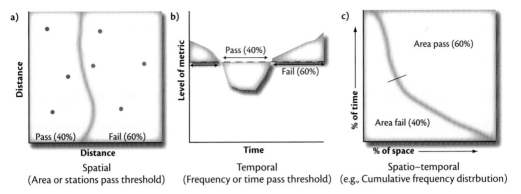

Figure 6.12. Multiple approaches can be used to assess compliance of a metric to a chosen threshold. These include a) determining the area of the water body in compliance (spatial), b) how frequently the parameter complies (temporal), and c) a combination of the two (spatio-temporal).

PIBI data to compare the results using different threshold values. Ultimately, it was determined that using a PIBI threshold of 3.0 improved the representativeness of the results by aligning the distributions of the two indices above and below the threshold value. This change had the added advantage of simultaneously standardizing the methods for these two subindices of the BHI and thereby making the methodology easier to understand and communicate.

Integrating indicators into overarching indices

Overarching indices give a much better integrated assessment (and therefore representative score) of an ecosystem's health than can be achieved using a single metric. These indices comprise multiple metrics that are ranked according to a threshold value and then averaged or, when there is adequate rationale for doing so, weighted differently before combining into one overarching index (Table 6.1).[25] For example, in the development of the BHI, the results from a combination of three metrics or subindices were area-weighted and combined, which in turn were averaged to create one overarching index (Figure 6.13). More specifically, three water quality indicators were ranked and averaged to formulate the water quality subindex, and three biotic metrics were averaged into a biotic subindex. The subindices were subsequently weighted by the surface areas of each reporting region, and the two composite subindices were averaged to calculate the overarching index, or BHI, for each of 15 separate reporting regions.

Table 6.1. Once threshold values are established for each metric, the assessment of those metrics compared to the threshold is performed.

Management objectives	Health indicator	Threshold values	Comparison of data to threshold
Achieve and maintain the water quality necessary to support the aquatic living resources of the Bay and its tributaries and protect human health.	Chlorophyll *a*	≤2.8 to ≤20.9 µg·l⁻¹	
	Dissolved oxygen	≥1.0 to ≥5.0 mg·l⁻¹	= Proportion of region that meets threshold values for each indicator
	Water clarity	≥0.65 to ≥2.0 m	
Preserve, protect, and restore those habitats and natural areas that are vital to the survival and diversity of the living resources of the Bay and its tributaries.	Bay grasses	Area (hectares)	= Area compared to goal
	Bottom dwellers	≥3 BIBI	= Proportion of region that meets threshold values for BIBI and PIBI
	Phytoplankton	≥3 PIBI	

Finding the balance—simple to complex indices

Multimetric health indices have become commonplace in resource and ecosystem management. The majority of these indices focus on stream macroinvertebrates and fish, but more recently, indices such as the BHI for Chesapeake Bay have been developed for estuarine environments using various water quality and biotic parameters. There are many parameters that can be included, and all need to be properly evaluated in terms of what they add to the robustness of the indices. Robustness refers to the ability of the indicator or index to perform well under a range of conditions. Although more simplistic indices may lack relevant parameters or the spatial and temporal resolution that make indices more robust or effective for regional comparisons, very complex indices may have indicators that do not necessarily contribute much to the robustness of the index. Hence, the main objective is to select the appropriate type and number of indicators that, when combined in an index, give a robust and accurate representation of an ecosystem's health and are understandable to the majority of users.

To weight or not to weight

There are advantages and disadvantages of weighting metrics (Table 6.2) that depend on whether you have chosen to use targets or relative ranking as your approach for measuring success or failure. Individual metrics can be weighted equally both within and among indices. However, this can be changed depending on the value of a particular index or perhaps the importance that a particular index brings to the spatially-explicit nature of the overarching index. For example, if the index being used is comprises of a relatively small number of samples, then the index could be weighted less than more robust indices that give better information in terms of regional comparisons. The rationale for the approach used in the creation of the BHI is that each subindex is an accurate representation of the abiotic (i.e., water quality)

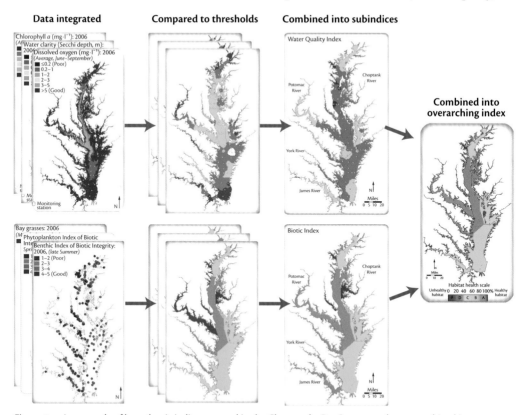

Figure 6.13. An example of how the six indicators used in the Chesapeake Bay Report card were combined into subindices and then the subindices combined into an overarching spatially explicit index.

Table 6.2. Advantages and disadvantages of different weighting methods used to determine index scores.

Approach	Advantages	Disadvantages
Equal weighting (index score is average of all indicators)	• Simple to understand and communicate • Do not have to justify weighting rationale	• Assumes all indicators are of equal importance
Use geometric mean (weight toward lowest score)	• Penalizes more imbalanced scores (i.e., geometric mean considers the evenness between component scores) • The more unbalanced, the lower the score	• More complicated and therefore harder to communicate
Weight according to importance to overall health	• If done correctly, provides a more accurate assessment than equal weighting	• How or what decisions are used to decide weighting dependent on who is present during initial meetings (i.e., bias)
Weight based on uncertainty of indicator score	• Less uncertainty of index scores than other methods	• Varying index scores from year to year according to uncertainty rather than changes in health • No uncertainty assessment for some indicators (e.g., aquatic grasses)
Only count worst score	• Simple to understand and communicate	• Assumes lowest score an accurate representation of ecosystem health • Loss of information if other indicators not included

and biotic conditions (i.e., phytoplankton, benthic organisms, and aquatic grasses) of Chesapeake Bay. Therefore, no one parameter was deemed more important than any other in determining the overarching BHI and equal weighting was the most simplistic and easiest method to communicate.

Testing the robustness of an index

A logical procedure for developing ecological indices includes data collection and synthesis, metric and threshold selection, index scoring, and validation. Typically, validation analysis involves data that were not used in the original calibration data set, or it involves bootstrapping or jackknifing (see Chapter 8 for more information on these techniques) of the validation data set to determine theoretical errors. However, in a looser context, other tests can be used to determine whether the index is measuring what it should be measuring. For instance, using the results of the BHI described previously, analyses of the relationship between the WQI and various configurations of land use and land cover (i.e., developed, agricultural, forest) were conducted to determine whether the index was responding to the nutrient loading (as one would expect because nutrient loading is creating the water quality impairments) in each reporting region

(Figure 6.14). This type of evaluation analysis was done using the WQI data for all reporting regions and by successively removing individual regions to determine the best relationship possible with the total of urban and agricultural land use and land cover in each reporting region. In figure 6.14, which uses 1995 data, the r² improved from 0.64 to 0.86 by removing two of the 15 regions from the relationship. The results of this analysis indicate that the WQI is quite robust as a health indicator (i.e., it is measuring what it should be measuring). By contrast, if the relationships had been very

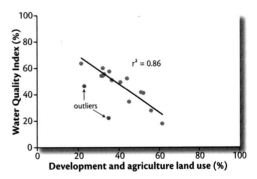

Figure 6.14. The significant relationship between the WQI and land use implies that the method for determining the WQI is sound (i.e., it is measuring what it should be measuring).

weak, then we could have used the results to determine what improvements to the index could be incorporated to strengthen the relationship.

Maximizing report card effectiveness

The high profile and sometimes controversial nature of report cards (especially where poor report card grades are given) necessitates special attention to the communication strategy (Figure 6.15). Your communication strategy (see Chapter 4) needs to consider the main messages that you want the report card to deliver, how to best deliver

the message, and how to reach a broad audience. In terms of report card messaging, the report card provides a great opportunity to communicate aspects, such as the overall health of a region, how one region compares to another, and how health may have changed from one year to another. The report card also provides a vehicle to communicate other related messages such as how much restoration effort is being undertaken or how the audience may help in restoration. Before releasing a report card, it is advisable to brief appropriate people and agencies about what the report card scores will be (with an embargo on their release)

Report cards based on relative ranking

Although calculating report card scores based on attaining targets is the preferred approach, this is not always possible because targets for some or all of the indicators may not be available. Alternatively, the relative ranking method is an approach that you may consider using until targets are available. This approach ranks each region from best to worst health and provides an ordinal grade based on the ranking. The limitation of this approach is that there is no absolute or definable health status in the manner that the target approach provides, although scientific interpretation of the indicator scores can be used to qualitatively discuss the health of each region.

The relative ranking approach was used to summarize the health of the Maryland Coastal Bays. This approach was adopted because targets were not available for many of the indicators used. Accordingly, a two-step process was used to determine the rank and ordinal score of each region. First, each indicator in each region was ranked and given a score based on the ranking. Second, ranking scores for all indicators monitored within a particular region were added together to give an overall ranking score for each reporting region, which was then used to list the regions from best to worst health condition. The results were presented in a color-coded table and map that enabled the audience to not only see the relative ranking of the regions (table), but also where these regions are located (map).[26] More recently, a report card using multiple thresholds was developed.[27]

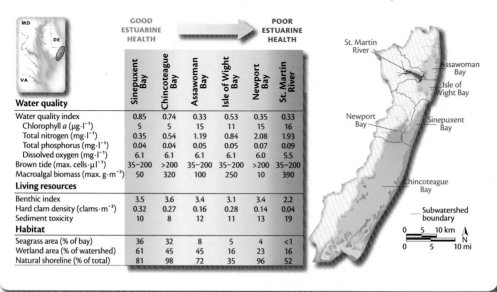

	Sinepuxent Bay	Chincoteague Bay	Assawoman Bay	Isle of Wight Bay	Newport Bay	St. Martin River
Water quality						
Water quality index	0.85	0.74	0.33	0.53	0.35	0.33
Chlorophyll *a* (µg·l⁻¹)	5	5	15	11	15	16
Total nitrogen (mg·l⁻¹)	0.35	0.54	1.19	0.84	2.08	1.93
Total phosphorus (mg·l⁻¹)	0.04	0.04	0.05	0.05	0.07	0.09
Dissolved oxygen (mg·l⁻¹)	6.1	6.1	6.1	6.1	6.0	5.5
Brown tide (max. cells·µl⁻¹)	35–200	>200	35–200	35–200	>200	35–200
Macroalgal biomass (max. g·m⁻²)	50	320	100	250	10	390
Living resources						
Benthic index	3.5	3.6	3.4	3.1	3.4	2.2
Hard clam density (clams·m⁻²)	0.32	0.27	0.16	0.28	0.14	0.04
Sediment toxicity	10	8	12	11	13	19
Habitat						
Seagrass area (% of bay)	36	32	8	5	4	<1
Wetland area (% of watershed)	61	45	45	16	23	16
Natural shoreline (% of total)	81	98	72	35	96	52

Figure 6.15. Report cards can generate media attention, getting the overall message to the public and highlighting issues of concern.

so that they have the opportunity to prepare appropriate responses. Working with people is far more productive than being provocative and uncooperative.

The impact of the report card, in terms of messaging and audience reached, will largely depend on how you interact with and use the news media (discussed in more detail in Chapter 4). Media events where reporters are invited to attend a briefing and record the unveiling of a report card (especially if the venue itself pertains to the report card) are particularly good at increasing exposure. A well-organized media event provides the opportunity to quickly and coherently get your messages across, while providing the media an opportunity to ask questions, conduct interviews, and get any visuals they may need for their story (e.g., photos of the waterway). Irrespective of whether you conduct a media briefing, it is still important to provide a press release, interviews, and answers to any questions the media may have.

Finally, your communication strategy needs to consider the types of products needed to reach the varying audiences. Although the report card is an effective means of getting a complex message out to a broad audience, the printed product is somewhat simple and needs to be supported by technical documents, newsletters, and website material. These documents need to provide a detailed account of the data and methods used, individual indicator scores, and interpretations and stories that explain what is being observed and why.

Ongoing development of robustness and improvement

Report card methods need improvement year after year. In the same manner that natural resource managers need to adapt monitoring efforts to changing requirements and scientific understanding, a report card should be continually improved and adapted as methods are enhanced, indicators are changed, and the monitoring program evolves. This approach is often counterintuitive for a high-profile product such as a report card where there are compelling reasons for the methods to be finalized before the report card is released, with little regard to when the product may be available (and thereby resulting in protracted delays). The challenge is finding the point at which the methods are rigorous and defensible enough to proceed with the release of the report card, while recognizing that the methods can be improved over time.

From a communications standpoint, this approach is beneficial because the product is available on a timely basis. However, it does introduce the challenge of explaining what effect, if any, method changes may have on interannual changes in the index score (see sidebar). Although the aim is to keep changes of report card methods to a minimum, cases will arise where it is necessary to make such changes.

The concept of constantly improving the report card pertains not only to the methods, but also to the manner in which the report card is communicated and promoted. The people responsible for releasing the report card need to continually seek better ways of presenting the content, engaging the news media, and expanding into new regions. The report card from Queensland, Australia, provides an overview

Addressing change in report card methods

- Be explicit that a grade change is due to changes in methods and not due to changes in the ecosystem's health.
- Provide details as to why the changes were made—at an appropriate location, such as a website.
- Conduct a retrospective analysis of previous year grades using the new methods such that the new grades can be put into historical perspective.

Building community knowledge

93

1998–1999

The report card grades are presented at a symposium (no physical report card). The grades are based on expert interpretation of monitoring results and the geographic coverage was limited to Moreton Bay and surrounding estuaries only.

2000

The first physical report card was produced and released to the public. A numerical ranking system was used, based on the ecological significance of the parameters. A broad diversity of ecosystem health indicators were included. The geographic cover was still limited to Moreton Bay region (20 grades provided for 20 regions identified). A media release took place, including local government officials (~eight local governments involved) and other stakeholders.

2001–2002

Major revisions to evaluation methods occurred, including a spatially explicit ecosystem health index approach, which was developed based on a select group of indicators. Boundaries of reporting regions were identified and based on residence time and water depth. Thirty-three grades were provided for the 33 regions identified and 20 local governments were involved. The report card included evaluation of management actions and expanded into northern regions and watersheds.

2003–2004

Changes to the report card grading methods were minimal. Reporting expanded into southern regions. Forty-five grades were provided for the 45 regions identified and approximately 20 local governments were involved. Changes largely focused on improving communication, including layout and presentation of the report card, and increasing media coverage (multiple, co-occurring media events—one in each major region).

2005–present

Minor refinement to methods continue to occur, including development of a biological health rating index. Presentation of the report card continues to improve, including the production of sub-region report cards and methods summary page.

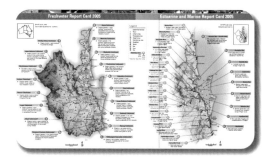

Figure 6.16. This figure shows the progression of an ecosystem health report card for the waterways of South East Queensland, Australia. Source: SEQ Healthy Waterways Partnership.

of how a report card evolved over an eight-year period (Figure 6.16).

In summary, report cards are a useful tool for any coastal assessment program, and the basic steps needed to create an effective, integrated report card include the following:

- Use a set of relevant and meaningful indicators and subindices that have sufficient spatial representation and ecosystem health-related thresholds.
- Create a ranking valuation scheme that employs a rigorous methodology and scientific analyses that allow for spatial (i.e., spatially explicit maps) and temporal (i.e., time series) comparisons and drill down capabilities (i.e., data transparency).
- Use evaluation and validation procedures to determine the robustness of your subindices and overarching health index.
- Implement an effective communication strategy that includes an annual reporting cycle with various communication products.

Chapters 5 and 6 provided methods of assessing past conditions. Chapter 7 the following chapter discusses how forecasting future conditions can be a major benefit to a coastal assessment program.

References

1. Bricker S, Longstaff B, Dennison W, Jones A, Boicourt K, Wicks C, Woerner J (2007) Effects of nutrient enrichment in the nation's estuaries: A decade of change. NOAA National Centers for Coastal Ocean Science Coastal Ocean Program Decision Analysis Series No. 26, Silver Spring, Maryland
2. Williams M, Longstaff B, Llansó R, Buchanan C, Dennison W (2009) Development and evaluation of a spatially-explicit index of Chesapeake Bay health. Mar Pollut Bull 59:14-25
3. Chester River Association, EcoCheck (2008) 2007 Chester River report card. Chester River Association, Chestertown, Maryland
4. U.S. Environmental Protection Agency (2000) Mid-Atlantic highland streams assessment. U.S. Environmental Protection Agency Region 3 EPA-903-R-00-015, Philadelphia, Pennsylvania
5. U.S. Environmental Protection Agency (2002) A framework for assessing and reporting on ecological condition: An SAB report. U.S. Environmental Protection Agency, Science Advisory Board EPA-EPEC-02-009, Washington, District of Columbia
6. Fancy SG, Gross JE, Carter SL (2008) Monitoring the condition of natural resources in US national parks. Environmental Monitoring and Assessment: Electronically published May 29, 2008.
7. Petersen JE, Kennedy VS, Dennison WC, Kemp WM (2009) Enclosed experimental ecosystems and scale: Tools for understanding and managing coastal ecosystems. Springer, New York, New York
8. McKee DJ, Atwell VV, Richmond HM, Freas WP, Rodriguez RM (1996) Review of national ambient air quality standards for ozone, assessment of scientific and technical information.

U.S Environmental Protection Office Air Quality Plan Standards Staff Paper EPA-452-R-96-007, Research Triangle Park, North Carolina
9. Kline LJ, Davis DD, Skelly JM, Savage JE, Ferdinand J (2008) Ozone sensitivity of 28 plant selections exposed to ozone under controlled conditions. Northwest Natur 15:57-66
10. Carruthers T, Carter S, Florkowski L, Runde J, Dennison W (2009) Rock Creek natural resource condition assessment, National Capital Region Network. National Park Service Natural Resource Report NPS-NCRN-NRR–2009-109. Fort Collins, Colorado
11. Wazniak CE, Hall MR, Carruthers TJB, Sturgis B, Dennison WC, Orth RJ (2007) Linking water quality to living resources in a mid-Atlantic lagoon system, USA. Ecol App 17:S64-S78
12. Lussier SM, da Silva SN, Charpentier M, Heltshe JF, Cormier SM, Klemm DJ, Chintala M, Jayaraman S (2008) The influence of suburban land use on habitat and biotic integrity of coastal Rhode Island streams. Environ Monit Assess 139:119-136
13. U.S. Environmental Protection Agency (2004) The Clean Air Act. U.S. Environmental Protection Agency, Washington, District of Columbia. http://epw.senate.gov/envlaws/cleanair.pdf
14. Townsend PA, Lookingbill TR, Kingdon CC, Gardner RH (In prep) Spatial pattern analysis for monitoring protected areas.
15. Bennetts RE, Gross JE, Cahill K, McIntyre C, Bingham BB, Hubbard A, Cameron L, Carter SL (2007) Linking monitoring to management and planning: assessment points as a generalized approach. The George Wright Forum 24(2):59-79
16. Hendricks J, Little J (2003) Thresholds for regional vulnerability analysis. Regional vulnerability assessment program. U.S. Environmental Protection Agency National Exposure Research Laboratory E243-05. www.nrac.wvu.edu/classes/resm493Q/files/final_stressor_threshold_table.pdf
17. Office of the Governor (2009) BayStat. Accessed 21 Jul. http://baystat.maryland.gov
18. Groffman PM, Baron JS, Blett T, Gold AJ, Goodman I, Gunderson LH, Levinson BM, Palmer MA, Paerl HW, Peterson GD, Poff NL, Rejeski DW, Reynolds JF, Turner MG, Weathers KC, Wiens J (2006) Ecological thresholds: The key to successful environmental management or an important concept with no practical application? Ecosystems 9:1-13
19. Biggs HC (2004) Promoting ecological research in national parks—a South African perspective. Ecol App 14:21-24
20. Jensen ME, Reynolds K, Andreasen J, Goodman IA (2000) A knowledge based approach to the assessment of watershed condition. Environ Monit Assess 64:271-283
21. Pantus FJ, Dennison WC (2005) Quantifying and evaluating ecosystem health: A case study from Moreton Bay, Australia. Enviro Manage 36:757-771
22. Lacouture RV, Johnson JM, Buchanan C, Marshall HG (2006) Phytoplankton Index of Biotic Integrity for Chesapeake Bay and its tidal tributaries. Estuaries Coasts 29:598-616
23. Buchanan C, Lacouture RV, Marshall HG, Olson M, Johnson J (2005) Phytoplankton reference communities for Chesapeake Bay and its tidal tributaries. Estuaries 28:138–159
24. U.S. Environmental Protection Agency (2003) Ambient water quality criteria for dissolved oxygen, water clarity and chlorophyll a for Chesapeake Bay and tidal tributaries. U.S. Environmental Protection Agency Office of Water EPA-903-R-03-002. Washington, District of Columbia

Building community knowledge

25. Lookingbill TR, Tellel SM, Schmit JP, Hilderbrand RH (in review) Synthesizing monitoring data for integrative assessment of protected areas. Ecol App

26. Wazniak C, Hall M, Cain C, Wilson D, Jesien R, Thomas J, Carruthers T, Dennison W (2004) State of the Maryland Coastal Bays. MD Dept Nat Res, MD Coast Bays Prog, Univ MD Ctr Env Sci, Maryland

27. EcoCheck (2009) 2008 Coastal Bays report card. Accessed 21 Jul. www.eco-check.org/reportcards/mcb/2009/

Further reading

Dennison WC, Abal EG (1999) Moreton Bay Study: A Scientific Basis for the Healthy Waterways Campaign. SE Queensland Water Quality Strategy, Brisbane.

EcoCheck (2009) National Oceanic and Atmospheric Administration and University of Maryland Center for Environmental Science. http://www.eco-check.org/

Ecosystem Health Monitoring Program (2009) http://www.ehmp.org

Helsinki Commission (2006) Development of tools for assessment of eutrophication in the Baltic Sea. Balt Sea Environ Proc No. 104. Helsinki, Finland. http://helcom.navigo.fi/stc/files/Publications/Proceedings/bsep104.pdf

University of California (2008) Institute of the Environment report card. UCLA College of Letters Sci Instit Env. http://www.ioe.ucla.edu/report-card-06.html

Gippsland Integrated Natural Resources Forum (2009) Report cards. Gippsland Integrated Nat Res Forum. http://www.ginrf.org.au/reportcard/list.asp

CHAPTER 7: ECOLOGICAL FORECASTS

BUILDING A PREDICTIVE CAPACITY TO GUIDE MANAGEMENT

David Jasinski, Ben J. Longstaff, and E. Caroline Wicks

If you can look into the seeds of time, and say which grain will grow and which will not, speak then to me.
—William Shakespeare, *MacBeth*

This chapter provides an overview of the process of developing, producing, and releasing an ecological forecast, which is supported by statistical analysis and models that underpin forecasts (see Chapters 8 and 9). Areas discussed in this chapter include why you may consider conducting ecological forecasting, some of the essential elements of a forecasting program, and some of the challenges you may face. Forecasting dissolved oxygen conditions in Chesapeake Bay, which aims to pull together all the essential elements of an effective forecasting program, is used as a case study. Ecological forecasting in this chapter is addressed as an operational component of ecosystem management and not as an exercise in analysis and modeling.

Ecological forecasting within a management framework

Analogous to weather forecasts, ecological forecasts predict and communicate future ecosystem traits in a manner that aims to inform the broader community, including scientists and resource managers. Like weather forecasts, ecological forecasts do not guarantee what is to come but offer scientifically sound estimations of what is likely to occur (Figure 7.1).

Ecological forecasting uses the detailed understanding of ecosystem processes, coupled with monitoring data, to develop quantitative models. These models are then used to forecast and communicate future ecological conditions. As you can see from this definition, ecological forecasting is a broad discipline, not only spanning across fields such as monitoring, modeling, management, and communication, but also across the various components of the ecosystem—physical, chemical, and biological. Ecological forecasting is considered to be a new and emerging discipline, particularly within coastal sciences. It is also expected that ecological forecasting will play a more important role in ecosystem management

Hydrometeorological Prediction Center

Figure 7.1. Ecological forecasting, like weather forecasts, aim to predict future condition. These forecasts do not guarantee what will occur but provide the best scientific estimate based on the most suitable models.

Definitions of ecological forecasting

"Ecological forecasts predict the impact of physical, chemical, biological, and human-induced change on ecosystems and their components."[1]

"... the process of predicting the state of the ecosystem services and natural capital, with fully specified uncertainties..."[2]

and policy decisions in the future.[2] In fact, the interaction between the scientific and management communities during the development and production of forecasts is one of the main reasons for undertaking ecological forecasting. By setting up a framework for communication between the scientists, who provide information, and managers, who apply it, the stage is set for a more functional assessment program.

Forecasting allows scientists to demonstrate an understanding of how an ecosystem operates, particularly in relation to variables that are of interest to managers. The entire forecasting effort can inform management, further justifying the sources and expense, beyond that for typical applications such as production of indicators because forecasting requires scientists to continuously evaluate the data.

Therefore, ecological forecasting is a relatively new discipline; there are few examples of operational forecast programs (i.e., those directly associated with decision-making) from which to assess successes and failures and the overall effect on improving the restoration and protection of

Forecasting uses prediction models

Prediction models can be used in one of two ways. The first is to predict a future condition of the system based on the current state of the system. The second is to predict the future condition of a system assuming changes in the management of that system. The latter is a scenario model and can be used to assess the potential effectiveness of various management activities when developing management plans. Scenario models gain more credibility from consistent, effective short-term forecasts (see Chapter 9).

coastal ecosystems. However, there are numerous initiatives currently under development that may rapidly change this situation, such as now-casting of sea nettles in Chesapeake Bay, forecasting the size of the summer hypoxic zone in the Gulf of Mexico (Figure 7.2), and forecasting impacts on shorebird habitat due to global climate change.[3] Interest in applying scientific knowledge of how natural systems work coupled with extensive data sets to develop tools to help us peer into the distant and not-so-distant future is increasing.

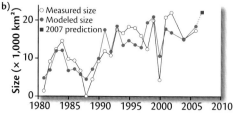

Figure 7.2. a) Illustration of watershed and hypoxic area. Summer hypoxia in the Gulf of Mexico is forecast using historical data. b) The hypoxia forecast for 2007 was 22,118 km², and the actual size was 20,461 km².[4]

Is forecasting for you?

Here we determine whether sufficient resources are available to conduct a forecasting effort and discuss benefits and uses of such a program. Based on this, you can determine whether an ecological forecasting effort fits within the needs of your coastal assessment program.

Considerations before starting ecological forecasting

Before committing to ecological forecasting, it is important to thoroughly assess the advantage of forecasting against other competing program needs. Forecasting does not necessarily need significant resources, but how much depends on a number of factors, such as the availability and status of a forecast model, whether additional data or information are needed, and the associated communication strategy. If a model is available, only minimal funds may be needed to populate and run the model when a forecast is required. On the other hand, if no model exists, it may be an expensive and time-consuming exercise to produce a working model. Model development can involve a significant analysis effort, which includes a lot of trial and error to achieve a model that yields satisfactory results. If data and information are needed to update or improve the model, additional collection may lead to significant resource (money and personnel) requirements. Communication of the forecast to stakeholders is a key factor in ecosystem assessment. The consideration of how you will communicate it, what materials will be produced (websites, bulletins, newsletters, etc.), and ancillary costs, such as printing, need to be addressed.

Reasons to make ecological forecasts

There are many potential benefits to ecological forecasting, ranging from informing management decisions to improving communication and outreach. One of the more common applications of ecological forecasting is providing early warning of events such as harmful algal blooms (HABs; Figure 7.3). Generally, for the purposes of forecasting, events are significant incidents of a relatively short-term nature that potentially have serious ecological consequences. If an event can be predicted, managers may be in a position to reduce economic impacts by warning the community of the impending event and therefore mitigating its impact. For example, in the Gulf of Mexico, the National Oceanic and Atmospheric Administration forecasts the location and intensity of red tide (a species of algae) blooms and the potential impacts on humans, marine mammals, and fish. This information is provided to natural resource managers in a bulletin, which is updated twice a week during the HAB season.[5] A red tide forecast model accurately describes the mechanisms behind red tide blooms in the South China Sea near Kat O, Hong Kong.[6] The researchers propose that this model can be used to warn fish farmers of potential blooms. The model has a lead time of three days, which would allow managers sufficient time to warn fish farmers of an impending bloom. Farmers, in turn, could then move potentially affected fish pens or adjust harvest times, if feasible. In this way forecasts can avert or lessen ecological and/or economic impacts.

Why forecast?

- Aid management decisions—where, when, and how to take action
- Provide an early warning system
- Foster interaction at the science–policy interface
- Help to set research agendas by improving understanding of the system
- Benefit communication programs—shift from reactive to proactive communication
- Benefit education by explaining cause-and-effect relationships

Ecological forecasts also have the potential to guide restoration, such as where and when to undertake a particular restoration activity. For example, in the Chesapeake Bay region, scientists are developing models to forecast changes in aquatic grass distribution over the summer. If an accurate model is developed, it could be used to determine the best locations and times for planting aquatic grasses for maximum survival potential. Scenario modeling exercises also benefit from accurate ecological forecasts. Effective implementation of ecological forecasts adds credibility to scenario models because scenario models within a given system are generally based on the same relationships as ecological forecasts.[7]

An important reason for undertaking ecological

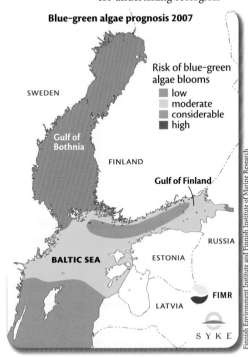

Figure 7.3. Forecasts act as an early warning system that can directly aid managers and stakeholders.

forecasting is to foster information exchange and interaction at the science–management interface. The process of developing forecast models, producing a forecast, and acting on the forecast can significantly improve communication between scientists and resource managers. Meetings and workshops should be held with all partners to work through important issues, such as the most important aspects of the ecosystem to aim to forecast, the appropriate spatial and temporal scales, and the levels of uncertainty acceptable for the intended purpose. This interaction aids in problem solving; setting research agendas; and identifying modeling, management, and monitoring priorities.[3]

Ecological forecasts also significantly benefit communication and outreach programs. By producing and publicizing a forecast, a communication program can change from being reactive (explaining why an event happened) to proactive (explaining why an event is likely to happen; Figure 7.4). This has numerous benefits, such as keeping the message focused, keeping management and target audiences engaged, and broadening the audience (Figure 7.5). As discussed at the end of this chapter, the Chesapeake Bay Program redesigned its communication strategy to incorporate forecasting of dissolved oxygen levels. By communicating the predicted summer dissolved oxygen condition, the Chesapeake Bay Program was able to explain not only why the

Caroline Wicks

Figure 7.5. Ecological forecasting, and the in-class exercises that demonstrate it, were taught to environmental educators in the Chesapeake Bay area.

conditions are expected to occur, but also what is being done to improve future conditions. In terms of educational purposes, forecasts can be useful to explain cause-and-effect relationships; provide context for understanding and explaining observed conditions; and explain gaps in knowledge and what is being done to reduce those gaps when the forecasts are incorrect.

Bringing together research, management, and communication

There are three main elements to an effective forecasting effort:

1) an engaged scientific community with access to data and resources to develop forecast models;

2) a management community with a strategy for restoration and protection efforts that includes the ability to act on ecological forecasts; and

3) a communications and outreach program that engages not only the scientific and management communities, but also the broader interested public (Figure 7.6).

Without every one of these components and open communication and feedback between individuals and agencies within these components the full potential of a forecasting program cannot be reached.

The role of research in an ecological forecasting program is based on three specific components: 1) understanding of ecosystem processes; 2) data

---

BAY JOURNAL • JUNE 2007

Average 'dead zone' predicted for this summer

Scientists predict the Bay's oxygen-depleted "dead zone" will be almost exactly average in size this year.

In their third annual forecast, they predict that from June through September, an average of 1.39 cubic kilometers—or 2.6 percent of the Bay's mainstem, will be anoxic—essentially having no oxygen. That makes it off-limits to almost all Bay creatures.

If that prediction holds up, 2007 would rank 11th when compared with the previous 22 summers, according to Dave Jasinski, a University of Maryland Center for Environmental Science analyst.

That would be worse than last summer when, on average, the amount of anoxic water in the Bay was 0.93 cubic kilometers, or 1.79 percent of the Bay's total volume. Last year was the seventh best year since Baywide water quality monitoring began in 1985.

But it would be a significant improvement from 2005, which was the fifth worst summer on record, when anoxic water covered 2.35 cubic kilometers along the bottom of the Chesapeake from the Bay Bridge to the Patuxent River.

The anoxia forecast is based on the historic relationship between spring flows from the Susquehanna River, nutrient loads from the upper Bay and the amount of anoxic water in the Bay.

Susquehanna river flows help to create a barrier, known as the pycnocline, between fresh water on the surface and salty ocean water on the bottom of the Bay. The nutrients fuel the growth of algae, much of which die and sink to the bottom where they are consumed by bacteria, which in turn use up oxygen. The pycnocline helps to prevent the bottom water from mixing with oxygen-rich water near the surface.

LOW DISSOLVED OXYGEN & BAY CREATURES

Bay scientists generally agree that dissolved oxygen concentrations of 5.0 milligrams per liter of water will allow the Bay's aquatic creatures to thrive. But dissolved oxygen needs vary from species to species. This table shows the oxygen levels needed for some of the Bay's most widely recognized species.

As concentrations fall below 5.0 mg/l, the situation becomes increasingly stressful to many of the Bay's inhabitants. Although some are more tolerant of low dissolved oxygen than others, concentrations can fall to the point where no animals can survive in some parts of the Bay. When the levels drop below 2.0 mg/l, that water is said to be "severely hypoxic," and when it drops below 0.2 mg/l that water is considered "anoxic."

STRIPED BASS: 5–6 mg/l   AMERICAN SHAD: 5 mg/l

MINIMUM OXYGEN REQUIREMENTS FOR KEY BAY SPECIES

YELLOW PERCH: 5 mg/l	HARD CLAM: 5 mg/l
BLUE CRAB: 3 mg/l	BAY ANCHOVY: 3 mg/l
SPOT: 2 mg/l	WORMS: 1 mg/l

Illustration by Sandra Janniche

from the last two summers have been remarkably accurate.

Because little can be done to influence flows, the Bay Program is seeking huge nutrient reductions from the Chesapeake's 64,000-square-mile watershed to reduce algae growth and improve water quality.

If the Bay Program's nutrient reduction goals were achieved, computer models suggest that anoxia would be-

potential for severe storms or hurricanes during the summer that could alleviate low oxygen conditions by mixing water in the Bay.

Forecasters at Colorado State University anticipate 17 named storms forming in the Atlantic basin between June 1 and Nov. 30. Nine of the 17 storms are predicted to become hurricanes, and of those nine, five are expected to develop into intense or

The Bay Journal, 06/07

Figure 7.4. Ecological forecasting can improve communication among scientists, managers, and the public.

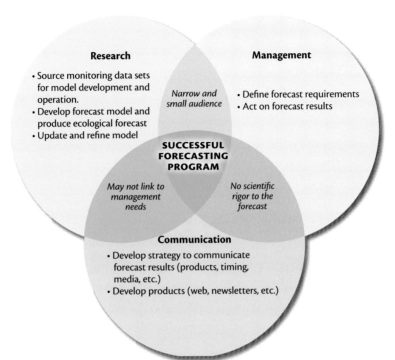

Figure 7.6. An effective forecasting program should have research, management, and communication represented.

analysis; and 3) predictive model development. Each of the three components is important. Understanding ecosystem processes is a complex endeavor. No process within an ecosystem is necessarily straightforward, and understanding how the variable you are interested in forecasting is affected by other variables within the system can take years of research. This effort can be aided by the modification and application of models developed for other systems. Usually, no scientific effort is wholly original, as there is always some application (hopefully credited) of the work of others in any research effort. For instance, if a management agency was interested in developing a forecast of the extent of low dissolved oxygen (hypoxia) in an estuary, there is a large body of evidence in the literature supporting the concept that summer hypoxia in estuaries is related to nutrient loading.[8,9] It is then possible to modify hypoxic prediction models from the literature to

fit the characteristics of a particular ecosystem. The current state of research on a given system may be such that this approach is the only realistic choice for the development of a forecast model.

The role of management in ecological forecasting programs is two-fold. First, as discussed previously, managers will be one of the primary users of the forecasts, so they need to help define forecast requirements, such as what parameters to forecast and what level of uncertainty is required if the forecast can be used for management decisions. The second major role of the management community is to act on the forecast, if necessary, which usually implies trying to mitigate the conditions or the effects of the conditions. Part of acting upon the forecast is allocating resources and directing researchers to collect the necessary data. It is important that forecast models predict something that is a management target and

You should consider forecasting when you have these elements:

- Access to monitoring data to produce a forecast model
- A conceptual understanding or hypothesis from which to develop a forecast model
- Resources, funds, and partner commitments for all components of the forecasting program
- Clear understanding of how your forecast effort will benefit all stakeholders
- A way to communicate the forecast (media releases, web sites, printed material, etc.)

be driven by a variable that managers can effect. An example might be an estuary with recurring summer hypoxia. Managers might be interested in knowing and communicating the extent of hypoxia each summer. However, this effort is only useful if the forecast model is driven by a variable managers can influence, such as nutrient load. Otherwise, the model is only communicating how bad things will get, not what people can do to prevent it. A forecasting effort may be problematic simply due to a lack of needed data. This may be the case more often than not, as few ecosystems in the world are monitored with the intensity and duration necessary to develop robust predictive models.

The role of the communication and outreach team is to ensure that the forecast reaches a broad audience and that the material is presented in a manner that will encourage people to read and understand the information being provided. This requires not only considering how to present the forecast results (see Chapters 3 and 4), but also providing material at the right level of complexity and content for the needs of the audience.

Components of an effective forecast

For a forecast to be effective and as accurate as possible, it needs to contain the appropriate scope and duration. The forecast should also address issues associated with model complexity and model assessment and subsequent improvement.

Defining the scope of your forecast— forecast duration and area

The scope of the forecast, both spatially and temporally, will vary according to the program needs and targeted ecosystem. The spatial and

temporal scale of your forecast needs to be one of the first decisions you make when designing a forecasting program. Spatial and temporal factors to consider include needs of the intended audience, in particular the management community that will use the forecast; level of detail of the supporting data; and accuracy and spatial and temporal extent of the forecast model. Ultimately, it is the available data that controls the spatial and temporal scale of the model as well as its accuracy.

Spatial scale

From Table 7.1 we can see that the spatial area covered by ecological forecasts can be as large as entire countries (e.g., forecasting distribution of zebra mussels within the entire United States) or as very small and localized as a region of shoreline or bay (e.g., forecasting the distribution of sea nettles in Chesapeake Bay). Scale is related to the phenomenon you are attempting to forecast; the data available to support the forecast model; and, most importantly, the purpose of the forecast. For example, a large-scale forecast may limit the ability for resource managers to act on the results of the forecast.

Temporal scale

Models can differ in the time frames in which they operate, in terms of not only how far into the future the prediction is made, but also what duration of time the forecast represents. How far into the future you aim to predict will obviously depend on the purpose of your forecast. It may be appropriate to predict events that could occur tomorrow (days), in the next season (weeks to months), or well into the future (years). Forecasts with extremely short time frames predict the likelihood of a given condition based on the current condition of its controlling factor(s). This

Table 7.1. Spatial and temporal scope of different forecasts from around the world.

Predicted variable	How far into future?	What is being predicted?	Duration	Spatial area
Sea nettle distribution[10]	Now	Presence/absence and density	Daily	Chesapeake Bay tidal waters
Harmful algal blooms[5]	Days	Presence/absence	Daily	Gulf of Mexico
Hypoxia[11]	Days to months	Presence/absence and size	None	Gulf of Mexico
Zebra mussel distribution[12]	Years to decades	Presence/absence	n/a	United States
Shorebird habitat[13]	50 to 100 years	Substantial losses	Forever	Humboldt, Delaware, North San Francisco, South San Francisco and Willapa Bays, and Bolivar Flats

type of prediction is referred to as *now-casting* and an example is the estimation of potential sea nettle distribution in Chesapeake Bay based on current water temperature and salinity distribution. The purpose of this now-casting program is to estimate the likelihood of an encounter with sea nettles in different regions of the bay.

Medium-term forecasts tend to predict conditions within a time frame of no longer than a year. The forecast of summer hypoxic conditions in the Gulf of Mexico is an example of a medium-term forecast. The size of the summer hypoxic area is calculated based on spring nutrient loads from the Mississippi River.[11] Long-range forecasts predict conditions in future years and often aim to predict the effects of management actions and inaction (e.g., shorebird habitat).

How far into the future you are forecasting will also have a strong bearing on the manner and speed in which proponents of the forecasting effort need to act. A forecast for conditions occurring within days will need to have a communication and management response strategy that is able to act quickly and with flexibility, such as web postings or e-mail updates. The communication and management approach for medium- and long-term forecasts allows for more time in which to develop communication products and management responses. Additionally, as more data become available to improve the forecast model, these longer-term forecasts have more potential to be updated as you come close to the actual date. Updating forecasts is commonly done by weather forecasters, who will constantly update the forecast as they get closer to the actual date of the prediction.

Forecast models—balancing model complexity and explanatory power

The models that are used to produce a forecast can vary significantly in complexity, from simple linear regressions to complex, spatially explicit, deterministic models (see Chapter 10). What model you ultimately use will depend on a number of factors and decisions, including the following:

- availability of pre-existing models or modeling research, resources, and data;
- specific needs of the forecast itself, such as the spatial and temporal scales; and
- the acceptable level of uncertainty.

Deciding on what level of model complexity may become a balance between providing the level of uncertainty required by managers and the benefits of being able to clearly explain how

Predicting the weather

Benjamin Franklin, scientist and inventor

Benjamin Franklin, one of the founding fathers of the United States, was an influential author, scientist, diplomat, and printer.[14] He was also one of the first people to make weather forecasts, which he published in his *Poor Richard's Almanacks*. These annual volumes were first published in 1732 and continued for 25 years. As with any forecaster, Franklin was concerned with the accuracy of his forecasts and offered this disclaimer in the 1732 edition of the almanac:

> "We modestly desire only the favourable Allowance of a day or two before and a day or two after the precise Day against which the Weather is set; and if it does not come to pass accordingly, let the Fault be laid upon the Printer, who... may have transpos'd or misplac'd it... And since, in spight of all I can say, People will give him great part of the Credit of making my Almanacks, 'tis but reasonable he should take some share of the Blame."
>
> —*Poor Richard's Almanack*, 1732

Franklin also made observations on weather, such as the movement of storms and the effects of volcanic eruptions on weather patterns. Franklin's work set the stage for weather forecasts that were based upon observation, not speculation.

Weather forecasts in *Poor Richard's Almanack*.

Complex model

Pros:
• Forecast uncertainty likely to be less than if a simpler model is used
Cons:
• 'Black box' approach—hard to explain/ little educational application
• Forecast is only benefit, not the process of generating the forecast

A balance between model complexity and explanatory power is needed

Simple model

Pros:
• Open and transparent approach— simplicity may encourage use
• Good explanatory power—easy to explain forecast/educational
Cons:
• Forecast uncertainty likely to be greater than if a more complex model is used

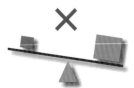

Figure 7.7. Forecasting models can have varying model complexity and explanatory power. The uncertainty or success of a model does not always depend on the complexity of the model.

and why a forecast is being produced (Figure 7.7). The complexity of a forecast model may therefore largely depend on its purpose or intended use—from direct implication on management decisions (preferably low uncertainty) to educational and outreach purposes (preferably low complexity). In many cases, a simple model may be preferable, as it appeals to a broader audience and is relatively quick to develop and explain. Additional complexity in forecast models may add incremental improvements in forecast accuracy and reduce uncertainty and, therefore, may be of more use to management. Simplicity ensures that cause-and-effect relationships will be understood because forecast models can be effective educational tools. Remember, sophisticated models do not necessarily guarantee predictive or decision-making success, and in some cases, decision-making may benefit from simpler explanatory methods.[15] It is important to keep in mind that additional model complexity does not guarantee reduced uncertainty. Each component that is added to a forecasting model has its own uncertainty that contributes to the overall uncertainty of the model. An example of resolving the conflict between model uncertainty and complexity can be seen in the development of the Chesapeake Bay dissolved oxygen forecast model. When the model was being developed, small incremental improvements to the regression model could be made by adding additional forcing functions. However, many of the additional forcing functions were rejected because the additional statistical benefit was considered small in relation to the increased difficulty in explaining and communicating how the forecast was generated.

The relationship among model uncertainty, communication, and the consequential role in management and research provides a useful framework for describing where a forecast can be of most value.[2,16] Figure 7.8 illustrates this framework and identifies where (management or research) the main role of the forecast should focus, depending on the associated uncertainty. Models with low uncertainty and high information content for managers have the most potential to influence decisions. At the other end of the continuum, models with high uncertainty are of less direct use to managers, yet they still serve to drive research questions aimed at reducing model uncertainty. Models between these two extremes have the potential to drive both management

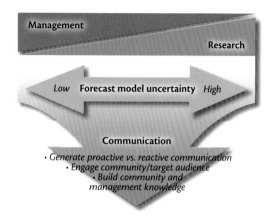

Figure 7.8. The model uncertainty can help determine whether the forecast should be used for research, management, or both. Regardless, communication is key.

decisions and research. Strengthening the link between management and research that evolves as people work together to resolve their individual needs is perhaps the most important reason for undertaking a forecasting effort.[3]

Although a forecast may have a high degree of uncertainty, it is still important to communicate the forecast, the proviso being that the uncertainties are clearly communicated and the reasons for producing the forecasts are clearly explained. To this end, public release of a forecast needs to include a variety of communication products, such as a newsletter, technical report, media release, presentation to media, and web material.

Recipe for success

- Include experts from scientific, management, and communication fields
- Be explicit with partners as to why you are starting a forecasting initiative
- Clearly define temporal and spatial limits of the forecast
- Make a start, but be ready for the forecast to be wrong
- Communicate the forecast and why the forecast may be wrong
- Keep forecast models relatively simple to increase communication potential
- Track the observed conditions and compare to the forecast
- Assess the accuracy of the forecast

Model assessment and improvement

An important component of any forecasting program should be the assessment and improvement of the model performance. The goal is a continual improvement of prediction accuracy. It might be best to think of this process as a cycle that begins with the release of the forecast prediction to management and the public (Figure 7.9). Information is given as to the variable you are forecasting, what you predict that condition will be, and (perhaps most importantly from a communications standpoint) what the controlling factors are that lead to the forecasted condition. It may also be

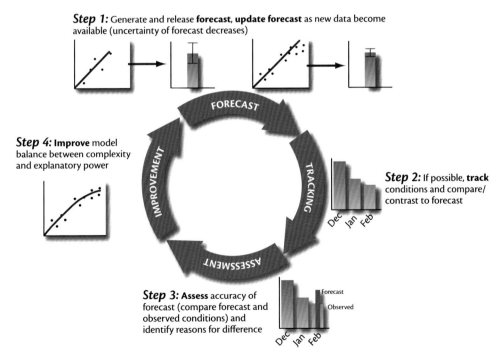

Step 1: Generate and release **forecast, update forecast** as new data become available (uncertainty of forecast decreases)

FORECAST

Step 4: Improve model balance between complexity and explanatory power

IMPROVEMENT

TRACKING

Step 2: If possible, **track** conditions and compare/contrast to forecast

ASSESSMENT

Step 3: Assess accuracy of forecast (compare forecast and observed conditions) and identify reasons for difference

Forecast
Observed

Figure 7.9. Continual assessment and improvement of the model is an important component of an effective forecasting effort.

Building community knowledge

possible to update the forecast as you approach the period you are predicting. This usually occurs because you will have more data to run in the model and, therefore, a better prediction of future conditions.

The next step in the cycle, if possible, is the monitoring of conditions over the time period that the forecast covers. This depends on the temporal resolution of your forecast. For instance, if the forecast is for conditions at a specific point in time this step would not be possible. However, for a forecast of the annual number of storms during the hurricane season,[17] the number of storms that occur as the season progresses is counted. This gives a general idea about how the model is performing in real time before the time period of the forecast is over. From a communications standpoint, the continuous updates of conditions keeps management and the public engaged.

After the time period of the forecast has passed, the forecast model performance can be evaluated. This includes a report back to managers and the public that contains a hypothesis as to why the forecast was inaccurate, if necessary.

Lastly, information gathered from assessing the model is used to help make improvements. Information gathered from recent studies in the targeted ecosystem or other ecosystems can also be used to help refine the model. Refinements can be as simple as changing how an input variable or variables are analyzed to adding a new input variable to completely change the type of model that is used. Although any improvement in model accuracy would be considered an improvement, remember to take model complexity into account.

Forecasts will not always be right—minimizing the consequences of an inaccurate forecast

Mistakes are the portals of discovery.

—James Joyce

As stated at the beginning of this chapter, ecological forecasts do not guarantee what is to

Pitfalls to avoid

Pitfall: Too much time and effort devoted to model development

Fix: Find balance between model development and benefits of releasing the forecast with an imperfect model

Pitfall: Reasons for conducting forecast not clearly communicated to stakeholders

Fix: Be very explicit about the benefits and reasons for forecasting

Pitfall: Forecasting becomes a routine exercise, not learning and improving from experience

Fix: Continually assess entire forecasting exercise, identify elements that succeed and repeat, identify elements that do not work and change

come but offer scientifically sound estimations of what is likely to occur. It is almost inevitable that if you start a program of ecological forecasting, you will at some stage provide a forecast that is either wrong or toward the outer margins of your uncertainty estimates (Figure 7.10). Although getting forecasts wrong is not uncommon (e.g., weather forecasts!), the success of your forecasting program may depend on how you prepare for and act on an inaccurate forecast. To avoid potential backlash for providing an inaccurate forecast and to ensure that stakeholders who may be acting upon the forecast do not waste time and effort, we suggest that you address each of the following:

- Minimize uncertainty of your forecast. As discussed previously, this involves balancing the uncertainty of your forecast model with model complexity. One approach to reduce the chance of incorrect forecasts is to provide updates as you get closer to the time frame you are predicting. This approach is similar to that used by meteorologists. They provide long-range forecasts that are often inaccurate, and give updates that generally are much more accurate closer to the time.
- Clearly explain the uncertainties—known and unknown—of your forecast to the target audience. Known uncertainties are the confidence limits of the forecast model. Unknown uncertainties include outside factors, such as weather events. Although these outside factors can have a definite influence on predicted variables, they are not themselves predictable. One of the common challenges of providing accurate ecological forecasts is accounting for effects of extreme weather events such as a large storm, flood, or drought, that a forecast model more than likely cannot account for. Be clear to your audience about what effect such an event may have on your forecast.
- Present your forecast at a level of accuracy that is relevant to its usefulness and intended

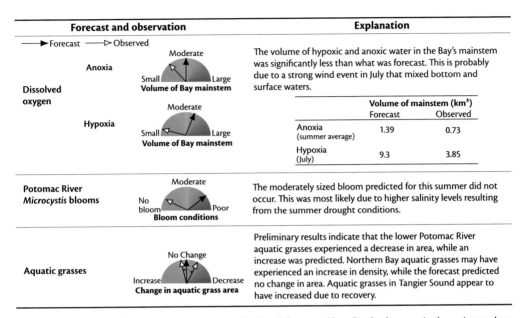

| Forecast and observation | Explanation |

Figure 7.10. In 2007, the Chesapeake Bay Program and EcoCheck forecasted low dissolved oxygen in the mainstem bay, HABs in the Potomac River, and aquatic grasses in three locations. However, the forecast was not accurate. This has still proved to be a good education and communication tool for the public. This table appeared in a publicly distributed newsletter.

use. It is important to understand that for many forecasts, spot-on accuracy of the exact magnitude or extent of a future condition may not be as important as correctly forecasting whether it will be mild, moderate, or severe or, even more simply, whether a condition is present or absent. For example, a hypothetical management agency issues a forecast that states that concentrations of a harmful algal in a particular bay during a given month will be 500±100 cells per liter on average. After data are collected for the month, it turns out that concentrations were only 300 cells per liter. The forecast was inaccurate in terms of concentrations but, more importantly, it accurately predicted that an HAB would occur. Ultimately, this may be more important to management and the community than predicting actual concentrations.

- If a forecast is wrong, explain why it was wrong and use it as a learning opportunity. While an incorrect forecast can at first appear to be a negative result, it can instead be used as a learning opportunity and have a positive outcome if addressed in the right way. If a forecast turns out to be inaccurate, this not only provides the basis for further research

and development, but also the opportunity to teach the audience about a particular aspect of the ecosystem that affects the forecast.

- A final and important consideration related to forecast accuracy is to avoid 'crying wolf', where your forecast repeatedly states an event is going to occur and it never does or not to the extent predicted. In the case of the red tide forecast in Hong Kong, if this model was implemented as an early warning system for fish farmers, false alarms could be costly if farmers are repeatedly taking evasive action for no reason.

Example of an effective forecasting effort: Dissolved oxygen forecast in Chesapeake Bay

Chesapeake Bay experiences persistent anoxia that occurs in the deeper waters of the bay each summer. This phenomenon affects the bay's wildlife and has been labeled the 'Dead Zone' by the media in the bay region. Due to the extensive data available for Chesapeake Bay, a strong relationship between the quantity of nutrients that enter the bay each spring and the volume of anoxic water the bay experiences each summer has been defined by several independent investigations. This relationship can be expressed by a simple linear predictive model. In late spring of 2005, the Chesapeake Bay Program began using a version of this model to forecast the average anoxic volume that the bay would experience the following summer (Figure 7.11). The anoxic model is based on the total nitrogen (TN) and total phosphorus (TP) load to the bay from the Susquehanna River from January to May plus the TN and TP load to the upper Chesapeake Bay from municipal and industrial point sources. The Susquehanna River is located at the northernmost part of the bay and supplies 50% of its freshwater. The dissolved oxygen forecast is a prediction of the average June to September volume of water with a dissolved oxygen concentration ≤0.2 mg·l⁻¹. After the final summer cruise in September, the actual average summer anoxic volume is calculated and compared with the forecasted volume (Figure 7.10). The dissolved oxygen forecast was made for the summers of 2005 to 2007 and proved to be accurate within the model's margin of error in 2005 and 2006. In 2007, a summer-long drought and July wind event decreased the anoxic volume below the margin of error predicted by the model. As stated earlier, the goal was not necessarily to forecast precision but to accurately predict whether the summer would have mild, moderate, or severe anoxia and to inform the public about the linkage between nutrients and anoxia.

The forecasting effort was initiated as part of the Chesapeake Bay Program's communication effort (Figure 7.12). In addition to dissolved oxygen, HAB occurrence and submerged aquatic vegetation abundance are forecasted. By informing management and the public about what summer conditions to expect and providing continual updates on these conditions throughout the summer, a higher level of engagement with the issues affecting the bay is maintained. Due to the dissolved oxygen forecast model being a simple linear relationship—the more nutrients that flow into the bay in the spring the more anoxia occurs in the summer—it is easy to explain and provides the basis for educating the public about why nutrients are bad for the bay. Additionally, forecasting has allowed scientists and managers to be proactive rather than reactive to emerging problems with bay health. In the past, resource managers had to scramble to explain problems with dissolved oxygen, HABs, and submerged aquatic vegetation as these issues emerged. Now that they are forecasting

these variables, they can set the stage for what conditions to expect.

The dissolved oxygen forecast includes research, management, and communication (i.e., the components needed for an operational, effective forecasting effort; Figure 7.12). The forecasting effort follows a timeline that starts in late spring with a press release, newsletter, and website containing forecasted conditions for the summer ahead. Conditions are tracked throughout the summer and posted on the Internet. Finally, in late October, a summer wrap-up newsletter is developed that evaluates the performance of the forecasts and attempts to explain any error in the predictions.

Step 1: Model the relationship between cause and effect.

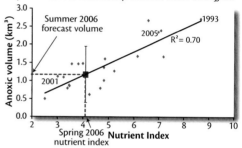

Step 2: Forecast the effect based on the model.

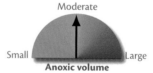

Step 3: Assess and improve the model for the next forecast.

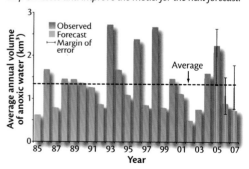

Figure 7.11. The steps taken during the forecasting of dissolved oxygen in the mainstem of Chesapeake Bay. Dissolved oxygen in Chesapeake Bay had most of the ingredients needed for an effective forecasting effort (see *Recipe for success* breakout box).

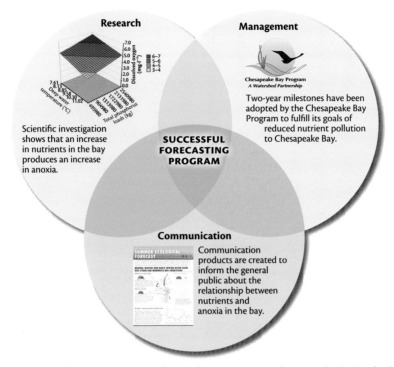

Figure 7.12. A diagram showing the interconnectivity of research, management, and communication involved in forecasting.

This chapter has given an overview of how to use ecological forecasting as a management tool. There are key attributes (e.g., defined spatial and temporal scales, simple forecast models) to a program that should be included, and some problems that you may come across (increased complexity, getting the forecast wrong). Ecological forecasting ideally should be part of a mature assessment program that has long-term data on which to base its models.

References

1. Committee on Environment and Natural Resources, Subcommittee on Ecological Systems (2001) Ecological forecasting: Agenda for the future. Washington, District of Columbia
2. Clark JS, Carpenter SR, Barber M, Collins S, Dobson A, Foley JA, Lodge DM, Pascual M, Pielke Jr R, Pfizer W, Pringle C, Reid WV, Rose KA, Sala O, Schlesinger WH, Wall DH, Wear D (2001) Ecological forecasts: An emerging imperative. Science 293:657–660
3. Valette-Silver NJ, Scavia D (2003) Ecological forecasting: New tools for coastal and ecosystem management. NOAA Technical Memorandum NOS-NCCOS-1
4. Turner RE, Rabalais NN, Justic D (2006) Predicting summer hypoxia in the northern Gulf of Mexico: Riverine N, P, and Si loading. Mar Pollut Bull 52:139–148
5. Stumpf RP, Culver MA (2003) Forecasting harmful algal blooms in the Gulf of Mexico. In: Valette-Silver NJ, Scavia

D (eds) Ecological forecasting: New tools for coastal and ecosystem management. NOAA Technical Memorandum NOS-NCCOS-1: 51–54
6. Lui GCS, Li WK, Leung KMY, Lee JHW, Jayawardena AW (2007) Modelling algal blooms using vector autoregressive model with exogenous variables and long memory filter. Ecol Model 200:130-138
7. Waycott M, Duarte C, Carruthers TJB, Orth RJ, Dennison WC, Olyarnik S, Calladine, A, Fourqurean JW, Heck Jr. KL, Hughes AR, Kendrick GA, Kenworthy JW, Short FT, Williams SL (2009) Accelerating loss of seagrasses across the globe threatens coastal ecosystems, Proc Natl Acad Sci U.S., p 1–5
8. Boicourt WC (1992) Influences of circulation processes on dissolved oxygen in Chesapeake Bay. In: Smith DE, Leffler M, Mackiernan G (eds) Oxygen dynamics in the Chesapeake Bay: A synthesis of recent research. Maryland Sea Grant Publication, College Park, Maryland, p 7-59
9. Hagy JD, Boynton W, Keefe C, Wood K (2004) Hypoxia in Chesapeake Bay, 1950-2001: Long-term change in relation to nutrient loading and river flow. Estuaries 27:634-658
10. Brown CW, Hood RR, Gross TF, Li Z, Decker MB, Purcell JE, Wang HV (2003) Nowcasting sea nettle distributions in the Chesapeake Bay: An overview. In: Valette-Silver NJ, Scavia D (eds) Ecological forecasting: New tools for coastal and ecosystem management. NOAA Technical Memorandum NOS-NCCOS-1, p 45–49
11. Scavia D, Rabalais NN, Turner RE, Justic D, Wiseman Jr W (2003) Predicting the response of Gulf of Mexico hypoxia to variations in Mississippi River nitrogen load. Limnol Oceanogr 48:951-956

Building community knowledge

12. Drake JM, Bossenbroek JM (2004) The potential distribution of zebra mussels in the United States. BioSciences 54:10

13. Galbraith H, Jones R, Park R, Clough J, Herrod-Julius S, Harrington B, Page G (2003) Global climate change and sea level rise: Potential losses of intertidal habitat for shorebirds. In: Valette-Silver NJ, Scavia D (eds) Ecological forecasting: New tools for coastal and ecosystem management. NOAA Technical Memorandum NOS-NCCOS-1, p 19–22

14. The Franklin Institute Science Museum (2009) The world of Benjamin Franklin. Accessed Jul 24. hwww.fi.edu/franklin/

15. Pielke Jr RA, Conant RT (2003) Best practices in prediction for decision-making: Lessons from the atmospheric and earth sciences. Ecology 84:1351-1358

16. Sarewitz D, Pielke Jr RA (1999) Prediction in science and policy. Technology in Society 21:121-133

17. Klotzbach P, Gray W (2007) Extended range forecast of Atlantic seasonal hurricane activity and U.S. landfall strike probability for 2007. Department of Atmospheric Science, Colorado State University. Accessed 20 Jul. typhoon.atmos.colostate.edu/forecasts/2007/april2007/

ENVIRONMENTAL INFORMATION

ANALYZING DATA TO GENERATE MEANINGFUL INFORMATION

The synthetic products discussed in the previous section are essential for building community knowledge and especially for providing tools for effective feedback among scientists, managers, and the general public. However, any synthesis is only as good as the information on which it is based, and the information available (through published materials and directly from scientists knowledgeable on a topic) completely relies on the raw scientific resources—the data. In this section, the process of turning data into information is considered, highlighting a number of approaches and techniques that can feed directly into syntheses and reporting frameworks as well as fulfilling specific requirements of appropriate and rigorous data analysis.

Environmental statistics: Statistics are a useful tool not only to assess the confidence in generating conclusions and gathering information from data, but also to provide dynamic and insightful ways to present data and develop explanations. Balancing simplicity and explanatory power is essential when using and applying statistics.

Environmental models: Models can assist in the understanding of elements of a system that cannot be directly observed either due to the spatial or temporal scale of the question or the interactions that can only be measured in isolation. By providing synthesis, analysis, simulation, and prediction, models can be a useful management tool.

Spatial analysis: One of the most effective ways to turn data into information is to provide relevant context, and presenting data on a map is an excellent way to help readers realize why they should care. Maps also place data in context to one another so that inferences and relationships can be determined. Often, this requires spatial analysis, which allows the calculation of confidence in an observed spatial pattern.

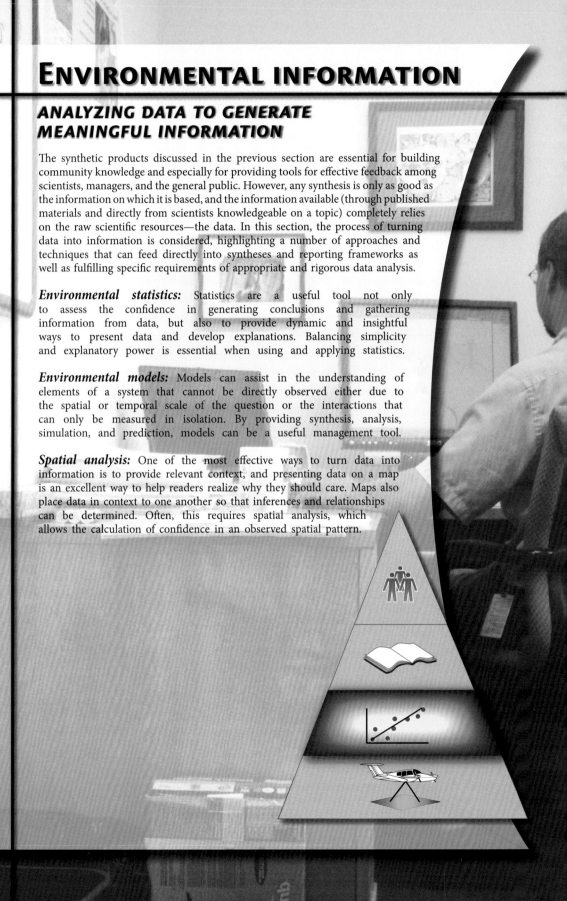

CHAPTER 8: ENVIRONMENTAL STATISTICS

BALANCING SIMPLICITY AND EXPLANATORY POWER

David G. Kimmel, Howard Townsend, Tim J.B. Carruthers, and Ben Fertig

There are no facts, only interpretations.
—Friedrich Nietzsche

One of the most important goals of a coastal assessment program is to increase the knowledge of individuals and agencies who make management decisions. Information must be presented in an easy-to-understand format and supported by quantitative analyses. Quantitative analyses often involve applying statistical techniques that are used to visualize, describe, and model data. Statistics allow scientists and managers to distill data into useful information and increase the amount of confidence they have in their conclusions (Figure 8.1). This chapter describes how to use statistics to strike a balance between explanatory power and complexity (Figure 8.2). This brief introduction should provide some guidance in using statistics to analyze data.

Statistics can build confidence

The mere mention of statistics often strikes fear into the heart of even the most seasoned scientist or manager. This chapter will hopefully alleviate some of these fears by presenting statistics in an applied context with examples that approximate real situations. The goal is to provide baseline information that will enable the reader to explore these topics in further detail. This chapter is not trying to teach a university-level statistics course. Mathematical statisticians who read this text might be appalled because it focuses primarily on the general aspects of how to apply statistics and statistical analysis and pays little attention to the mathematical underpinnings of the analyses. Readers should consult the texts listed at the end of this chapter to ensure that they are applying a particular statistical method correctly.

The chapter begins with a short section on the role statistics play in describing data. Then, the chapter moves on to graphing data and lessons learned from these graphs. Quantitative descriptions of data come next, including simple descriptors of central tendency and variability. Some time is spent describing methods for detecting trends and patterns in data because many coastal assessment activities include long-term data

Analyzing environmental data

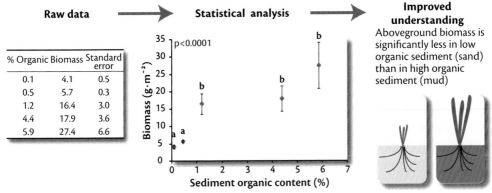

% Organic	Biomass	Standard error
0.1	4.1	0.5
0.5	5.7	0.3
1.2	16.4	3.0
4.4	17.9	3.6
5.9	27.4	6.6

Improved understanding
Aboveground biomass is significantly less in low organic sediment (sand) than in high organic sediment (mud)

Figure 8.1. Statistics help to explain raw data and lead to improved understanding of a system. In this example, statistical analysis of seagrass data led to improved understanding of the relationship between sediment organic content and seagrass biomass.[1]

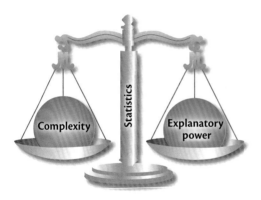

Figure 8.2. By balancing complexity and explanatory power, statistics allow users to make quantitative arguments based on their research.

sets. The next goal is to provide a brief introduction to statistical modeling, including information on when to apply different kinds of statistical tests and making predictions with models. Finally, some suggestions on the presentation of statistical information in reports and presentations is offered.

In addition to presenting a basic outline of statistical methods, this chapter also attempts to infuse a philosophy about the proper use of statistics. Keeping in mind the quote from Nietzsche that begins this chapter, users of statistics should keep in mind that two approaches to using statistics exist:

- "Like other occult techniques of divination, the statistical method has a private jargon deliberately contrived to obscure its methods from non-practitioners"—G.O. Ashley
- Using statistics as a tool for making principled quantitative arguments

Resource managers and scientists should be in the business of providing principled quantitative information and want to steer clear of obfuscation. If they find themselves going down a path of obfuscation, then they should stop, regroup, and make sure that in the application of statistics they truly understand what they have done, why they have done it, and clearly communicate that to the audience.

Statistics synthesize data and report information

The primary reason scientists and managers use statistics is to describe scientific findings or make inferences about a system using data collected from the system. Statistics is an important tool that can synthesize larger data sets into easier to explain numbers and account for randomness in observations of nature. In other words, statistics is the discipline that deals with turning data (numbers) into information.

Descriptive statistics are used to provide quantitative information about a data set. Central tendency (mean and median) and dispersion (variance and standard deviation) are two commonly computed descriptors of data. This information is often very useful to display in graphical form, which can eliminate the use of long tables of data values (Figure 8.3).

Inferential statistics (or statistical models) are used to detect correlation or patterns in the data. In other words, does a particular variable of interest (dependent variable) change in response to one (or more) other variables (independent variable)? This can also be stated as the changes to the dependent variable are not due to random chance and are related to one or more variables. A myriad of statistical tests are designed to test hypotheses that are simply a variance on the main theme: Can I detect an effect that is not due to random variability?

Minimizing errors and selecting samples

All statistics ultimately assess variability in data. Variability in data can be caused by a variety of factors, including variables of interest, variables not of interest, and randomness (variability with no discernible cause).

It is often necessary to minimize effort (for financial and time constraints), but also maximize confidence in the conclusion. With that in mind, data collection systems need to ensure that data are sufficient for providing explanatory power and are representative of the system observed. To achieve this, you ideally know what questions

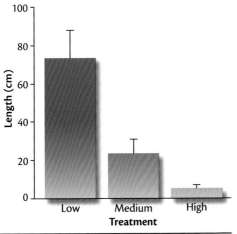

Treatment	Average length (cm)	Standard deviation
Low	72.63	15.43
Medium	23.41	8.04
High	5.00	2.25

Figure 8.3. Central tendency and dispersion can be more effectively displayed as a graph, eliminating the need for long tables of data values.

are to be answered (or hypotheses to be tested) about the system, and then a power analysis can be performed. A power analysis (see next paragraph) allows the user to optimize the study by helping to pick an appropriate sample size needed to detect a statistically significant effect.

Statistical errors
In making statistical inferences about a system based on a sample, the user is likely to make two types of errors, conveniently named Type I and Type II errors. Type I (or α) error is finding differences that exist in the sample but do not actually exist in the system, and Type II (or β) error is not finding differences in the system that actually exist. Typically, the α-error level is set at 0.05 (the significant p-value), thus allowing the user to have some certainty that they have found effects that are not just artifacts of sampling; however, often (but wrongly) the β-error level is ignored. A power analysis helps to ensure that an effect has not been missed or that a difference actually exists. The statistical power of a study depends on the sample size, strength of an effect, variability, and the α-error level. A large enough sample will minimize the Type I and II errors. However, be aware that a large sample size can show effects that are statistically

Key terms
Sampling error—Because statistical analyses are based on samples from a population or system and not the whole system, the results from the sample need to be generalized to the population. In making statistical inferences about a system based on a sample, the user is likely to make two types of errors, conveniently named Type I and Type II error.

Type I (or α) error—Finding differences that exist in the sample, but that do not actually exist in the system. The results of a statistical test are often considered *significant* if the results surpass some confidence threshold probability. Typically, the α-error level is set at 0.05 (the significant p-value), thus allowing the user to have some certainty that there are some meaningful effects that are not just artifacts of sampling; however, often (but wrongly) the β-error level is ignored.

Type II (or β) error—Not finding a statistically significant difference in a sample that actually exists in the larger population.

Confidence—The ability of a statistical analysis to avoid Type I error.

Power—The ability of a statistical analysis to avoid Type II error.

Effect size—An index that describes the magnitude of difference between treatments. The index used will vary depending on the desired analysis.

Power analysis—An analysis that enables the user to ensure that they have an adequate sample size to navigate between Type I and Type II errors for a given ability to measure a desired effect size. The equations for performing a power analysis depend on the statistical test to be performed. Consult a bio-statistician (or other quantitatively oriented scientist or analyst) for assistance.

significant but not meaningful. Typically, resource constraints lead to data-limited situations, so it is necessary to find a balance between Type I and

II errors by being thoughtful about the α-error level is set. (See "Sanctity of the p-value" for more information.) For example, if managers want to conduct a study to test the effectiveness of sewage treatment plant improvements on the proportion of harmful algae in a coastal bay, they would need to determine how many water samples have to be collected to determine whether they have a statistically (and ecologically) meaningful reduction in harmful algae before and after the new treatment plant goes online. The goal of putting the new plant into place is to reduce the proportion of harmful algal species by 10% (thereby decreasing the likelihood of blooms dramatically).

The baseline density (before the sewage treatment plant) is so high that small climatic events (e.g., high rainfall) can easily result in increased nutrients and a harmful algal bloom. Ideally, the study would be designed such that a sufficient number of samples are collected to calculate an effect size (or detectable difference) in the proportion of harmful algal species that is 10%, for example, with 95% confidence and 80% power (Figure 8.4). However, knowing the high cost of sampling and analyzing samples, government officials are agreeable to adjusting the desired confidence and power levels. Before initiating the study, the managers would want to put together some information on a power analysis to determine the required sample size.

Using the power analysis graph, the sample size necessary for 80% power and 95% confidence is around 700 samples. In consulting with the treatment plant officials, the managers may work to adjust sample size based on desired power, confidence, and resources available for work.

Another factor that affects the power analysis is the effect size (or detectable difference). Imagine that the treatment plant managers were under constant constraints and were obligated to do some improvements, but they were only mandated to reduce the proportion of harmful algal species by 3%, and plant upgrades for further reduction would become prohibitively expensive. In this case, a new power analysis graph could be generated (Figure 8.4b). Note that the graph has the same shape as Figure 8.4a; however, much larger sample sizes would be necessary for a smaller detectable difference, resulting in a more expensive study. The treatment plant managers might prefer to spend more on a study than on construction and maintenance of plant upgrades.

Many methods exist for determining an appropriate sample size; one simple method uses random resampling (bootstrapping) of previously collected data (Figure 8.5). In this example, samples of benthic microalgae (known to be highly variable) were used to determine that between 6 and 12 replicate samples were required to allow confident assessment of differences between sites.

Representative samples
Another important factor for answering questions in science is ensuring a representative sample (Figure 8.6). The target population or system must be defined by relying on logic and good judgment. Make sure that system is defined in a way that

a)

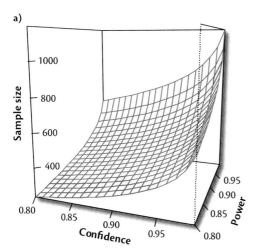

b)

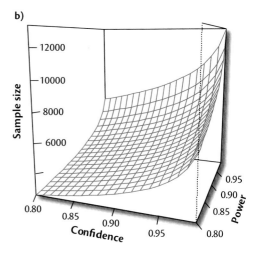

Figure 8.4. Using data from a pilot study, a researcher can make estimates of variability (standard error) associated with different sample sizes. a) This technique may demonstrate that a study may be conducted with much lower necessary samples sizes than b) what are determined with conventional power analysis.

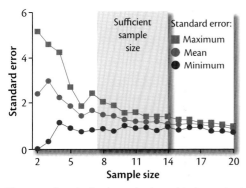

Figure 8.5. Sample size determination using the method of Day and Quinn,[2] after Grinham et al.[3] From 30 sediment chlorophyll determinations, each sample size was randomly sampled 10 times, the standard error of each sample determined, and the maximum, minimum, and mean standard error sampled.

aligns with the purpose behind conducting the study. Sampling methods can be considered as either *probability* or *non-probability*. In probability samples, each item in the system has some known chance of being selected. Probability-based sampling includes random sampling, systematic sampling, stratified sampling, and cluster sampling. Non-probability sampling is systematic, but with a random start (Table 8.1). Such methods include

convenience, judgment, quota, and snowball sampling (Table 8.1). Using sampling based on probability allows you to calculate sampling error, or the degree to which a sample does not accurately reflect the system. When drawing inferences about a population from a sample, results should be reported as a range of values to reflect the inherent uncertainty introduced by sampling. Using non-probability methods, the extent to which the sample differs from the population cannot be calculated.

Imagine that you are in charge of a monitoring program that has been given a mandate by a state agency to collect data on a small estuary. There is a small budget and a list of parameters that must be measured. It is up to you to decide how much data to collect and when to collect it.

The first place to begin is to find out why the agency wishes to monitor this estuary. In particular, is there a specific question needing to be answered? Often, simply knowing what the data will be used for can go a long way toward developing a monitoring program. For example, if an agency is interested in knowing how much phytoplankton is present in the lake each spring, then clearly one does not need to institute a year-round sampling program. The agency may also be interested in only one section of the lake, so therefore, the sampling can be restricted on a spatial scale.

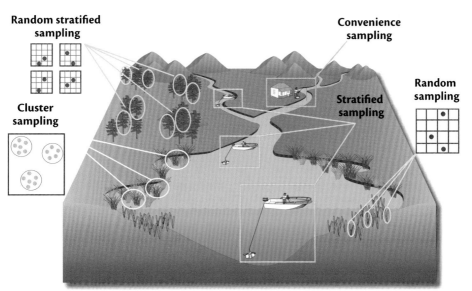

Figure 8.6. Sampling method is based on available resources, data required, and analyses conducted. For descriptions of various sampling methods see Table 8.1.

Table 8.1. Description of the different major sampling methods.

Probability–based methods	Non–probability-based methods
Random sampling: Each item or individual in the population has an equal (non-zero) probability of being chosen for the sample. Minimal bias is introduced with this method except for cases in which all items in the population are not identified (e.g., the population is large, individuals are difficult to identify).	*Convenience sampling:* Items are selected from those that are readily available. This is appropriate to use for exploratory work, where generalizations about a population are not necessary. Researchers might use this method to get a handle on likely results so that they can develop a plan and budget for a more thorough investigation.
Systematic sampling: Items are listed in no particular order and every n^{th} item is selected, where n is selected to ensure that items are in equal intervals depending on sample size. If the list has no inherent order, then this is equivalent to simple random sampling but may be easier to perform. This is equivalent to randomly listing 1,000 names and selecting every 10th name.	*Judgment sampling:* Researchers draw a sample based on their judgment. For example, a researcher may want to make inferences about all the tributaries in a river system but draws a sample from one tributary. In this case, the researcher must be confident (and able to convince others) that this tributary is representative of all.
Stratified random sampling: Items are grouped based on some common characteristic, and probability of selection depends on the proportion that strata represent in the whole population. This is a desirable method because it reduces variability in the statistical analysis due to sampling error. See the sidebar on Simpson's paradox for pitfalls with stratified sampling to avoid. This is equivalent to putting different numbers of names in different size hats and pulling out names in equal proportions from each hat.	*Quota sampling:* This is similar to stratified random sampling, in which the researcher identifies strata and proportions to represent the population but then uses convenience or judgment sampling. The same caveats for convenience and judgment sampling apply.
Cluster sampling: In this method, rather than drawing a sample based on items, the sampling unit is a collection, or cluster, of elements. Once clusters have been selected, then every item in the cluster can be measured. Alternatively, a random sample of items within a cluster can be measured, this is known as two-stage cluster sampling. One might use this method to study disease in oyster populations, where one would randomly sample oyster bars, but could not draw a random sample of oysters without first identifying clusters (or oyster bars).	*Snowball sampling:* This method is used when items with the desired characteristics are difficult to encounter in the population. Often, one item is identified and its connection to others used to find other items with similar characteristics. This method makes it difficult to determine whether a researcher has identified an appropriate cross-section of the population, so generalizations based on this method are tenuous. This method, for example, may be used to conduct a study on clam disease in an instance where clam beds are not well-defined. In this case, one could not develop an adequate frame for a random sample but would need to find a few clams that might lead the researcher to others in the area.

The sanctity of the p–value

The output of most statistical programs that use traditional (parametric) analyses will show a p-value. There is often considerable confusion concerning the interpretation and meaning of p-values. Some of this confusion is alleviated by first defining what a p-value represents and offering some advice on interpretation.

A p-value is a measure of probability and ranges from zero to one. Probability is the relative possibility that an event will occur, as expressed by the ratio of the number of actual occurrences to the total number of possible occurrences. For example, assume that two populations have been measured and a mean calculated for each one. A simple statistical question to ask is: Do the populations have the same mean? This is the null hypothesis. The appropriate statistical test is selected and the

answer is determined, which is contained in the p-value. In this hypothetical example, a p-value of 0.04 was calculated. Strictly interpreted, this means that if the two populations were sampled at-random repeatedly, it is expected that a smaller difference between the two means would be found 96% of the time and a larger difference between the two means 4% of the time. It does not mean that there is a 96% chance that there is a real difference between the means. This is the expectation under the null hypothesis for a test.

College statistics reminds us that a p-value below 0.05 is significant. This is a common convention, but has no absolute meaning. In fact, it is an artifact of the age when p-values were in tables and not easily calculated. Modern computing allows us to calculate exact p-values. To take a real example, a study of sediment microalgal abundance demonstrates a case where a highly significant p–value has relatively little ecological significance. Figure 8.7 shows abundance over time in field sampling sites and some laboratory mesocosms taken from the same sediment at time zero. Sums of squares are equal to the Mean Squares (MS) times the degrees of freedom (DF) and have the useful attribute that they are additive. A rule-of-thumb approach to assessing the importance of one component in an Analysis of Variance (ANOVA) model can be estimated by finding the total sum of squares (SS) and then calculating the %SS for each term in the model. The strictly correct way to do this is using the relative MS variation.[4] However, that approach is much more labor intensive. Back to the example, it is clear that between sampling times, there was highly significant variation (p=0.0001) and also that between treatments there was highly significant variation (p=0.0005). Looking at the graph (Figure 8.7) shows this to make sense. However, looking at the %SS variation, the *time* term accounts for (approximately) 27% of the variation that is explained by the total ANOVA model, whereas the *treatment* term accounts for only (approximately) 7% (Figure 8.7). The overall conclusion then is that the difference between treatments is small compared to the differences measured over time—an ecological statement that the p-values provided little insight into. It is important to note the final choice of interpretation lies with the analyst.

> ### Pitfalls to avoid
>
> - Too much complexity (it does not necessarily mean more information)
> - Be careful when calculating means—Simpson's paradox
> - Saying too much or over-interpreting the data
> - Poor use of statistics programs as they can be a black box— garbage in and garbage out

There are other approaches of model selection and inference besides the classic null hypothesis significance testing approach. A current trend in analysis among quantitative ecologists is to use other methods such as maximum likelihood estimation in combination with the Information Theoretic Approach (sensu Burnham and Anderson)[5] and Bayesian approaches.

Graphing data

The basic idea of statistics is to describe and understand variability in data. Therefore, the first thing to do is graph the data. Graph the data in as many ways as possible. Simply looking at the data helps to see any potential patterns in the data. Any obvious patterns in the data should be apparent, and these patterns can suggest analyses that may be appropriate. In addition, looking at the data allows you to understand how they are distributed. Understanding distribution is important for applying the proper tests. It is important to note that most data collected will not be normally distributed. The normal distribution is a particular distribution used in parametric statistics. The mean is zero, the variance is 1, and the shape of the curve is often described as a bell, and, thus, is known as the bell curve.

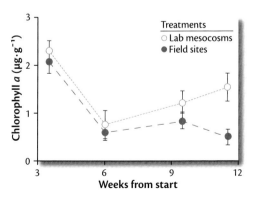

Source	DF	MS	F–value	p–value	SS	%SS var
Time	3	33.19	53.87	0.0001	99.57	27
Treatment	1	23.83	25.15	0.0005	23.83	7
Site (Tr)	10	0.95	2.58	0.0046	9.50	3
Time x Tr	3	6.22	10.09	0.0001	18.66	5
Time x Site (Tr)	30	0.62	1.68	0.0143	18.60	5
Error	528	0.37			195.36	53
				Total SS	365.52	

Figure 8.7. Abundance of benthic microalgae in surface sediments in mesocosms and field sites over 12 weeks. Table shows results of ANOVA analysis and calculation of Sums of Squares (SS) and %SS variation.[6]

Moving beyond the mean—descriptive statistics

Once the data have been graphed, start by using descriptive statistics to summarize the data. The first step in doing this is to describe the data using measures of central tendency and dispersion. The central tendency can also be described as an expected value in that if a single datum was randomly drawn from all of the data, it is expected that the datum's value will equal the value of the measure of central tendency plus some disperson around the central tendency. In actuality, that would not be the case, and the datum's value would reasonably lie within a range of values or the measure of dispersion. The arithmetic mean and standard deviation is commonly used to measure the central tendency and dispersion; however, some other simple options can be beneficial in particular circumstances (Table 8.2).

A slew of data has been collected, what should be reported? The mean, the median, or something else? What should be reported depends on the message trying to be conveyed. The two graphs in Figure 8.8 show the different ways to present central tendency of the collected data and what message is being conveyed.

The chosen measure of central tendency can be very important, for example, when comparing it to a management or regulatory threshold. In the following hypothetical example of more than a

> *Everything should be made as simple as possible but not simpler.*
> —Albert Einstein

decade of total phosphorus (TP) requirements, the mean is above the threshold for management because there were three occasions with very high values in 11 years of data. (Note that 75% of the values were acceptable, i.e., below the threshold, Figure 8.8). A more valid interpretation is perhaps provided by the median and the maximum (Figure 8.8). Generally, concentrations are acceptable; however, some occasions result in very high pulses of nutrients into the example waterway.

Analyzing trends

An agency contacts you and wants to know whether there are any trends in some long-term

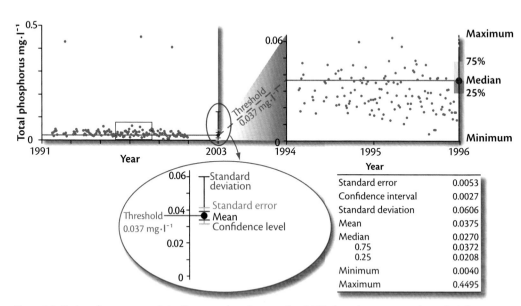

Figure 8.8. Choice of summary statistics (i.e., central tendency and variability) used to report study results is important. These two graphs of total phosophorus data show two ways to present central tendency. The left graph uses the mean, and displays 75% of the points were below the threshold. The graph on right shows how the median and maximum can be used to show a perhaps more valid interpretation of the data. Different measures of central tendency may differ slightly; however, such differences may have implications for policy and regulations. (Hypothetical example)

Table 8.2. The various ways to measure expected values.

Measure of central tendency (expected value)		Measure of dispersion	When to use
Median	Middle value in an ordered list	Range difference between the 25th and 75th percentile	Small data sets or when extreme events are of no interest, the median is not a good estimator of central tendency
Mode	Most common value in a list	Semi-interquartile range: 0.5 (Q1-Q3)	Larger data sets, that are not normally distributed
Arithmetic mean	Add up all the values in the list and divide by the number of values in the list.	Standard deviation, variance $$\overline{x} = \frac{1}{n} \sum_{i=1}^{n} x_i$$	Must meet normality assumption, then can be used for small data sets; if normality assumption is not met, should have larger sample size
Geometric mean	This minimizes the effect of extreme values on the measurement of central tendency. Multiply all the values together and take the nth root of the product.	Standard deviation, variance $$\overline{x} = \sqrt[n]{\prod_{i=1}^{n} x_i}$$	Appropriate for averaging ratios from log normal data
Harmonic mean	This method is very important for calculating averages of rates.	Standard deviation, variance $$\overline{x} = \frac{n}{\sum_{i=1}^{n} \frac{1}{x_i}}$$	Appropriate for averaging rates and proportions

In these equations, $\overline{x}$ is the mean value of x; x_i is the index of each value (x) of all the items in the sample; and n is the number of items in the sample. Σ (sigma) signifies that all the items in the list should be added up, and $\prod$ (pi) indicates that all the items in the list should be multiplied together. Finally $\sqrt[n]{\ }$ indicates that the nth root of a value should be calculated (if n=2, then take the square root; if n=3, then take the cube root, etc.) When it becomes necessary to calculate measures of central tendency and dispersion for non-normally distributed data (e.g., binomially, Poisson), different formulas are used. Consult a mathematical statistical text (or a statistician) for more information.

monitoring data they have been collecting. When monitoring data reaches an adequate length, this question becomes common. The first thing to do, as always, is to graph the data. Graphing the data will begin to tell the story of the information that's been gathered. However, to be confident in the conclusions, further analysis is required. Thus, two ways to analyze the data are explored: 1) linear trend analysis and 2) non-linear trend analysis.

Linear trend analysis

The most common trend analysis is a linear trend analysis. Regression is used to fit a linear model to the data. For example, Figure 8.9 shows a linear fit to a long-term record of TP. In Figure 8.9a, the trend analysis is straightforward. Let us see what happens when we extend the data to the year 2000.

Now, a linear fit does not really tell the full story (Figure 8.9b). Clearly, there was a long-term increase in phosphorus concentration, but something happened in the mid-1980s. This

event was a ban on phosphorus-based detergents, which led to a dramatic decline in the amount of TP in the river. As a result, there was a rapid decline in phosphorus concentrations and then little change in phosphorus concentrations over the past 20 years. A linear fit to these data would indicate a slight downward trend over the entire record; however, that is clearly not the case. The lesson to be learned from this example is that simply applying a best-fit line to the data can be misleading. The next section will discuss how to deal with this problem.

Non-linear analysis

It is important to explore the data thoroughly and to think non-linearly. The next example shows a comparison of two trend calculations for total nitrogen (TN), TP and chlorophyll *a* (chl-*a*) (Figure 8.10). An initial analysis with linear trends applied to the data showed mostly decreasing or non-significant trends for most of the sites, with one exception. Using a non-linear, quadratic fit to the

Analyzing environmental data

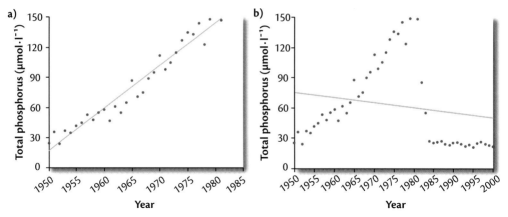

Figure 8.9. Linear trend analysis. a) A linear model is fit to the data. b) When the time frame is extended, the linear fit no longer applies. Often, the application of a best-fit line can be misleading.

data shows vastly different results. Using non-linear analysis, the majority of sites show a pattern of previous decline but current increase. Both of the examples were chosen to show that data may change over time and that the frame of reference used to show trends is very important. This needs to be kept in mind when analyzing monitoring data for trends.

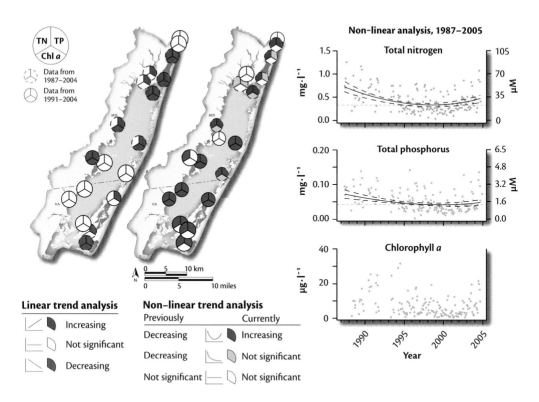

Figure 8.10. Linear vs. quadratic analyses can result in vastly different conclusions regarding trends, in this case, in the water quality of the Maryland Coastal Bays.[7]

Models are useful for stakeholders

Why would someone want to create a model instead of just simply performing statistical analysis using standard techniques? For simple models, it is probably not worth the trouble, so generally statistical models are used when inferential statistics are performed rather than descriptive statistics. For more complex analysis, developing models helps to clearly demonstrate what the user is thinking. In other words, management decisions rely on plans that necessitate some assumptions about causes and effects in a system. Models require mathematical formalization of the assumptions and provide structure for organizing relationships, and assumptions are made explicitly. This formalization ensures objectivity and transparency for stakeholders. Rather than having multiple stakeholders with multiple informal models and varying implicit assumptions in their heads (mental models), a formal mathematical model can be reviewed and scrutinized by all stakeholders, thereby ensuring fair representation for all.

Understanding statistical models

All statistical analyses are mathematical models. Often it is not implicitly stated that a mathematical model is created, but they are. When students calculate an average in math class, it is a modeling exercise because any statistical analysis is a model.

For example, a simple arithmetic mean (the average) can be expressed as a mathematical model:

$$E(X) = x + \varepsilon$$

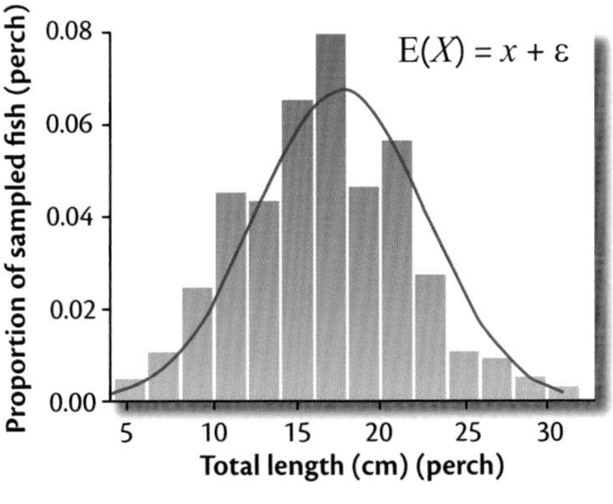

Figure 8.11. Size distribution of sampled fish. Orange line represents arithmetic mean. (Hypothetical example).

In words, this translates to "the expected value, $E(X)$, of any object of the data set X is the mean, x, plus some error term, ε ." This is in essence the underlying mathematical model for simple descriptive statistics. Using a hypothetical example, measure the lengths of fish of different ages (1–5 years) and from different salinities (5 ppt–20 ppt) in experimental tanks (Figure 8.11). By calculating the mean and standard deviation of the length data, it is known that the sample likely came from a population that can be modeled (denoted by orange line) as normally distributed, with a mean length of 16.5 cm and standard deviation of 4 cm. This corresponds to the function, where the expected value, $E(X)$, of any perch length is the mean value, x, and the associated error (standard deviation), ε.

A more complex model, for example, would be a simple linear regression model:

$$E(y) = \beta_o + \beta_1 x_1 + \varepsilon$$

In words this translates to, "the expected value, $E(y)$, of any object of the data set y is the average value, x, multiplied by some effect factor, β, plus some error term, ε." Or, the dependent (or outcome) variable, $E(y)$, is a function of the independent (or explanatory) variable, x, with some residuals, ε. This is, in essence, the underlying mathematical model for simple univariate statistics.

In the fish example, the model is made more complicated by investigating the relationship between length and age. By knowing the age of the fish a more specific expected value, $E(y)$, can be determined (Figure 8.12). In effect, the normal distribution model above is broken up into several smaller normal distribution models for each age (Figure 8.12).

Rather than summarizing the data (read, create a model) as a series of smaller normal distribution curves, the linear equation form is used. With this, the fish lengths, y, are now calculated as a function of fish ages, x_1, and have some errors, known as residuals, that demonstrate that nature cannot be perfectly explained with math. It is helpful to attempt to graphically represent nature and use the model as a single line (Figure 8.13).

One or more outcome variables can be described with one or more explanatory variables and effect factors. This requires more data and more effort on the part of the statistician.

$$E(y_i) = \beta_o + \beta_1 x_1 + \beta_2 x_2 + \varepsilon$$

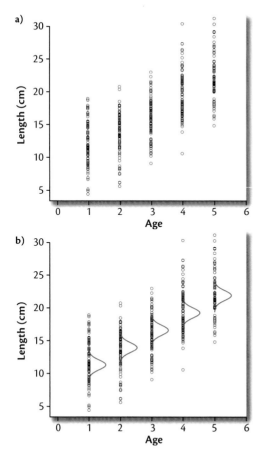

Figure 8.12. a) The length data from Figure 8.11 can be further broken out by age of subjects. By knowing the age of the fish, a more specific expected value occurs, E(y). b) In effect, the normal distribution model above is broken up into several smaller normal distribution models for each age. (Hypothetical example.)

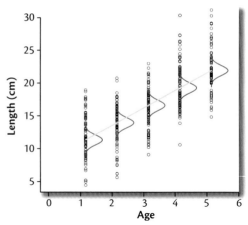

Figure 8.13. The line depicts a mathematical model that summarizes the relationship between fish lengths as it relates to their ages. (Hypothetical example.)

could have also been fish weight measurements and used that as an additional y variable. Similarly, the amount of food provided to each perch could have been manipulated, and this would have been an additional x variable to add to the model.

The βs of the model are parameters that are estimated from the data and are used to quantify the strength of the relationship between the explanatory and predictor variables. Typical methods of parameter estimation include classical least squares, maximum likelihood, and Bayesian. Suffice it to say that the strength of the relationships and the number of explanatory variables in the model can be used to assess the model. The model relationships can then be

Rather than using a simple linear equation, the user now has to use a multiple linear regression equation, but the same principles hold, just with an additional variable—salinity, denoted as x_2, to help explain the variability in perch length. Instead of a line to represent the data, connect two lines orthogonally to develop a plane that summarizes the data (Figure 8.14).

There can rapidly be more variables in a model that can be easily represented and these ideas could be extended virtually indefinitely (though you have to be careful about overparameterizing the model). This progression of models and graphs at least illustrates the idea that there can be additional explanatory variables (the xs) as well as outcome variables (the ys). With this perch example, there

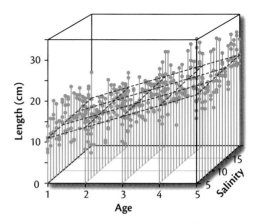

Figure 8.14. The plane depicts a mathematial model that summarizes the relationship between fish lengths as it relates to their ages and the average salinity of the tank the fish inhabited. (Hypothetical example.)

Simpson's paradox

Simpson's paradox is an effect that arises from combining group data that were sampled in a stratified manner. In the following hypothetical example, a number of diseased oysters were surveyed in the upper, middle, and lower Chesapeake Bay in waters from zero to two meters and two to four meters. From the inital sampling, it appears that more diseased oysters are present in two to four meters of water. However, when the data are combined, it appears that there is slightly more disease prevalence in zero to two meters of water. Which is the correct answer? In this case, the combined data ignore the fact that the sampling occurred in three separate bay regions. The baywide mean must reflect this fact, and the combined mean must be weighted for each location. That is, the percentage for each region must count for one-third of the total mean; otherwise, some regions will be over- or underrepresented. If this is done, the result is: 28.5% for zero to two meters and 30.1% for two to four meters depth, which is more consistent with the uncombined data.

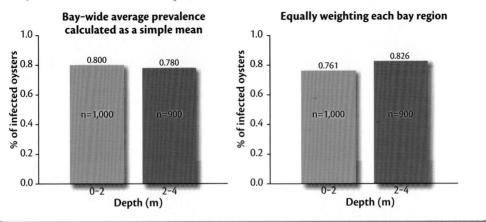

used to make predictions, forecasts, and projections, but paying attention to prior thought and the conservative use of explanatory variables is necessary to make meaningful predictive models. Remember the balance between explanatory power and complexity as we go on to consider predictive ability.

The purpose of these few equations is to show that the math underlying statistics is fairly straightforward and nothing to worry about. The math used to estimate the parameter values in these equations can be hairy, but generally, computer software deals with that (see "Software available" at the end of this chapter).

Various types of analysis

Ultimately, the majority of what people learned in a statistics course or multivariate statistics course is based on this sort of modeling and an understanding of whether you want to explore differences in data sets or relationships. In addition, to decide what sort of tools are needed, an understanding of whether the data are discrete, ordinal, or continuous is needed (Table 8.3).

Data are considered to be discrete if they can be classified into two or more mutually exclusive groups with no order (yes/no, small/medium/large, red/blue/green, etc.). Data are considered to be ordinal if they can be classified into two or more mutually exclusive groups with order, but the interval between the groups is undefined (e.g., a scale of 1 to 10 describing how much you enjoy a movie). Data are considered to be continuous if they can be classified in two or more mutually exclusive groups with order and with a regular interval between them (length measurements, weight measurements, etc.). Continuous data can take on any value with a distribution.

Comparing simple to complex models

Resource managers often have high expectations of large data sets and it is quite possible to develop very complex models to address these questions. The challenge with complex models is that you can often have models that overfit the data. That is to say, the model describes the data you have at hand but would not do a good job of describing another

Analyzing environmental data

Table 8.3. Select anaylsis based on type of data collected and the relationship under investigation.

X Independent or predictor variable(s)	Y Dependent, outcome, or criterion variable(s)	Recommended analysis
1 continuous	1 continuous	Pearson correlation, Spearman correlation, simple linear regression
1 continuous	1 dichotomous	Logistic regression
1 ordinal	1 ordinal	Spearman rank-order correlation
1 discrete	1 discrete	χ^2 test
1+ continuous	1 continuous	Multiple regression
1 discrete	1 continuous	One-way ANOVA, or t-test if x is dichotomous
1 dichotomous	1 ordinal	Mann-Whitney U
1 discrete	1 ordinal	Kruskal–Wallis
2+ discrete	1 continuous	Factorial ANOVA
1+ discrete & 1+ continuous	1 continuous	Analysis of covariance (ANCOVA)
1+ discrete	2+ continuous	Multivariate ANOVA
1+ discrete & 1+ continuous	2+ continuous	Multivariate ANCOVA
2+ continuous	1+ discrete	Discriminant function analysis, logistic regression, generalized linear models (GLM), generalized additive models (GAM)
0 (inferred existence)	2+ continuous	Factor analysis/principal Components analysis
2+ continuous	2+ continuous	Canonical correlation

data set sampled from the population or system of interest. Building complex models may allow you to incorporate factors of interest; however, they may cause you to lose general explanatory power. One should strive for parsimony of explanations in order to achieve a balance between complexity and general explanatory power.

Detecting data patterns—multivariate statistics

It is often the case during monitoring efforts that you collect many different variables but have no real idea of how they are related. Are there distinct patterns in the data (i.e., are multiple parameters showing similar variability during a particular time period)? Do particular variables respond in a similar fashion to some forcing factor? These types of questions are too complex for univariate statistics because multiple variables are being examined, so other methods must be used. Although multivariate statistics may sound complicated, they are simply extensions of methods with which we are already acquainted. Two different cases for detecting patterns are examined next: 1) multiple independent variables and the detection of inter-relationships among them and 2) one (or more) dependent variables responding to multiple independent variables.

Finding inter–relationships

Using the decision tree like that presented in Figure 8.15, it is clear that there are multiple statistical methods designed to find interrelationships among the data. Here is an example of analyzing water quality monitoring data using multivariate techniques. These data have multiple independent variables. In this case, the goal was to monitor and compare current ecosystem health status. Data were collected on two occasions (May and July) from four areas of Maryland's Coastal Bays: St. Martin River, Public Landing, Johnson Bay, and southern Chincoteague Bay. A suite of variables were measured (salinity, temperature, Secchi depth, TN, and TP) from each of 100 sites randomly distributed across the four regions (Figure 8.16).

Once all the data were collected and tabulated, any gaps in the data were eliminated by only including sites where all variables were able to be measured. To focus on how each data point compared to the mean, the data were standardized; that is, the mean of each variable was subtracted from the data value. Because there were multiple independent variables on different scales, the Multidimensional Scaling (MDS) technique was the most appropriate for analysis. This technique is nonparametric, so it does not rely on a set mean and standard deviation. The MDS had an acceptable

Univariate data—quantitative data

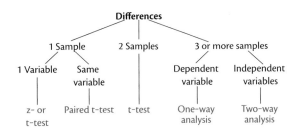

Univariate data—categorical data

1 Variable

χ^2 goodness of fit

Variables

χ^2 contingency table

Multivariate data

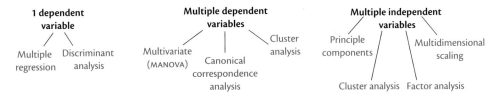

Figure 8.15. A decision tree that can be used to determine which model fulfills your research needs.

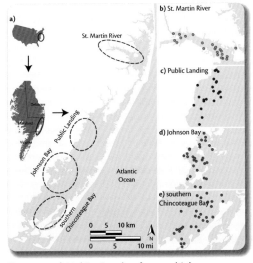

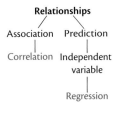

Figure 8.16. a) Multivariate data from multiple independent variables of water quality were collected from four regions of Maryland's Coastal Bays b) St. Martin River, c) Public Landing, d) Johnson Bay, and e) southern Chincoteague Bay.[7]

stress level of 0.14 (less than the threshold stress level of 0.15). See the textbooks referenced at the end of this chapter for more information about this process.

The MDS output provides two pieces of information. The MDS plot (Figure 8.17a), when analyzed with respect to both region (color) and collection date (shape), can show how each measured variable responded to region and collection date. Position on the graph indicates the strength of the relationship such that data closer together are more similar. The MDS plot indicates that water quality variables differed by region because data in each color cluster together. For example, water quality variables at sites in southern Chincoteague Bay (blue) were more similar to other sites in southern Chincoteague Bay than sites at Public Landing (brown). Public Landing was the most homogenous because data cluster together the tightest, close to the origin of the MDS axes. Furthermore, since data from both May (square) and July (circle) are randomly distributed, the data do not vary by collection date. This means

a)

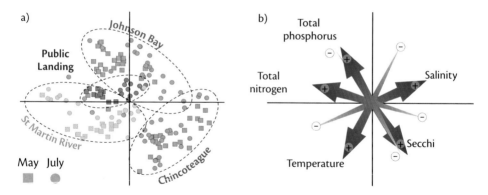

b)

Figure 8.17. a) MDS analysis plot with respect to region (color) and time (shape) shows how the data respond to each. b) Principle axis correlation shows relationship between measured variables.[8]

that sampling time did not have as big of an influence on these data as did sampling region.[8]

The second piece of information about the variables measured can be gleaned from the principle axis correlation plot (Figure 8.17b). Each variable is assigned an axis. Axes pointing in similar directions (i.e., the same quadrant) are positively correlated to one another, whereas axes pointing in opposite directions (i.e., diagonal quadrants) are inversely related. Axes at right angles (i.e., adjacent quadrants) are unrelated. In this example, TN and TP are positively correlated, and are both inversely related to Secchi depth. Meanwhile, all three (TN, TP, and Secchi depth) are unrelated to salinity and temperature (but salinity and temperature are inversely related to each other). Overall, MDS provides a powerful tool for identifying inter-relationships among multiple independent variables and condensing the results into plots that visually indicate the story of these data.

Making predictions

Using statistics and models, we can attempt to make predictions. When developing models to make a forecast, it is useful to develop some measure that demonstrates the uncertainty in the model. For simple models, confidence limits about the regression line can be used to estimate the uncertainty in the model and any predictions made from the model (Figure 8.18).

When the National Weather Service (NWS) makes predictions about hurricanes, the uncertainty in predicting the hurricane's path is illustrated using a cone that envelopes the most likely predicted path (Figure 8.19). Note that the farther out the predictions are made, the greater

the uncertainty in the estimated path. Predictions beyond three to five days in many cases are not very informative because of the high degree of uncertainty. The NWS is continually working to improve the quality and accuracy of hurricane predictions.

Hurricane and other complex weather and climate models have only recently (20–30 years) become highly reliable. Similar models for ecological systems are not available. At this stage, only relatively simplistic forecasting models are feasible for ecological systems. These models are more effectively used for creating scenarios for policy exploration. See Chapter 7 for more information.

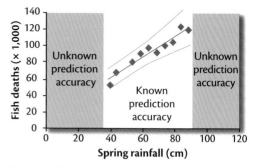

Figure 8.18. The inner line represents the regression equation, and the outer line represents the uncertainty around the relationship (95% confidence limits). A linear regression equation is a useful tool for estimating future outcomes. However, projections beyond what has been previously observed are more uncertain and likely to be highly inaccurate. (Hypothetical example).

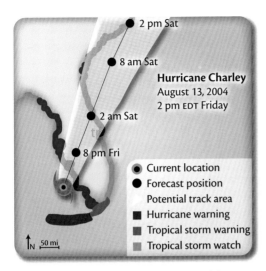

2 pm Sat

8 am Sat

Hurricane Charley
August 13, 2004
2 pm EDT Friday

2 am Sat

8 pm Fri

● Current location
● Forecast position
◢ Potential track area
■ Hurricane warning
■ Tropical storm warning
■ Tropical storm watch

↑N 50 mi

Figure 8.19. Forecasts using more complex models are possible, but as the implications for forecast uncertainty increase, the need to communicate such uncertainty increases.[9]

Effective visual presentation of statistics assists understanding

Statistics are essential for the independent assessment of the validity of trends observed or hypothesized in data sets. However, it is often difficult for readers to link statistical summaries presented in complex tables with the general conclusions discussed. Visual presentations can greatly assist in clarifying these linkages by synthesizing large or complex analyses in the context of the issues being discussed.

One way visual summaries can assist is the presentation of many different types of data (and associated analyses) adjacent to each other to show how the different results combine to provide key messages or conclusions. In an example from the Yucatan peninsula, six tables and four ANOVAS are presented to emphasize geographic, seasonal, and long-term trends in seagrass nutrient data to show the take-home message from the data (note the explicit links to the data tables in the figure legend; Figure 8.20).

Visual presentation of statistical results provides clarity, helps in focusing on the key messages, and provides a basis for the reader to assess the validity of results and a context for clear interpretation. In some cases, good visual presentation assists in the use of complete analysis results to clearly explain conclusions. A good example is a study assessing species relationships

Reporting medical care

Florence Nightingale, nurse and mathematician

Noel Collection

Florence Nightingale, a pioneer in nursing and talented mathematician, used statistics to report on medical care conditions during the Crimean War. Her innovative presentations, which included rose diagrams, were given to members of the British Parliament.[10] These presentations illustrated the seasonal sources of patient deaths in the military field hospital she managed during the war. Her visual presentation of information was so effective, it could be understood by people who were not familiar with traditional statistical reports.

Later in her career, Nightingale went to India where she conducted an extensive statistical study of sanitation in rural areas.[10] She and her studies were instrumental in improving medical and public health services.

In 1859, Nightingale was the first female member elected to the Royal Statistical Society.[10]

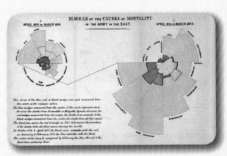

Nightingale created this rose diagram in 1858 to describe the causes of death in military field hospitals. She also demonstrated that social phenomena could be objectively measured with mathematical analysis. Her revolutionary ways of displaying data helped to communicate information to the public. In the diagram above, the blue wedges represent deaths from preventable diseases, the red wedges represent deaths from wounds, and the grey wedges represent all other causes of death.[11]

Analyzing environmental data

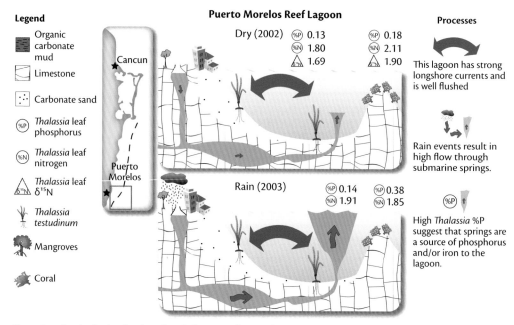

Figure 8.20. Synthetic visualization of analysis summarizes nutrient processes in a tropical seagrass meadow. Explicit links to analysis and data tables (not presented here) are given in the figure legend.[12]

within the seagrass genus *Halophila*, using DNA data. The data collection, data analysis, and the message are all complex in this case but have been clearly presented to show significant groupings and how these relate to both morphology of individuals and sampling location (Figure 8.21). For example, the multi-leaved samples (e.g., *H. beccari*) are an early branch in the analysis and, therefore, are the most primitive forms, and *H. decipiens* from the Caribbean and the Indo-Pacific are not genetically differentiable, suggesting that this species' global distribution is relatively recent. Clear presentation of statistical results can be used as an effective tool in the explanation of complex messages.

Applying statistics

Some of the most important concepts in this statistics chapter are:
- Statistics are to be used to synthesize information and make quantitative arguments with confidence.
- Proper sampling or experimental design is necessary to ensure that the collected data can be analyzed.
- Before you do anything else, in order to have a better feel for any potential patterns or problems in the data set, graph the data.

- Strike a balance between simplicity and complexity when modeling the data.
- The data should tell a story that makes sense ecologically (or biologically, or chemically, etc.) in addition to being supported by quantitative analysis (statistics).
- Clear visualization of results can turn statistics into an important tool for presenting (and not just validating) key hypotheses and conclusions.

"A statistical analysis, properly conducted, is a delicate dissection of uncertainties, a surgery of suppositions." –MJ Mulroney

References
1. Wicks EC, Koch EW, O'Neil JM, Elliston K (2009) Effects of sediment organic content and hydrodynamic conditions on the growth and distribution of *Zostera marina*. Mar Ecol Prog Ser 378:71-80
2. Day RW, Quinn GP (1998) Comparison of treatments after an analysis of variance in ecology. Ecol Monogr 59:433-463
3. Grinham AR, Carruthers TJB, Fisher PL, Udy JW, Dennison WC (2007) Accurately measuring the abundance of benthic microalgae in spatially variable habitats. Limnol Oceanogr Methods 5:119-125
4. Underwood AJ (1997) Experiments in ecology: Their logical design and interpretation using analysis of variance. Cambridge University Press, Cambridge, Massachusetts
5. Kendrick GA, Jacoby CA, Heinemann D (1996) Benthic microalgae: Comparisons of chlorophyll *a* in mesocosms and field sites. Hydrobiologia 326/327:283-289

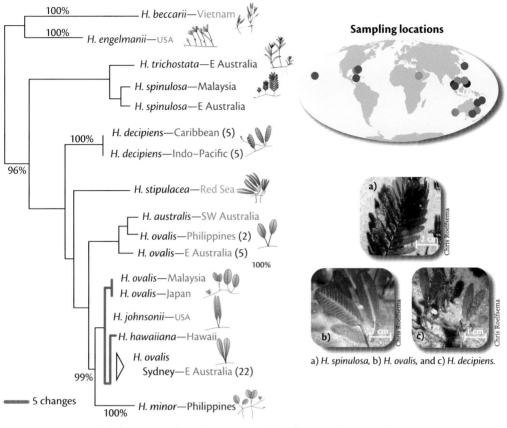

Sampling locations

a) *H. spinulosa*, b) *H. ovalis*, and c) *H. decipiens*.

Figure 8.21. Summary of phylogenetic analysis of DNA sequence data, showing relationships between collection sites and genetic similarities. The xx% at branching points on the tree indicate how many times a particular branch was produced from 500 reruns of the analysis on subsets of the total data set (>75% is good, >90% is a strong relationship for phylogenetic analyses). Clustering may be based on similarites or dissimiliarites among the data.[13]

6. Burnham KP, Anderson DR (2002) Model selection and multimodel inference: a practical information-theoretic approach. Springer, New York, New York

7. Wazniak CE, Hall MR, Carruthers TJB, Sturgis B, Dennison WC, Orth RJ (2007) Linking water quality to living resources in a mid-Atlantic lagoon system, U.S.A. Ecol Appl 17:564-578

8. Fertig B, Carruthers TJB, Dennison WC, Jones AB, Pantus F, Longstaff B (2009) Oyster and macroalgae bioindicators detect elevated δ^{15}N in Maryland's Coastal Bays. Estuaries Coasts 32(4):773-786

9. Sharp DW, Spratt SM, Hagemeyer BC, Jacobs DL (2006) Major land-falling hurricanes as mesoscale convective systems: A paradigm shift for WFO operations. Amer Meteorological Soc, 23rd conference on severe local storms, presentation

10. Audain C (2006) Biographies of women in mathematics: Florence Nightingale. Accessed 12 Dec. www.agnesscott.edu/Lriddle/WOMEN

11. Nightingale F (1858) Notes on matters affecting the health, efficiency and hospital administration of the British Army: Founded chiefly on the experience of the Late War. Harrison and Sons.

12. Carruthers TJB, van Tussenbroek BI, Dennison WC (2005) Influence of submarine springs and wastewater on nutrient dynamics of Caribbean seagrass meadows. Estuar Coast Shelf Sci 64:191-199

13. Waycott M, Freshwater DW, York RA, Calladine A, Kenworthy WJ (2002) Evolutionary trends in the seagrass genus *Halophila (Thouars)*: Insights from molecular phylogeny. Bull Mar Sci 71:1299-1308

Further reading

Burnham KP, Anderson DR (1998) Model selection and inference: A practical information-theoretic approach. Springer-Verlag Telos, New York, New York

Cleveland WS (1993) Visualizing data. Hobart Press, New York, New York

Dobson AJ, Barnett A (2008) An introduction to generalized linear models, 3rd edition. Chapman & Hall/CRC, Boca Raton, Florida

Gelman A, Carlin JB, Stern HS, Rubin DB (2003) Bayesian data analysis. (Texts in Statistical Science Series.) Chapman and Hall/CRC, Boca Raton, Florida

Analyzing environmental data

Grimm, LG (1995) Reading and understanding multivariate statistics. American Pyschological Association, Washington, District of Columbia

Motulsky H (1995) Intuitive biostatistics. Oxford University Press, New York, New York

Scheaffer RL, Mendenhall W, Ott RL (1996) Elementary survey sampling, 5th edition. Duxbury Press, New York, New York

Sokal RR, Rohlf FJ (1994) Biometry. WH Freeman, New York, New York

van Belle G (2002) Statistical rules of thumb. Wiley, Hoboken, New Jersey

Wood S (2006) Generalized additive models: An introduction with R, 1st edition. Chapman & Hall/CRC, Boca Raton, Florida

Zar J (1998) Biostatistical analysis, 4th edition. Prentice Hall, Upper Saddle River, New Jersey

Software available

SAS—Cary, North Carolina: SAS Institute, Inc.

Microsoft Office Excel—Microsoft Corporation (or other spreadsheet software)

S+—Tibco Software Inc., Palo Alto, California

Mathematica—Wolfram Research Inc., Champaign, Illinois

R—R Development Core Team. R: A language and environment for statistical computing. R Foundation for Statistical Computing, Vienna, Austria

Statistica—StatSoft, Tulsa, Oklahoma

SigmaPlot—SPS Software Inc., Chicago, Illinois

CHAPTER 9: ENVIRONMENTAL MODELS

PROVIDING SYNTHESIS, ANALYSIS, SIMULATION, AND PREDICTION

Todd Lookingbill, Tim J.B. Carruthers, Jeremy M. Testa,
William K. Nuttle, and Gary Shenk

All models are wrong but some are useful.
—George E.P. Box

Models can act as an interface among scientists, managers, and the public to build a shared understanding of the status and trends of coastal resources (Figure 9.1). Environmental models can be an effective way of synthesizing large quantities of environmental data. These models can assume a variety of forms and be used to address many different types of research questions. The concept of environmental models has already been introduced in the previous chapter on

statistical analyses (see Chapter 8). This chapter provides more in-depth discussion of model utility, formulation, and evaluation.

Model utility—the many roles that models play

One common application of environmental models is simply to identify and characterize patterns in data. These patterns can be analyzed to evaluate hypotheses about how the system functions. An improved understanding of ecosystem function through the use of models can be useful in

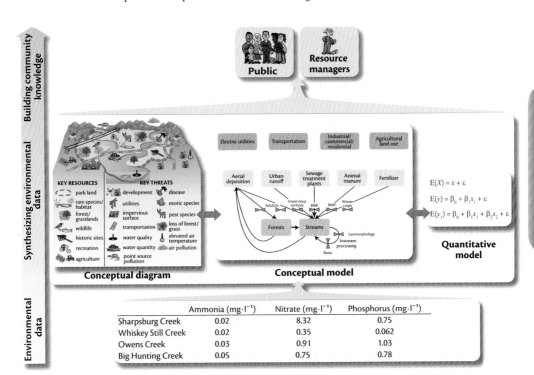

Figure 9.1. Environmental models synthesize information and increase understanding of the status of coastal resources.

quantifying the cause and effect relationships underlying ecological assessments. For example, zooplankton are a key component in the food web. The quantity of zooplankton living in an estuary determines the size of the fish population that an estuary can support, but zooplankton are difficult to measure. Instead, scientists can use a model of the food web to infer the quantity of zooplankton present from measurements of plankton and fish. In this way, scientists use mathematical models to fill a gap in their knowledge about an important component of the ecosystem and generate information about a system parameter that cannot be directly measured.

Models and prediction

Predictive models extend our understanding of the ecosystem beyond the limits of available data. Model predictions can be used either to describe future conditions of the resource or to reconstruct past changes. This capability serves three purposes. First, simple predictive models can be used to express the null hypothesis that variations will continue in response to unchanging outside forces. Second, model predictions can be tested against new observations to validate the underlying conceptual framework. Finally, predictive models can be used to map the expected normal range of variation in the ecosystem (e.g., as a result of the inherent variability of climate-driven processes).

> ### Why we use environmental models
>
> *Synthesize*—summarize and describe raw data
> *Analyze*—compare alternative theories and concepts
> *Simulate*—conduct virtual experiments
> *Predict*—project future changes

Models and virtual experiments

Models also play a valuable role in providing a means to conduct virtual experiments on systems where it would be otherwise impossible or unethical to conduct controlled manipulations. These types of modeling activities may be associated with proposed restoration or management scenarios. In this role, models provide a valuable tool for assessing the economic and environmental trade-offs that may arise from new management or policy decisions. For example, efforts to improve and protect estuarine water quality frequently focus on the load of nutrients contributed from its watershed (Figure 9.2). However, nutrient loads cannot be measured directly. Instead, they are calculated as the product of measured inflow from rivers and streams and measured nutrient concentrations. The Fluxmaster model, developed by the U.S. Geological Survey,

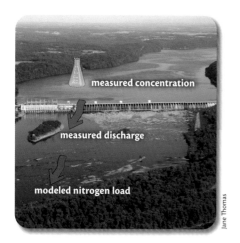

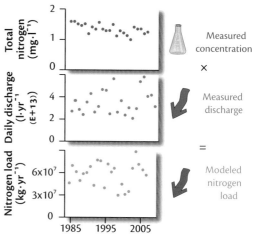

Figure 9.2. Nutrient loading from large watersheds cannot be measured directly. Models are used to estimate loads from measurements of inflow rates 🗲 and nutrient concentrations 🧪 . Models can also be used to evaluate the effects of proposed management practices designed to reduce nutrients entering streams and rivers. The data represents modeled nitrogen load at Conowingo Dam on the Susquehanna River. Source: *va.water.usgs.gov/chesbay/RIMP/loads.html*.

Recipe for success

- Be question driven; do not let the model drive the process
- Identify the appropriate model for the inferences you wish to draw
- Model at an appropriate scale for the process being represented and inferences to be drawn
- Get stakeholder input on the development of the model

takes the calculation of nutrient loads one step further to improve the information provided to managers. Using this model, the effect of short-term variations in freshwater inflow can be statistically removed from the estimated nutrient loads. With this source of variation removed, the model provides a clearer picture of the effect of management activities in the watershed. Thus, managers can use the model output from these experiments in an adaptive management context to learn from and revise future plans of action.[1]

This chapter discusses how the conceptual foundation described previously in this book can be used to help guide the selection and design of useful quantitative models. We describe the subtle balancing act required in choosing a mathematical formulation that satisfies trade-offs among precision, generality, and realism. Of course, the usefulness of a model can be evaluated only relative to the specifics of the intended application. We provide four common environmental models that span a gradient in temporal, spatial, and functional resolution. Finally, we provide an extended case study that applies differing modeling formulations to the challenge of forecasting salinity in Florida Bay and considers the performance of the different models based on common criteria for model evaluation.

Detailed conceptual models provide the foundation for successful quantitative models

A large upfront investment in conceptual diagrams and models is a valuable first step in creating quantitative models. As discussed in previous chapters, initial scoping can be used to identify and describe the structural elements (e.g., habitats, species, communities) and key processes of the system (e.g., disturbances, biogeochemical cycles, physics, threats). Conceptual diagrams can provide

Creating an integrative approach

Howard T. Odum, ecologist

Howard Odum created a novel definition of ecology as the study of large entities (ecosystems) at the "natural level of integration."[2] He aimed to classify large ecosystems and then make predictive generalizations about these ecosystems.

He communicated his new ideas effectively, frequently using tangible analogies to electrical or mechanical systems.[2] Flow of carbon was analogous to the flow of electrons, a charging capacitor to the storage of biomass, and so on. Eventually, Odum generalized these symbols, and they became their own ecological language. This thinking allowed understanding of flows and pools of energy within an ecological system and provided insight into potential deficits, leading to new insights into ecosystem function. When combined to form systems diagrams, these symbols were considered by Odum and others to be the language of the "macroscope". He believed that reducing ecosystem complexities to flows of energy permitted the discovery of general ecosystem principles.[2]

Odum opened new fields in ecology by providing a framework to describe and therefore model and predict complex ecological processes.[2]

Fuel-subsidized solar conversion

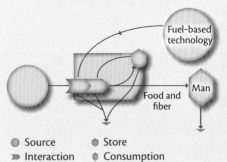

A symbols and system diagram involving fuel-subsidized solar conversion.

a central focus in the scoping effort and can help to clarify thinking. Words can be ambiguous, but an image provides both context and synthesis. The process of developing conceptual diagrams can be used to shed light on monitoring objectives, critical resources, priority threats, and relationships among these system components (Figure 9.3).

Although conceptual diagrams provide a dynamic communication tool for scientists, managers, and stakeholders, conceptual models can be used to develop a more formal framework for organizing data and guiding the calculations that lead to quantitative, mathematical models (Figure 9.4). Conceptual ecological models can take the form of any combination of narratives, tables, or graphical depictions.[4,5] The models continue the process of formalizing our understanding of how things work. This understanding is expressed as concepts about the underlying mechanics of the ecosystem that can later be quantitatively implemented and parameterized in mathematical form.

Conceptual models are similar to conceptual diagrams in that they are abstractions of reality frequently based on incomplete information. As such, they often do not represent finished products but are based on concepts that can and probably will change as monitoring provides new knowledge about the ecosystem. Thus, the models can be regarded as provisional and adaptive and should be continually challenged in terms of their ability to capture reality and their utility for management.

Model formulation—the nuts and bolts of quantitative models

Once the has been established, implementing a quantitative model involves choosing the specific form and functions used to represent the ecosystem components. The interdisciplinary nature of ecological assessments has produced a truly dizzying array of models that vary in purpose and structure. These differences must be considered as part of the model selection process.

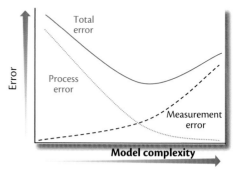

Figure 9.4. There are several trade-offs associated with the level of complexity included in models. Error associated with omitting key systems processes (process error) might be reduced at the cost of including new error associated with data collection (measurement error) and estimation of parameters and mathematical relationships of unknown importance.[6,7]

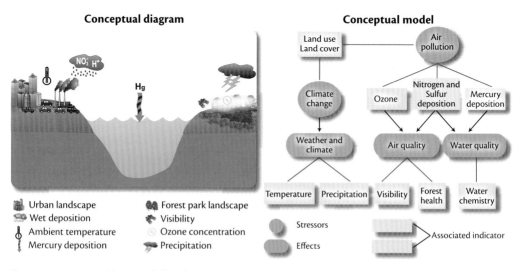

Figure 9.3. A conceptual framework describing critical components and linkages for a monitoring program for the National Park Service National Capital Region Network.[3]

Process error (e):
Inherent variability of feature being measured (e.g., natural variation that will not be captured in model)

Measurement error (o):
Error associated with data collection (e.g., attributes of the input data)

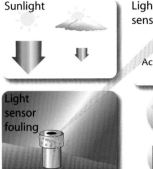

Sunlight

Light sensor

Light sensor fouling

Actually measures electric potential difference

Parameter error (p):
Uncertainty in parameter estimates (e.g., measuring electric potential difference to estimate light intensity)

Structural error (s):
Error associated with model formulation (e.g., choice of modeling method)

Figure 9.5. Using the measurement of of underwater light as an example. Four different sources of error that should be considered in model selection: Total model error = process error (e) + measurement error (o) + parameter error (p) + structural error(s).[8,9]

Striking a balance

Unfortunately, there is no single best model for all coastal assessment program questions. Selecting a modeling approach often comes down to striking a balance between model complexity and other characteristics that may be important to the program, including precision, generality, and realism.[10]

With improved modeling tools at our disposal, models have become easier to build, with a trend toward increasing model complexity. However, a complex model is not necessarily preferable to a carefully formulated simple model. For example, the

Table 9.1. Models can be grouped according to a number of criteria related to their structure.[9,11-13]

Simple models	vs.	Complex models
• Can be easily built and easily discarded and replaced • Can be readily understood and compared • Can facilitate communication to broad audiences		• Can consider non-linear processes (including thresholds) • Can include positive feedbacks • Can investigate contagious processes/spatial fluxes
Empirical (statistical) models	vs.	**Mechanistic (process) models**
• Describe relationships between different variables without characterizing the underlying mechanics responsible for the relationships		• Explain underlying mechanics responsible for relationships between different variables
Deterministic models	vs.	**Stochastic models**
• Do not include uncertainty in the input parameters • Always provide the same output		• Include uncertainty in the input parameters, usually through probability distributions • Can provide a range of output values
Analytical models	vs.	**Simulation models**
• Use mathematical expressions to represent the connections in a system • Predict system behavior from a set of parameters and initial conditions		• Generate a sample of scenarios, with only part of the system being mathematically modeled • Are used when simple analytic representations of the system are not possible
Static models	vs.	**Dynamic models**
• Represent variables that do not change through time.		• Capture temporal change
Non-spatial models	vs.	**Spatial models**
• Make predictions using independent variables measured without regard to spatial location (e.g., outputs could be pie charts)		• Create spatially structured output • Incorporate neighborhood effects and/or simulate the fluxes of materials, organisms, energy, etc., directly into the model

Analyzing environmental data

inclusion of additional processes or relationships in a model requires additional parameters. Each parameter brings with it a potentially new source of error (Figure 9.5). Errors are associated with the selection of model formulation used to quantify relationships, the measurement of the input data, and the estimation of the parameters (Figure 9.5). The net effect of increasing model complexity can be to decrease the accuracy of model predictions, as errors associated with leaving processes out ('sins of omission') are replaced by errors associated with including processes that are poorly measured, unmeasured, or unmeasurable ('sins of commission').[9]

Overly simple models, in contrast, may not capture critical ecosystem properties and processes. Though easier to interpret, they can lack realism. Nevertheless, simple models have considerable advantages: They can be easily built and easily discarded and replaced, they can be readily understood and compared, and they can be presented to and generally understood by broad audiences.[13] In coastal assessment programs, time is often a limiting resource. For example, management decisions cannot be delayed for the time it might take to implement, calibrate, and verify a state-of-the-art hydrodynamic water quality model. Ockham's Razor provides valuable guidance here.

In addition to the simple versus complex dichotomy, several other structural contrasts help to bring some order to the vast assortment of modeling options (Table 9.1, previous page). Model utility ultimately depends on the specific resources, constraints, and objectives (i.e., the purpose) of the assessment program. The domain of applicability of a model describes the set of conditions for which a model is useful.[14] Different model structures have different domains of applicability, and careful model selection entails consideration of how different candidate models treat space, time, and

Ockham's Razor

Ockham's Razor is a popular rule in science stating that the simplest of competing theories is usually preferable.

function. For example, if the primary purpose of a coastal assessment program is to identify nutrient hotspots in an estuary, a spatially explicit model would be appropriate. However, if the purpose is to track overall trends in nutrient loads following a change in management policy, a greater emphasis might be placed on the dynamic properties of the model.

The following pages present four common quantitative model formulations that span a gradient in spatial, temporal, and functional resolution. The approaches range from simple, statistical correlation models to complex, physically based, process simulation models (Figure 9.6). This representative sample provides a flavor of the breadth of modeling options available for coastal assessment programs. Each model description is

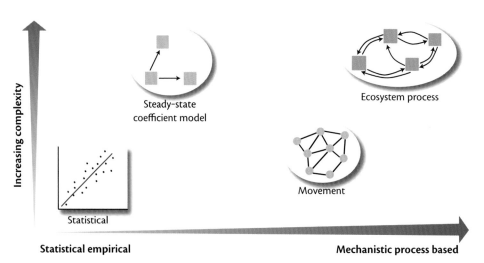

Figure 9.6. Models of varying complexity and formulation can be used to investigate a range of research questions.

accompanied by a graphic depicting its general domain of applicability (space, time, function) and an example application of the approach.

Correlation models

Definition: Use statistical analyses to identify critical relationships between attributes
Examples: Regression, multivariate ordination

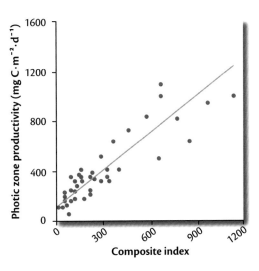

Figure 9.7. Empirical regression models have been widely used to model primary productivity for estuaries throughout the world. The above data illustrate the correlation between phytoplankton net production and a composite index of chlorophyll *a* concentration, optical depth, and surface irradiance in San Francisco Bay.[16]

At their most basic level, many models for coastal assessment are purely statistical and take advantage of the strong correlation between environmental parameters of interest (e.g., photic zone productivity) and more easily measured proxy variables (e.g.,photic zone productivity and composite index; Figure 9.7). These models can be rather simple in formulation, but are extremely powerful when extrapolated to allow prediction of unobserved events. They are also frequently referred to as empirical models, recognizing their reliance on available data.

A number of statistical tools can be used to formulate these models. These range from simple linear regression to more complicated analytical techniques, such as multivariate and time series statistical procedures. Statistical correlation analysis also can be used both as a screening technique to identify potential cause-and-effect relationships and as the first test of hypothesized relationships. However, correlation alone does not indicate that a cause-and-effect relationship exists.

When explanatory variables are spatially structured, the model can be considered spatially implicit, and output can be mapped. For example, relatively few data points gathered from meteorological stations are often used to build simple "lapse rate" regression models to describe the relationship between temperature and elevation. Recent advances in technology, including portable *in situ* sampling devices (see Chapter 12), allow for higher density monitoring networks to be placed in difficult-to-reach locations. As a result of these increased data,

the potential to generate higher resolution maps using statistical models has greatly improved (Figure 9.8). Geographic information systems (GIS) and remote sensing platforms (see Chapter 13) have also played prominent roles in improving statistical mapping capabilities.

These types of models are quite effective for representing ecological processes that have spatial structure but do not depend on spatial interactions. They are considerably less effective for modeling processes with a high spatial contagion (i.e., what happens at one point in space depends on the dynamic state of neighboring points), such as the spread of disturbances.

Movement models

Definition: Depict dispersal or other types of movements across space.
Examples: Diffusion models, network models

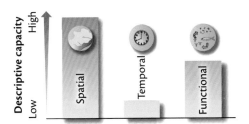

Analyzing environmental data

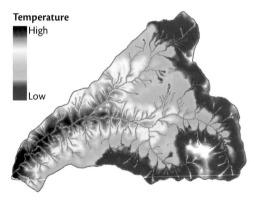

Temperature
High

Low

Figure 9.8. The output of regression models that use predictor variables with spatial patterns can be mapped even if spatial location is not explicitly included in the model. Here temperature is modeled as a function of elevation, slope aspect, and distance from stream.[15]

Movement models can range in complexity from simple GIS-based estimates of potential movement corridors to individual-based dispersal simulators. Network models, which apply the mathematics of graph theory, are examples of movement models that can be mathematically complex but require limited calibration of mechanistic processes.

Crude environment networks (i.e., graphs) can be generated with little to no direct observations of actual movement. A graph comprises a set of nodes representing the center of environmental patches and a corresponding set of edges that represent connectivity between nodes (Figure 9.9). Patches that are considered connected by some type of ecological flux (e.g., dispersal of organisms) are represented by drawing an edge between their respective nodes. Thus, the model has a minimum requirement of only two pieces of data: a spatial

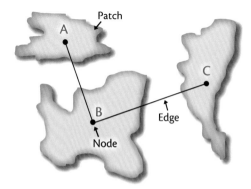

Figure 9.9. A connected graph illustrating graph patches, nodes, and edges. Patch A is directly connected to B and indirectly connected to C.

map of patches (e.g., coral reefs, oyster bars) and a method for defining movement between patches (e.g., wind, gravity, currents).

A network (e.g., the coral reefs of the South Pacific) would be considered fully connected if every node could be reached from every other node via some pathway of connected patches (Figure 9.10). In addition to quantifying overall connectivity, the graph model can be used to identify nodes within the network of special importance, such as stepping-stone or critical source habitat for interpatch dispersal.[17] The approach has proven extremely successful for modeling the functional characteristics of an ecosystem from the perspective of the physical distribution of natural resources.

Steady-state coefficient models

Definition: Use derived or measured terms (coefficients) to quantify flows between defined compartments.

Example: Patuxent River Estuarine Box-Model

Between simple statistical models and fully process-based mechanistic models are a class of models called steady-state coefficient models, which are relatively simple but offer some functional dynamics. For example, box-models are used in coastal ecosystems to compute advective and diffusive transports of salt, nutrients, and other key variables from commonly available hydrologic and hydrographic data (e.g., salinity and freshwater inputs). To construct a box-model, a system is first divided into defined volumes; or "boxes." Then, coefficients of the exchange between boxes are derived from mass-balances of salt and water for each box.

There are many excellent examples of the application of box-modeling to coastal systems.[19,21,22] In an application for the Patuxent River estuary,[22] a box-model was used to examine the effects of sewage treatment upgrades on two key ecological processes (Figure 9.11): 1) dissolved inorganic nitrogen (DIN) transport

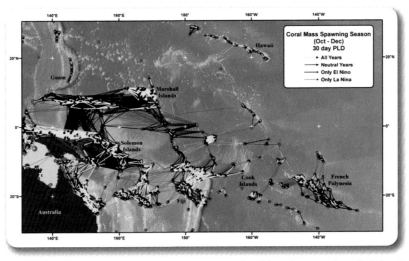

Figure 9.10. South Pacific showing potential connections among coral reefs based on a 30-day pelagic larval duration during the coral spawning season of an El Niño (1997), La Niña (1999), and a neutral year (2001). Unique connections occur during the El Niño event.[18]

into three regions of the estuary and 2) the net production rate of dissolved oxygen in the surface layer of the lower estuary, which is an index of net ecosystem productivity (photosynthesis–respiration). It was discovered that following sewage treatment upgrades to remove DIN from discharge, the physical transport of DIN into the lower estuary from the middle estuary declined significantly (Figure 9.11b), but modeled net oxygen production rates (and chlorophyll a) in this region increased over time (Figure 9.11c). This seemingly contradictory result was explained by

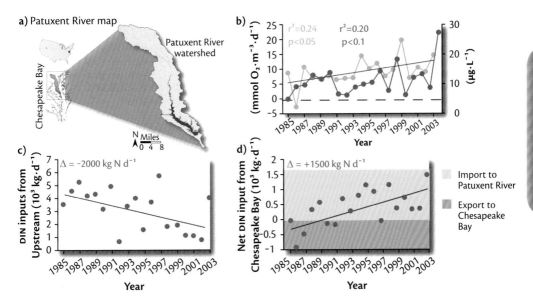

Figure 9.11. a) Map of the Patuxent River estuary. b) Time series (1985–2003) of chlorophyll a (dark green) and net O_2 production (light green) shown in the surface layer of the lower Patuxent estuary. c) Box-model-computed DIN transport from the middle to lower estuary has declined significantly from 1985–2003. d) Net DIN transport into the lower estuary from Chesapeake Bay has increased significantly during the same time period.[22]

Analyzing environmental data

an increase in the physical inputs of DIN into the estuary from Chesapeake Bay over the same time period (Figure 9.11d), which nearly offset the DIN reductions achieved by sewage treatment upgrades. The outcome from this relatively simple modeling exercise identified the need for whole ecosystem restoration and water quality management strategies.

Ecosystem process models

Definition: Represent physically based processes in a spatially explicit framework.
Example: Chesapeake Bay Estuarine Model

At the extreme end of the complexity gradient are ecosystem process models. At a minimum, these mechanistic, physically based models use the principle of mass conservation. Hydraulic and hydrodynamic models use both the conservation of mass and conservation of momentum. Models of water quality use the laws of chemistry, and so on.

The Chesapeake Bay Estuarine Model is an example that is spatially explicit, deterministic, and mechanistic (see Table 9.1). It is used to examine the effects of nutrient and sediment loads in the bay. The Estuarine Model is built on

Figure 9.13. In the Estuary Model, the Chesapeake Bay is represented by almost 13,000 computational cells that average 1.5 square miles in area. The cells are stacked up to 15 layers in the deepest areas of the bay.

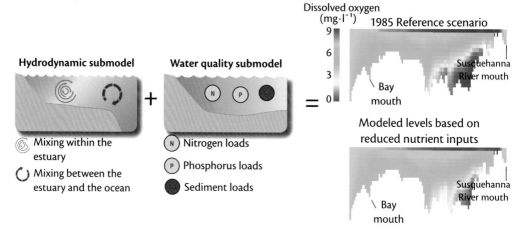

Figure 9.12. Information from the hydrodynamic and water quality submodels of the estuarine model are combined to simulate the effects of nutrient load reduction on future water quality conditions, such as dissolved oxygen levels.[23]

two submodels: the hydrodynamic submodel and the water quality submodel (Figure 9.12), which share the same computational grid that consists of 12,961 model cells (Figure 9.13). The hydrodynamic submodel simulates the mixing of estuarine waters with coastal ocean waters, and the mixing of water within Chesapeake Bay. The Water Quality Model simulates the fate of nutrients and sediments in the bay and the response of water quality through chemical and biological processes for 24 state variables, such as water temperature, salinity, and nutrients.[24]

These models are particularly useful for prediction because they represent physical processes observed in the world. Predictions with mechanistic models are based on explicit representation of the causes and mechanisms at work in the ecosystem. Explicit representation of cause-and-effect based on general principles increases confidence in the ability of a model to predict the behavior of the system beyond the limits of available observations. For example, the Estuarine Model forecasts changes in the health of the bay (measured by the percentage of the bay that meets set water quality standards) if nutrients are increased or decreased to specific levels. The models are also good for simulating different management scenarios. Currently, the Estuarine Model is being directed toward the examination of potential further nutrient and sediment reductions to fully restore the water quality required for the bay's living resources.

Model evaluation—structured assessment of model performance

Matching the appropriate model structure to the purpose of the modeling activity is aided by a strict set of criteria for model evaluation (Table 9.2). Testing models with these criteria reveals patterns in the behavior of the models, the system being studied, and the interrelationship of the two.

The following case study illustrates a multilayered approach to the problem of predicting salinity fluctuations in Florida Bay. Salinity prediction tests our knowledge of processes that drive water flow and mixing in an estuary. These processes are essential to maintaining the structure and function of estuarine and coastal ecosystems.

Case study—evaluating alternative models of Florida Bay salinity

In Florida Bay and other estuaries in South Florida the interest in salinity prediction is motivated by managers' need to anticipate what effects regional water management decisions will have on the region's living resources. Salinity is the key characteristic of habitat in estuarine and coastal ecosystems that is sensitive to changes in regional hydrology. Salinity is an aspect of water quality that controls the composition and geographic distribution of submerged aquatic and wetland communities and affects the life history of most estuarine animal species.

Table 9.2. Criteria considered for evaluation of models.[25]

Portability	The model should be widely available for evaluation and application. This requirement also extends to the documentation and data needed to apply the model. Simulation models that require specialized computing equipment, (e.g., access to parallel processing or a supercomputer facility) are not widely available.
Validity	The predictive capability of the model is generally known and accepted. An important aspect of validation is the existence of a data set that is generally accepted to represent the variation in the system that the model is intended to explain.
Fidelity	The model is consistent with understood mechanisms of cause-and-effect within the limitations of the underlying model formulation. This condition reflects one of the characteristics of an ideal ecological indicator and challenges model builders to become familiar with and extend the current state of understanding of the ecosystem.
Focus	Model results relate directly to the ecosystem attributes defined as performance measures. For example, salinity is a physical attribute that links to other biological components of estuarine ecosystems. However, different attributes of salinity variation may have different ecological effects. Linking different attributes of salinity to ecological indicators might be best approached by using different models rather than by relying on a single predictive model for salinity.
Ease of use	Model results can be obtained quickly within the time allotted for analysis of alternatives. For example, if a Monte Carlo approach is used to map ecosystem response in a probabilistic sense, then models must be capable of iteratively rerunning a large number of simulations with randomized inputs. Attention must be paid to the computational facilities needed to run the models and to the presentation of simulation results.

Analyzing environmental data

Regional water management in South Florida has altered natural timing and patterns of freshwater inflow to estuaries. Water no longer moves slowly from north to south down the peninsula. Instead, stormwater now drains quickly away from the Everglades wetlands in the center to the Caloosahatchee and St. Lucie estuaries on the west and east coasts (Figure 9.14). Planned changes in the regional system would restore more natural flow patterns, decreasing drainage to the west and the east and increasing the inflow of freshwater to Florida Bay and the southwest coast. Water managers rely on simulated future conditions in the estuaries, based on salinity predictions, to guide their decisions.

The influence of other regional drivers complicates efforts to restore and maintain estuarine ecosystems. In addition to changes in water management, conditions in Florida Bay are affected by rising sea level, climate change, and episodic events. We evaluate four models and three alternative model formulations in terms of their ability to support restoration and management of the Florida Bay ecosystem (Table 9.3).

Modeling approaches considered for Florida Bay

Multivariate linear regression (MLR)— Determine statistical relationships between different ecological components

Mass balance—Account for the inputs and outputs of water from basins delineated by geomorphological features

3-D Hydrodynamic—Determine hydrodynamics of a system in one, two, or three dimensions

Statistical models

The statistical models predict salinity directly from patterns of variation in related drivers, such as rainfall and streamflow. Salinity in Florida Bay responds to variation in regional rainfall on two time scales. Rainfall over the Everglades wetlands, upstream from the bay, drives variations in water levels, and freshwater inflow to the bay. These are

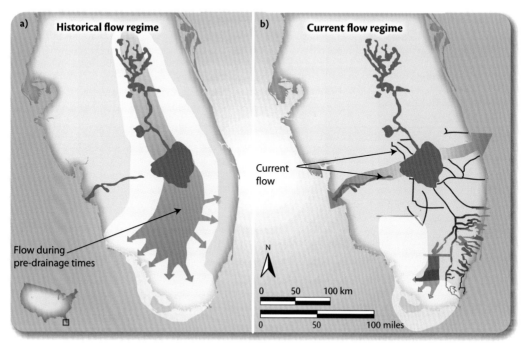

Figure 9.14. A comparison of current and historical flow regimes through the Everglades wetlands, showing how water that once flowed south into the Everglades is now directed to the east and west. a) Historical water flow through the Everglades wetlands. b) Current water flow regime. Based on information provided by the South Florida Water Management District, *www.evergladesplan.org/docs/fs_fl_bay_feas_study.pdf*.

Table 9.3. Comparison of the models used to investigate salinity changes in Florida Bay.[28,30-33]

Model name	Model type	Simulated parameters	Spatial domain	Grid size	Simulation temporal domain
Multivariate Linear Regression MLR[1]	Statistical	Salinity	Florida Bay, Whitewater Bay, southwest Gulf coast, Manatee Bay, Barnes Sound	N/A	1965–2000, daily
Four box[2]	Mass balance	Salinity	Florida Bay	Regional	1993–1998, monthly
FATHOM[3]	Mass balance	Salinity	Florida Bay, Manatee Sound, Barnes Sound	Open-water basins	1965–2000, monthly
EFDC[4]	3-D hydrodynamic	Salinity	Florida Bay, Whitewater Bay, southwest Gulf coast, Manatee Bay, Barnes Sound	Variable	1965–2000, daily

responsible for changes in salinity over seasonal and longer time scales. Local rainfall in the bay and wind-driven currents are responsible for driving day-to-day and week-to-week changes in salinity. Researchers captured these relationships in multivariate linear regression (MLR) models and applied the models to construct an extended 36-year time series of estimated daily salinity from long-term data on wind, rainfall, wetland water levels, and sea level (Figure 9.15).[26,27]

Error statistics computed from predictions of the MLR models revealed differences in characteristics of salinity between inshore and open water locations. The fidelity between model predictions and measured salinity provides insight into the behavior of the estuary that is not well represented in the model or the data available for input to the model. Values of the coefficient of determination

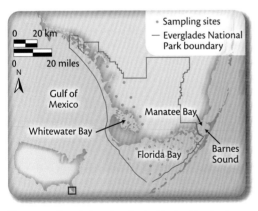

Figure 9.15. Sample locations in the Marine Monitoring Network used for the MLR models in the Everglades National Park.[28]

(r^2) and the Nash-Sutcliffe efficiency statistic were lower (meaning less fidelity between calculated and measured salinity values) in the following inshore bays: Joe Bay, Little Madeira Bay, Terrapin Bay, and Garfield Bight. The discrepancy relates to greater influence of short-term, day-to-day variation in salinity. Therefore, local rainfall and wind conditions exert greater influence on salinity variation at inshore locations. The ability to predict this variation is limited by a lack of data that accurately characterizes these local drivers.

Mass-balance models

Mass-balance models are the simplest form of mechanistic salinity models. Two mass-balance models have been implemented in Florida Bay – the Four-box model and FATHOM. Both calculate changes in salinity by dividing the bay into discrete regions and keeping account of changes over time in the mass of water and salt contained in each. This involves estimating freshwater fluxes into and out of each region and calculating salt fluxes related to advection and exchange of water between regions within the bay and between the bay and the coastal ocean.

The four-box model divides the bay into four regions (Figure 9.16).[29] These delineate areas that have similar characteristics of water quality, including salinity, sediment, and ecological communities. Input data consist of estimated monthly rainfall for each region and amounts of freshwater inflow into the northeast and central regions from the Everglades wetlands. Long-term salinity data provides information about the variation of salinity along the boundary with the Gulf of Mexico.

Analyzing environmental data

The four-box model was developed as a tool to estimate residence time and evaporation from the bay from available data on other freshwater fluxes and observed fluctuations in salinity. Parameters in the model describe the seasonal pattern of evaporation and the mean tidal exchange between regions. Initially, the values of these parameters are unknown. Values are estimated through calibration, that is, through an automated process that selects the set of values that minimizes differences between calculated and measured salinity over a specific period of time. Errors in calculated salinity values over a different period tests the predictive capability of the calibrated model. The standard error of prediction with the four-box model is about 2 practical salinity units (psu) over all four regions. The calculated exchange fluxes and evaporation rates provide information that is critical to understanding processes that control nutrient concentration and the onset of plankton blooms.

The bathymetry of Florida Bay divides the bay into a series of basins, and this provides a natural framework for mass-balance accounting. The FATHOM mass-balance model divides the bay into about 40 regions (Figure 9.17) based on the position of banks and shallows that fill the bay.[31,32] Freshwater fluxes are estimated from available data, as for the four-box model. However, in contrast to the four-box model, the FATHOM model uses highly detailed bathymetric data to define the volumes of the basins and the geometry of the banks that separate them.

The FATHOM model uses simple hydraulic flow (Mannings) equations to calculate the

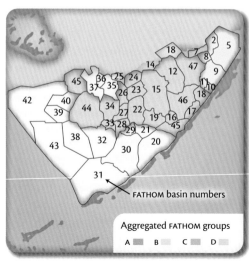

Figure 9.17. Map identifying the basins and the aggregated regions used in FATHOM for salinity calculations.[32]

exchange fluxes between basins. At each time step, the FATHOM model solves for discharge in uniform, hydraulic flow across each bank based on information on the depth of water, bank width and bottom roughness, and the difference in water levels between the upstream and downstream basins. By this mechanism, the influence of tidal forcing and month-to-month changes in sea level in the Gulf of Mexico propagates into the bay and drives the exchange of water and salt among basins.

Due to its greater spatial resolution (when compared to the four-box model), the FATHOM model has been used to investigate the sensitivity of salinity to changes in freshwater inflow from the Everglades wetlands.[30] Of particular interest are conditions that promote the formation of hypersaline conditions in the central region of the bay. Managers at the South Florida Water Management District have used the FATHOM model to establish minimum limits on freshwater inflow required to avoid serious harm to the bay's ecology.

Hydrodynamic models

Hydrodynamic models form the core of a comprehensive estuarine modeling program. These models provide the most detailed prediction of conditions in an estuary. However, the quantity and quality of available data impose the same limits on the implementation of hydrodynamic models as on the other types of models.

Implementation of the Environmental Fluid Dynamics Code (EFDC) model serves as a recent example of the implementation of a hydrodynamic

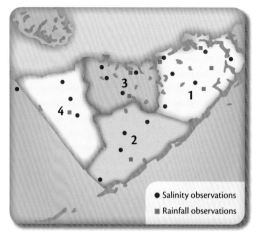

Figure 9.16. The four box model divides Florida Bay into regions based on observed patterns in water quality.[30,34]

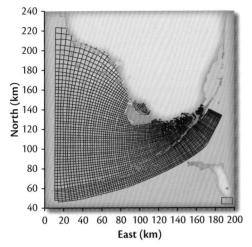

Figure 9.18. Spatial grid used in the Environmental Fluid Dynamics Code model.[35]

model in Florida Bay. The EFDC is a general-purpose model for simulating surface water bodies represented in one, two, or three dimensions. This model represents physical characteristics of the water body on a spatial grid comprising stretched or sigma coordinates in the vertical and Cartesian or curvilinear, orthogonal coordinates in the horizontal (Figure 9.18). The code solves three-dimensional, vertically hydrostatic, free surface, turbulent-averaged equations of motion for a variable density fluid. Dynamically coupled transport equations for turbulent kinetic energy, turbulent length scale, salinity, and temperature are also solved. In addition, the EFDC model allows for tide-driven drying and wetting of shallow areas by a mass conservation scheme.

For application in Florida Bay, the domain of the EFDC model takes in a large area of the south Florida shelf outside the mouth of the bay. The model was configured using National Oceanic and Atmospheric Administration (NOAA) and United States Geological Survey (USGS) bathymetry. Open-boundary conditions include tides and sea level, salinity, and temperature. Surface heat exchange is calculated based on spatially varying wind and atmospheric data. Estimates of inflows, salinity, and temperature for canal, creek, and river discharges are applied as inputs along the northern boundary of the bay and the southwest Florida coast.

At the present stage of development, EFDC calculations capture key characteristics of water movement, but results of salinity calculations are mixed. Calculated water level fluctuations exhibit a shift in the tidal regime from macrotidal in the western areas to microtidal in the central and northeast regions. This transition reflects the attenuation of tidal energy in flow over the bay's shallow banks. In the central and northeast regions water level fluctuations are driven locally by wind and globally by fluctuations in sea level in the Gulf of Mexico. Errors in salinity calculations by the EFDC model are larger than those for the statistical and mass-balance models, but work continues to improve the implementation of the EFDC model.

Model comparison

Each of the models described here was developed to fulfill a particular need for salinity prediction in Florida Bay. Comparison between models must take into account a number of desired qualities not simply how well the calculated salinity values match observations. The choice of which model to use as a tool for data analysis or to evaluate wide-ranging proposals for water management will give consideration to portability, focus, and

Pitfalls to avoid

- Modeling in isolation
- Believing that the model is reality
- Combining processes that occur at differing scales
- Adding unnecessary complexity to the model
- Using higher-or lower-resolution models than are necessary

Table 9.4. Evaluation scores for Florida Bay salinity and hydrology models (1= poor, 5= very good).[25]

Model	Portability	Validity	Fidelity	Focus	Ease of use
MLR	5	5	5	5	5
Four box	3	4	4	3	5
FATHOM	3	5	4	5	4
EFDC	2	5	3	5	3

ease of use as well as fidelity and validity of the model (Table 9.4).

Because of their relative simplicity, the development and application of statistical and mass-balance models have preceded hydrodynamic models. FATHOM and the multivariate linear regression models have been used widely to evaluate the effects of various water management alternatives on the bay. Development of the EFDC hydrodynamic model continues toward the ultimate goal of a comprehensive simulation model capable of tracing the influence of freshwater flows from the Everglades wetlands through Florida Bay and out onto the Florida Shelf. Even after this is accomplished, the statistical and mass-balance models will likely remain in use for planning-level decisions on a regional basis.

References

1. Christensen NL, Bartuska AM, Brown JH, Carpenter S, D'Antonio C, Francis R, Franklin JF, MacMahon JA, Noss RN, Parsons DJ, Peterson CH, Turner MG, Woodmansee RG (1996) The report of the Ecological Society of America committee on the scientific basis for ecosystem management. Ecol Appl 6:665-691
2. Cleveland CJ (2008) Odum, Howard T. Accessed 16 May. www.eoearth.org/article/Odum%2C_Howard_T
3. Lookingbill TR (2005) Conceptual ecological models. In: Monitoring Plan: National Capital Region Network of the National Park Service. Washington, DC. Prepared for NPS I&M Program
4. Noon BR (2003) Conceptual issues in monitoring ecological resources. In: Busch ED, Trexler JC (eds) Monitoring ecosystems: Interdisciplinary approaches for evaluating ecoregional initiatives. Island Press, Washington, District of Columbia, p 27-71
5. Lookingbill TR, Gardner RH, Townsend PA, Carter SL (2007) Conceptual models as hypotheses in monitoring of urban landscapes. J Environ Manage 40:210-222
6. Lookingbill TR, Gardner RH, Wainger LA, Tague CL (2008) Landscape modeling. In: Jorgensen SE, Fath BD (eds) Encylopedia of Ecology. Elsevier, Oxford, UK, p 2108-2116
7. O'Neill RV (1973) Error analysis of ecological models. In: Nelson DJ (ed) Radionuclides in ecosystems. National Technical Information Service, Springfield, Virginia, p 898-908
8. O'Neill RV, Gardner RH (1979) Sources of uncertainty in ecological models. In: Zeigler BP, Elzas MS, Kliv GJ, Oren TI (eds) Methodology in systems modelling and simlulation. North-Holland Publishing, Amsterdam, The Netherlands, p 447-463
9. Peters DPC, Herrick JE, Urban DL, Gardner RH, Breshears DD (2004) Strategies for ecological extrapolation. Oikos 106:627-636
10. Levins R (1966) The strategy of model building in population ecology. Amer Sci 54:421-431
11. Hilborn R, Mangel M (1997) The ecological detective: Confronting models with data. Princeton University Press, Princeton, New Jersey
12. Jackson LJ, Trebitz AS, Cottingham KL (2000) An introduction to the practice of ecological modeling. BioSci 50:694-706
13. Pace ML (2002) The utility of simple models in ecosystem science. In: Canham CD, Cole JC, Lauenroth WK (eds) Model in ecosystem science. Princeton University Press, Princeton, New Jersey, p 49-62
14. Cale WG, O'Neill RV, Shugart HH (1983) Development and application of desirable ecological models. Ecol Model 18:171-186
15. Lookingbill TR, Urban DL (2003) Spatial estimation of air temperature differences for landscape-scale studies in montane environments. Agricul Forest Meteor 114:141-151
16. Cole BE, Cloern JE (1987) An empirical model for estimating phytoplankton productivity in estuaries. Mar Eco Prog Ser 36:299-305
17. Urban D, Keitt T (2001) Landscape connectivity: A graph-theoretic perspective. Ecology 82:1205-1218
18. Treml EA, Halpin PN, Urban DL, Pratson LF (2008) Modeling population connectivity by ocean currents; graph-theoretic approach for marine conservation. Landscape Ecol 23:19-36
19. Wulff F, Stigebrandt A (1989) A timed-dependent budget model for nutrients in the Baltic Sea. Global Biogeochem Cycles 3:63-78
20. Smith SV, Hollibaugh JT, Dollar SJ, Vink S (1991) Tomales Bay metabolism C-N-P stoichiometry and ecosystem heterotrophy at the land–sea interface. Est Coast Shelf Sci 33:223-257
21. Gazeau F, Gattuso J-P, Middelburg JJ, Brion N, Schiettecatte L-S, Frankignoulle M, Borges AV (2005) Planktonic and whole system metabolism in a nutrient-rich estuary (the Scheldt Estuary). Estuaries 28:868-883
22. Testa JM, Kemp WM (2008) Variability of biogeochemical processes and physical transport in a partially stratified estuary: A box-modeling analysis. Mar Ecol Prog Ser 356:63-79
23. Chesapeake Bay Program (2005) Chesapeake Bay environmental models. Integration & Application Network, www.ian.umces.edu/communication/newsletters/2005/models/
24. Cerco C, Cole T (1993) Three-dimensional eutrophication model of Chesapeake Bay. J Environ Eng 119: 1006–1025
25. Marshall III FE, Smith D, Nuttle WK (2006) Simulating and forecasting salinity in Florida Bay: A review of models. Critical Ecosystems Initiative (CESI), Cooperative Agreement #-CA-H5284-05-0006, submitted to Everglades National Park 110609
26. Marshall III FE, Smith D, Nickerson D (2003) Salinity simulation models for north Florida Bay Everglades National Park. Cetacean Logic Foundation, Inc., New Smyrna Beach, Florida, p 41
27. Marshall III FE (2003) IOP salinity analysis using statistical models. Cetacean Logic Foundation, Inc., New Smyrna Beach, Florida, p 35
28. Marshall III FE (2005) ICU runs summary report for southern estuaries subteam of RECOVER. Environmental Consulting & Technology, Inc., New Smyrna Beach, Florida
29. Kelble CR, Johns EM, Nuttle WK, Lee TN, Smith RH, Ortner PB (2007) Salinity patterns of Florida Bay. Estuar Coast Shelf Sci 71:318-334
30. Nuttle WK, Fourqurean JW, Cosby BJ, Zieman JC, Robblee MB (2000) The influence of net freshwater supply on salinity in Florida Bay. Water Resources Research 36:1805-1822

31. Cosby BJ, Nuttle WK, Fourqurean JW (1999) FATHOM: Model description and initial application to Florida Bay.

32. Cosby BW, Nuttle WK, Marshall F (2005) FATHOM enhancements and implementation to support development of MFL for Florida Bay. Environmental Consulting & Technology, Inc., South Florida Water Management District #C-C-15975-WO05-05, New Smyrna Beach, Florida

33. Hamrick JM, Moustafa MZ (2003) Florida Bay hydrodynamic and salinity model analysis. In: Florida Bay Program & Abstracts, Joint Conference on the Science and Restoration of the Greater Everglades and Florida Bay Ecosystem, University of Florida/IFAS, Gainesville, Florida

34. Boyer JN, Fourqurean JW, Jones RD (1997) Spatial characterization of water quality in Florida Bay and Whitewater Bay by multivariate analyses: Zones of similar influence. Estuaries 20:743-758

35. Hamrick JM, Zhen-Gang J (2008) Coupled hydrodynamic and water quality modeling of Florida Bay. In: Program and abstract book, 2008 Florida Bay and Adjacent Marine Systems Science Conference, University of Florida/IFAS, Gainesville, Florida

Further reading

Calabrese JM, Fagan WF (2004) A comparison-shopper's guide to connectivity metrics. Front Ecol Environ 2:529-536

CROGEE (2002) Florida Bay research programs and their relation to the comprehensive Everglades restoration plan. National Academies Press,Washington, District of Columbia

Gentile JH, Harwell MA, Cropper W, Harwell CC, DeAngelis D, Davis S, Ogden JC, Lirman D (2001) Ecological conceptual models: A framework and case study on ecosystem management for South Florida sustainability. Sci Total Environ 274:231-253

Hayes B (2000) Graph theory in practice; part I. Amer Sci 88:9-13

Analyzing environmental data

Chapter 10: Spatial analysis

Making maps and using spatial analyses

R. Heath Kelsey and Ben J. Longstaff

Maps are human representations of the world.
—Peter Whitfield

Although spatial analysis is technically a component of statistical analysis and environmental modeling, the important role it plays, or should play, in coastal assessment programs warrants specific attention in its own separate chapter. This chapter provides some of the basic principles for producing effective maps through to the process of undertaking complex spatial analyses.

Spatial analysis: An essential tool for coastal assessment

Spatial analysis is the process of investigating ways that information in relation as a function of space or location either in relation to each other or to other features, such as pollution sources. The aim of spatial analysis is to identify and understand patterns and regularities, and this can be achieved using a variety of geographic information systems (GIS) and statistical and mathematical approaches (Figure 10.1). These approaches range from simple and intuitive to highly technical. An important result of spatial analysis is often the ability to present information as maps, which if presented well, are very effective tools for communicating information. However, spatial analyses may be more encompassing than maps alone. Its techniques represent important tools in the assessment toolbox, useful at any stage of a coastal assessment program. It is important to note that a thorough understanding of the data used in spatial analysis is a necessity, and caution must be exercised when interpreting data or generating new information. This issue will be discussed later in this chapter.

Choosing the right tool for a particular spatial analysis question depends on the data available and the specifics of the question. Typically, spatial data are available for very specific locations or points (point data), linear representations

Sample data set					
Site	Month	Lat°	Long°	DO	Sal
A	March	39.7	76.7	8	5
A	March			7	7
A	March			7	6
B	May	38.7	77.7	6	13
B	May			6	16
B	May			7	15

DO=dissolved oxygen, Sal=salinity

Maps

Single data sources (point data alone)

Data integration (point, line, and polygon data sources)

Spatially analyzed

Spatial analysis

Spatial and statistical output
$(Y=f(\text{proximity } Xy))$

Pure statistical/model output
$(Y=B_0+B_1X_1,...B_2X_2)$

Figure 10.1. Spatial analysis covers a broad spectrum of skills and applications from mapping simple data sets to in-depth statistical analysis.

Analyzing environmental data

(line data), regions (polygon data), or grids (raster data) (Table 10.1). Each data type has unique qualities that make it suitable in some instances and less suitable in others. For example, point data often present the most precise representation of data location (e.g., sampling results at specific sites), but because one cannot sample every location, point data may provide an incomplete picture of measured parameters. For example, it is often difficult to infer concentrations of a water quality parameter at locations between the specific sampling sites where it has been measured. In some cases, it may be possible to use interpolation techniques to develop a continuous surface from the point data. These analyses can be helpful in visualizing patterns not immediately apparent and can suggest particular areas of concern or even sources of pollutants.

GIS is more than map-making

Although GIS is often thought of as primarily a computerized mapping system, the functionality of most GIS software allows in-depth analyses of spatial relationships. A formal definition of GIS would include the analysis and management of spatially referenced data.

The power of maps

Maps can convey spatially referenced data in a holistic way that immediately informs readers, viewers, and researchers about the complex patterns that would be difficult or even impossible to observe otherwise. The simplicity of maps also makes them an excellent tool for crossing cultural, social, and scientific barriers that may otherwise prevent sharing of scientific information. For example, villagers in the highlands of Papua, New Guinea, viewed, for the first time, a spatial representation of their land as part of a participatory rural appraisal exercise (Figure 10.2). The map, drawn by everyone in the village who wished to participate, displayed previously unseen spatial relationships, such as the locations of toilet

Table 10.1. Selecting the appropriate data type and resolution will make the results of monitoring more valuable.

Type		Positive attributes	Drawbacks
Vector: Data comprise discrete coordinates that can be represented as points or connected to create lines and polygons.			
Point—a pair of x and y coordinates defining a single location		Spatially precise representation of data values at specific locations; if represented well, can imply patterns or associations	Information on areas not represented normally implied but not presented
Line—a sequence of connected points defined by x and y coordinates		Discrete representation of boundaries, good intuitive representation of gradients and areas	Regional boundaries depicted, but areas not quantified
Polygon—a closed set of lines defined by x and y coordinates		Area representations of data values and patterns	Scale dependent, variability within area not represented
Raster: Data consist of a grid of cells in continuous space.			
Grid—defined by the number of rows and columns, cell size, and coordinates		Good representation of area and spatial variability	Larger file size, depends on resolution of underlying data used to create the grid

areas in relation to rivers and the changing extent of remaining rainforest.

Geographic presentation of data on maps can be used to clearly illustrate features such as sources of pollution or hotspots of impacts, patterns, processes, or even levels of compliance relative to thresholds or criteria. However, there is a science and art to producing maps that are easy to understand and will have the greatest effect. We recommend a three-step process: production of a draft map, working map, and final product (Figure 10.3). Choices of colors, scale, and symbols are some of the important elements to consider when producing a map. It is well worth investing time and effort into the presentation of a map, especially if the map is going to be used many times. For example, a consistent look between maps and parameters helps the reader to focus on differences in the data or information being conveyed rather than on differences in the maps format or color.

Heath Kelsey

Figure 10.2. Villagers in Papua, New Guinea, collectively create a map of their land. Maps cross cultural, social, and scientific barriers.

Visualize the environment using interpolated maps

One important disadvantage of mapping point data alone is that spatial patterns may not be easily identified. When important features such

as transition zones, patterns, and boundaries are difficult to visualize with point data alone, the use of interpolation techniques can provide estimates of the conditions between data points (Table 10.2).

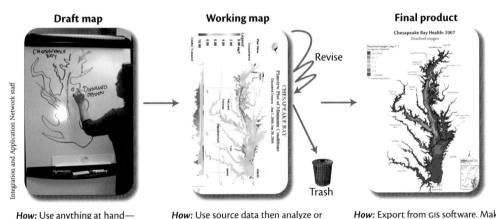

Draft map   **Working map**   Revise   Trash   **Final product**

Integration and Application Network staff

Analyzing environmental data

How: Use anything at hand—paper, whiteboard, etc.

Why:
• Explore ideas and options
• Draft a map on which working maps and final products are based

How: Use source data then analyze or model data and display in GIS or similar software.

Why:
• Exploratory analysis
• Rapid turnaround and short-lived products
• Preparation for final product

How: Export from GIS software. Make final adjustments in graphic software. Ensure that all map elements are present, appropriate color ranges, etc.

Why:
• Important that map is understandable to audience

Figure 10.3. Maps convey spatially referenced data in a manner that immediately informs the audience. Therefore, care should be taken in the development of maps. Source of maps: Chesapeake Bay Program; EcoCheck.

Selecting interpolated surfaces

Various methods to interpolate surfaces from point data are available. Caution should be used when selecting one for a particular data set. A detailed exploratory evaluation of the data should be undertaken to evaluate the best choice. Popular options include kriging, inverse distance weighting, and radial basis functions. Each methods has options that depend on the data resolution and variability and goals of the analysis. Consultation with a spatial analyst familiar with geospatial statistics may be required to use the most appropriate method.

With a specifically designed sampling regime and spatial analysis software, interpolated surfaces can provide a far more illuminating output than point data alone. An important consideration in producing these maps is ensuring that the associated uncertainties of the interpolations are minimized and clearly presented so that the user has a clear understanding of the data confidence.

Detecting changes in the zones of impact

Functional zones are geographic entities with similar structural and functional characteristics, such as habitat types, ecological processes, and anthropogenic impacts. These zones provide a framework from which a spatially explicit monitoring program can be designed and

Table 10.2. Interpolation techniques can develop a continuous surface from point data. These analyses can be helpful in visualizing patterns not immediately apparent. However, each technique has advantages and disadvantages, and researchers must consider which method will apply best to their investigation.[1]

	Point data	Spatial interpolation
Advantages	• It is easy to map with limited GIS skills.	• Spatial patterns and gradients are easy to visualize.
	• Maps can be produced routinely and in batches.	• Some methods can produce uncertainty estimates.
	• Fewer sampling stations mean resources required or more resources to increase temporal resolution.	• Surface area statistics (e.g., area of compliance) can be calculated.
Disadvantages	• It is hard to detect, interpret, and illustrate spatial patterns.	• An expert with advanced GIS and spatial statistics skills is required.
	• Measurements are valid at the sampling location only.	• Process is time consuming because maps are usually produced individually (no batch processing).
	• Surface area calculations/assessment are not possible.	• Good spatial coverage of sampling stations is needed to minimize uncertainty of spatial prediction.
		• Increased computing power for producing large data sets may be needed.
		• Sampling design needs to be optimized to show patterns and reduce uncertainty.
Example		

Maryland Coastal Bays

Total nitrogen 2003–2005 Annual (Jan–Dec)

● Excellent: <0.55 mg·l⁻¹
● Good: 0.56–0.64 mg·l⁻¹
△ Poor: 0.65–1 mg·l⁻¹
▦ Degraded 1–2 mg·l⁻¹
■ Very degraded: >2 mg·l⁻¹

Total nitrogen June 11–12, 2004

■ Excellent: <0.55 mg·l⁻¹
▦ Good: 0.56–0.64 mg·l⁻¹
▦ Poor: 0.65–1 mg·l⁻¹

0   5   10 km
N 0   5   10 miles

implemented with the aim of detecting whether the zones are changing in response to human activities. The concept of monitoring functional zones was first used in Moreton Bay, Australia, where the monitoring program was designed to detect changes in water quality and critical habitats, such as seagrass and coral.[2] Defining the types and extent of functional zones was based on a conceptual understanding of the bay, which was based on the most recent research and monitoring findings. A conceptual diagram illustrates four broad zones in the estuarine and marine portions of the bay and the main sources of pollutants into each (Figure 10.4). To detect changes in the zones, a spatially explicit monitoring program was designed so that the zones of impact could be identified and tracked over time with a known degree of uncertainty. Water quality parameters, such as chlorophyll *a* and total nitrogen concentration, were measured each month to track seasonal changes in the zones of impact and after major events, such as floods. The data were summarized annually in a report card that calculated what proportion of the bay's surface area was meeting established criteria. The annual criteria assessment for the report card provided a frequent and integrated assessment on the changes of area of impact.

If the spatial density of sampling stations is enough to interpolate the data with sufficient precision (see preceding discussion on interpolation methods), spatial patterns can be discerned that may have important implications to understanding system processes and management.

Recipe for success

- Always consider presenting your information on a map
- Use maps at all stages of your assessment and analysis program from developing ideas to exploring and interpreting data to reporting results
- Conduct simple GIS analysis in-house, which can be done with minimal training; however, engage a GIS specialist for complex spatial analysis questions
- Provide spatial interpolations of your data, if possible
- Remember, that obtaining the data and GIS layers you need for the spatial analysis can be the biggest and most time-consuming challenges
- Use data with the appropriate spatial and temporal resolution for the question
- Be aware of error associated with the data and products and report uncertainty
- Put extra time into the final maps and other products; contact a science communication specialist, if necessary

For example, spatially intensive samples and interpolation of sewage nitrogen in Moreton Bay helped to identify two distinct sewage plumes, which was contrary to the initial belief that impacts were due to a single source (Figure 10.5)

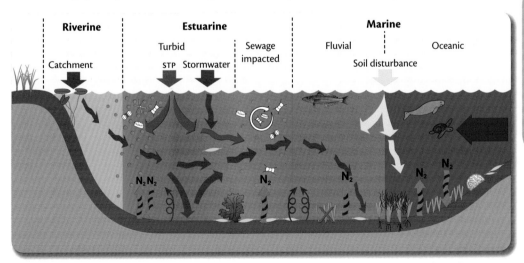

Figure 10.4. The functional zones in Moreton Bay influenced by changes in water quality. Conceptualizing these zones helped to develop criteria for an ecosystem health monitoring program.[2]

Analyzing environmental data

and the decline in plume size in subsequent years after wastewater treatment plant nitrogen reduction. Similarly, by tracking the spatial extent of impact zones, it is possible to determine whether management actions are taking effect—a different approach than assessing factors such as concentration alone.

Optimize spatial sampling strategy

Characterizing the spatial variability of a region enables the sampling strategy to be designed so that an optimal array of stations (number and location) is established for spatial interpolation. The number and location of sampling stations will largely depend on the spatial variability of the environment and the precision of the interpolation required. For example, only a few sampling stations are required in a homogenous area for a spatial prediction of high precision, whereas significantly more stations would be required in a spatially variable area for a similar level of precision. Optimizing spatial sampling frequency is a four-step process (Figure 10.6), which can be repeated, if necessary, to reflect the varying spatial patterns that can occur over time.

Data integration to combine diverse data sources and types

With the ever-increasing supply of data, data types, and data sources comes the challenge of analyzing all the information that invariably has different spatial and temporal densities and uncertainties. Spatial analysis, particularly GIS representations, can provide a framework for integrating these multiple data sources (Figure 10.7). Data from various sources and formats can be overlaid and analyzed and results presented. One of the most desirable outcomes of simple overlays is the suggestion of potential causes of observed conditions that can then be more rigorously tested with other analyses.

An important characteristic of all spatial data is spatial resolution. Spatial resolution can be thought of as the data density—a grid with the extent presenting values for every 1 x 1 meter square (1 m cell size) has a higher spatial resolution than a similar grid presenting values for every 5 x 5 meter square (5 m cell size). All values within the 5 m cell are generalized to present one value for the entire grid cell. There may be variability of the data value within the 5 m cell that is apparent (and helpful) in the 1 m cell. Data of all types can be presented with varying spatial resolution, and knowledge and awareness of the spatial resolution of data are important considerations when making inferences and performing analyses.

It can be tempting to always use data with higher spatial resolution in investigating causes of observed conditions, but this is not always advisable; higher resolutions can create unnecessary data management issues. For example, a raster data set containing water temperature

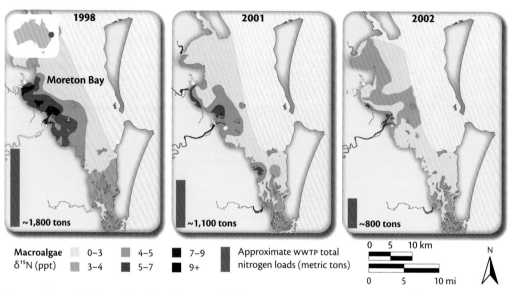

Figure 10.5. Interpolated maps show change in nitrogen distribution in Moreton Bay after WWTP upgrades.[3]

Step 1: Oversample the monitoring region. Assign sampling stations coordinates, with a greater number of stations randomly assigned in regions where increased precision is required. Within a short period of time, measure parameters at each of the assigned stations.

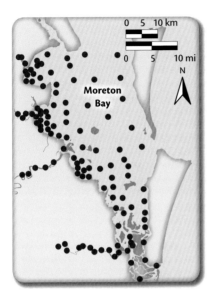

Step 2: Determine the uncertainty of the spatial interpolations. Compute predictive coefficient of variations for each parameter for a variety of sampling scenarios, ranging from all stations to a small subset.

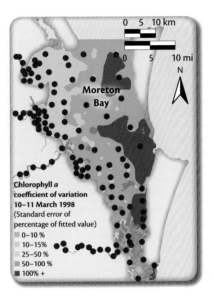

Step 3: Design sampling station frequency. Decision is based on the level of uncertainty required, uncertainty of the sampling scenarios, availability of resources to conduct monitoring, and incorporation of existing stations to ensure that long-term data sets are retained.

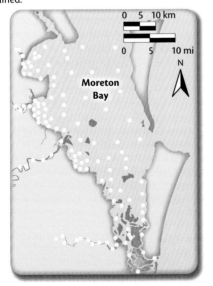

Step 4: Monitor, map, and review. Use assigned stations for routine monitoring program. Map parameters and associated coefficient of variations. Periodically review maps to ensure that you are still obtaining required coefficient of variations.

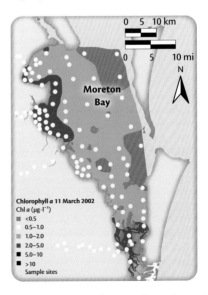

Figure 10.6. Optimizing spatial sampling frequency is a four-step process. The number and location of sampling stations will largely depend on the spatial variability of the environment and the precision of the interpolation required.[4]

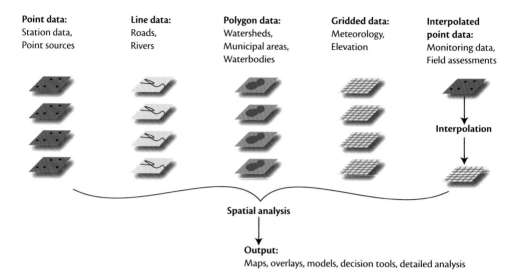

Point data:	Line data:	Polygon data:	Gridded data:	Interpolated point data:
Station data, Point sources	Roads, Rivers	Watersheds, Municipal areas, Waterbodies	Meteorology, Elevation	Monitoring data, Field assessments

Interpolation

Spatial analysis

Output:
Maps, overlays, models, decision tools, detailed analysis

Figure 10.7. A diagram depicting the theory behind combining a diversity of data sets through spatial analysis.

values for every one meter square of the entire Atlantic Ocean would be an extremely large and unwieldy data file. Moreover, it is difficult to justify needing information of water temperature with such high resolution for such a large area. For a large area, water temperature data for a 10-km grid cell may be sufficient to reveal patterns important at the ocean scale.

However, regardless of the data type and resolution, each data set can be brought into a single spatial domain and the spatial relationships examined. For instance, raster data presenting land use can be overlaid with line data for watershed boundaries, polygon data for urban area limits, and point data for local environmental agency sampling locations. Examining these data in tabular form may provide no insight into the processes affecting the study area, whereas evaluating them spatially may illuminate important patterns and processes.

Garbage in, garbage out: Analyses are only as good as the data

All data have a certain amount of uncertainty and limitations that need to be recognized. Data that are too limited in either accuracy or spatial resolution cannot support inference or analysis at higher resolution.

For example, elevation data from two sources were used to develop Digital Elevation Models (DEMS), watershed boundaries, and potential stream locations for the same location in a Maryland river (Figure 10.8). The left DEM consists

of 30 m x 30 m grid cells and was created by the National Hydrology Database maintained by the United States Geological Survey (USGS), and available for the entire United States. The right DEM has 2 m x 2 m grid cells and was created by the State of Maryland from Light Detection and Ranging (LIDAR) data. LIDAR data are typically collected from airplanes using laser emissions similar to sonar applications. Laser pulses are reflected

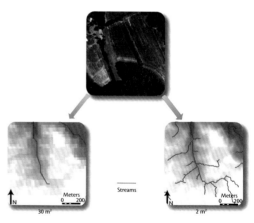

Figure 10.8. DEMS and resulting stream delineations for the same area but that are derived from data of different resolutions. The image on the left has elevation data for every 30 m x 30 m grid cell, and the right image has elevation data for every 2 m x 2 m cell. More detailed stream delineations are possible using the higher resolution data in the image. Source: ned.usgs.gov and dnrweb.dnr.state.md.us/gis/data/lidar.

from the ground surface, and time elapsed for the return of each pulse is equated to relative elevation. Instrument location and elevation are calculated using Global Positioning System (GPS) equipment. The laser pulses can be very closely spaced, creating a detailed model of the terrain.

In each case, flow direction and accumulations were calculated based on the elevation in each cell. Flow accumulations over a specified threshold were classified as "streams." The higher resolution DEM supports a much more detailed representation of surface flow accumulation and the subsequent stream network. In this example, we can see how the resolution of the underlying data set ultimately affects the output product for a very small area (Figure 10.8). If the area were much larger, perhaps for a major river system, the higher resolution may not provide much additional information, but could dramatically increase data file size and processing times (Figure 10.8).

There are also several sources of potential error in each case; in each DEM, error is associated with applying a single elevation value to all locations within the grid cell. Obviously, there will be some

elevation variation within that grid cell that is not represented, and this effect is more pronounced in the lower resolution data. There is also error associated with the data that were used to generate the DEMs. Both the topographic data used to create the left DEM and the LIDAR data used to generate the more detailed DEM will have at least some error associated with them. These errors may be small but still should be recognized, and a close examination of available metadata is always a good idea. Ground-truthing (verifying data by measuring conditions at an actual location) can be performed to increase confidence in the data as well.

Spatial analysis can be an essential tool for coastal assessment

Overlaying spatial data sets from several sources can create new information by enabling patterns to emerge that would not have been visible otherwise. A simple example would be adding spatial information to tabular data of water quality information and plotting it on a map. A pattern may emerge that suggests that water quality may

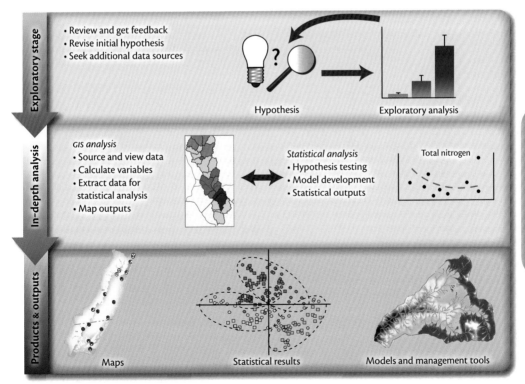

Figure 10.9. Spatial relationships can be further investigated through a three-step process that begins with exploration and ends with communication products.

be degraded near a particular pollution source or specific area, but how do we move beyond the suggestion of a relationship to a more rigorous evaluation of cause and effect? Conceptually, we can follow the general steps outlined in Figure 10.9 to move from an exploration of potential relationships to a thorough assessment.

A first step might include an exploratory phase, where stress and outcome data are plotted together; a second step may include more in-depth analysis of particular variables and statistical analysis; and a final step would include the production of statistical and map products that convey the findings of your analyses. Using these steps as a guide, we will follow a case study in a small estuary in South Carolina, USA, where potential bacterial pollution sources were evaluated. The state health department wanted to determine whether septic tanks that had not been switched over to the sewage system installed in the area in the past decade or so were contributing to the high fecal coliform bacteria counts in the estuary.

Exploratory stage

During an exploratory data evaluation phase, preliminary looks at all of the relevant data through spatial overlays may reveal interesting patterns that we might want to evaluate further. Feedback and discussion with managers, ecologists, or other relevant parties may suggest additional hypotheses as well.

In this example, fecal coliform bacteria concentrations in the estuary were available through historical data collected by shellfish regulating agencies and were plotted with data representing several hypothesized sources of fecal pollution, including septic systems, sewage system components, and urban land use (Figure 10.10).[5] Murrells Inlet, South Carolina, is primarily residential but has some light industry, commercial areas, restaurants, and marinas and boat landings. Although the area has a public sewer system, there were still many homes that had not been connected at the time of the study. It had been hypothesized that the source of high bacteria concentrations observed in the estuary was sewage leaking from aging or malfunctioning septic tanks, especially in the northern part of the estuary. The regulating agency needed to have better information regarding the sources of bacteria if it was to force homes to remove septic tanks and become connected to the sewer system.

The overlay of septic tanks and bacteria data showed that several of the stations with routinely

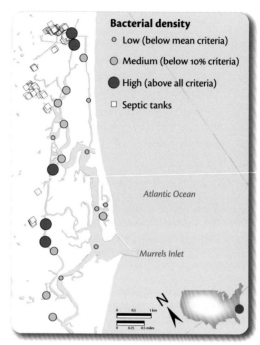

Figure 10.10. Bacteria concentrations appear to be higher near areas where septic tanks are located, Murrels Inlet, South Carolina.[5]

high bacteria counts were near areas with remaining septic tanks, clearly suggesting that septic tanks may be a likely source for the high bacteria levels observed. To evaluate this further, the hypothesis was then tested against other potential hypotheses and sources for the bacteria in the estuary.

In-depth analysis

More detailed statistical analyses may require calculation of variables using GIS or data acquired from additional sources. In this case, other potential sources of fecal pollution in the estuary included runoff from urban areas, domestic animals, marinas and boat landings (where sewage handling facilities were located), and sewage system components with unnoticed malfunctions (Figure 10.11). To develop parameters to test land use and related effects, spatial data were obtained from local agencies, other researchers, and the U.S. Census Bureau. In some cases (GPS) units were used to obtain precise locations for important features, such as sewage system lift stations or small marinas. Using GIS, distances were calculated from each sampling station to marinas and boat landings, outfalls from drainage basins, and nearest

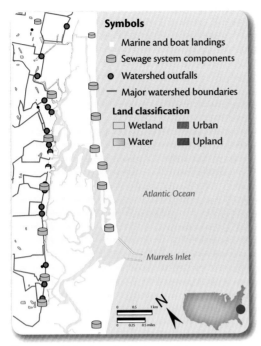

Symbols

☐ Marine and boat landings
⬡ Sewage system components
● Watershed outfalls
— Major watershed boundaries

Land classification
☐ Wetland ▨ Urban
▨ Water ▨ Upland

Atlantic Ocean

Murrels Inlet

Figure 10.11. Other hypothesized potential sources in Murrels Inlet for observed bacteria concentrations included marinas and boat landings, runoff from urban areas, and malfunctioning sewage system components.[5]

urban and non-urban land uses. These distances were inversely weighted with numbers of boats at the marinas, number of septic tanks in the outfall catchment, and so forth. (Figure 10.12).

To account for runoff-driven sources like domestic animal waste or urban areas,

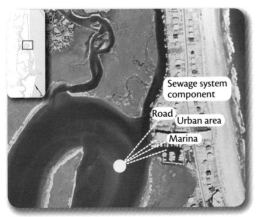

Figure 10.12. White line shows calculation of weighted inverse distance to nearest marina for Station 04–04 in Murrells Inlet, South Carolina.[5]

Linking cholera to drinking water

John Snow, physician

John Snow was a British physician and is considered one of the fathers of epidemiology for his work in tracing the source of a cholera outbreak in Soho, Westminster, England, in 1854.

By talking to local residents, he identified the source of the outbreak as the public water pump on Broad Street.[6] Although Snow's chemical and microscope examination of a sample of the water was not able to conclusively prove its danger, his studies of the pattern of the disease were convincing enough to persuade the local council to disable the well pump.[6] Snow used a spot map to illustrate how cases of cholera were centered around the pump (see map below, red circle). He also made solid use of statistics to illustrate the connection between the quality of the water and cholera cases by linking water from sewage-polluted sections of the Thames River to homes with an increased incidence of cholera.

Snow's study was a major event in the history of public health and is one of the first examples of using spatial data for human health and water quality management.[6]

Analyzing environmental data

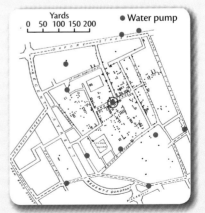

Map depicting locations of well pumps and cholera cases.[6]

precipitation data for the days preceding sampling were obtained from historical data from the nearest weather station. Additional water quality information, such as salinity, water temperature, tide cycle stage, and general weather conditions were also collected at the time of bacterial sampling.

Each parameter became a variable in a statistical analysis. In this case, relatively simple regression techniques were used to evaluate the relationships between the various parameters of interest while accounting for important environmental variables, such as salinity and water temperature.

The results of the analyses suggested that after salinity, precipitation was probably the most important contributing factor for fecal pollution in the estuary and that proximity to urban land uses was associated with higher fecal coliform bacteria concentration. The analysis also showed that septic tanks were not strong indicators of fecal pollution in and of themselves. The combination of results suggested that urban runoff potentially carrying pet waste was perhaps the biggest contributing factor for the fecal pollution in the estuary.

To assess these results, a bacterial source tracking study was undertaken to determine whether the type of animal source contributing the bacteria could be identified.[7] Using a microbiology-based technique called Antibiotic Resistance Analysis (ARA), bacteria sources from the sewer system were compared to bacteria collected at the sampling stations. Like the statistical modeling, results from this analysis suggested that most of the bacteria were probably not from human sources and, therefore, probably not from the septic tanks. Taken together, the two analyses presented strong evidence that the source of much of the bacteria was from nonhuman sources—potentially pets.

Output products

After completing the analysis, products were prepared that described the findings graphically as well as statistically. Maps showing the spatial relationships of antibiotic resistance and potential sources were prepared. These maps illustrate areas likely affected by human sources of fecal pollution, which were compared to the original fecal pollution maps (Figure 10.13). The majority of sampling sites had low antibiotic resistance index scores, especially those sites where bacteria counts were highest, suggesting that most of the fecal pollution was from non-human sources.

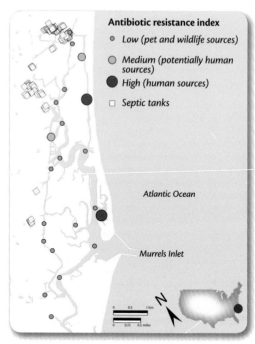

Figure 10.13. Antibiotic Resistance Analysis results suggested that humans are not the source of bacteria at the stations nearest septic tanks.[5]

Regression results were simply presented to demonstrate the most important effects on fecal pollution in the estuary. As a result of these analyses, the local management areas

Pitfalls to avoid

- Asking too much of your data—using data improperly and getting misleading results
- Not being aware of data aggregation issues when combining data
- Not considering or attempting to display data on map
- Over-interpreting your results, not being aware, considering or reporting the error or uncertainty of the spatial analysis
- Giving insufficient time and effort given to producing the final map
- Not including map elements, such as a key, scale, and labels
- Assuming that higher resolution is always better—computation time and data management issues unnecessarily burdensome

did not attempt to persuade homeowners with septic tanks to become connected to the sewage system. Instead, efforts were refocused on pet waste—a "poop-and-scoop" education and cleanup campaign was incorporated into the local management plan.

References

1. Dennison WC, Thomas JE, Cain CJ, Carruthers TJB, Hall MR, Jesien RV, Wazniak CE, Wilson DE (2009) Shifting sands: Environmental and cultural change in Maryland's coastal bays. IAN Press, Cambridge, Maryland
2. Abal EG, Dennison WC, Greenfield PF (2001) Managing the Brisbane River and Moreton Bay: An integrated research/ management program to reduce impacts on an Australian estuary. Water Sci Technol 43(9):57-70
3. Costanzo SD, Udy J, Longstaff B, Jones A (2005) Using nitrogen stable isotope ratios (δ^{15}N) of macroalgae to determine the effectiveness of sewage upgrades: Changes in the extent of sewage plumes over four years in Moreton Bay, Australia. Mar Pollut Bull 51:212-217
4. Toscas P (2008) Spatial modelling of the probability of obtaining a detectable concentration of ammonia in Moreton Bay, Australia. Environ Monit Assess 137:379-385
5. Kelsey RH, Porter DE, Scott GI, White DL, Neet MJ (2004) Measuring land use effects on fecal pollution using GIS and regression modeling. J Exp Mar Biol Ecol 298:197-209
6. Johnson S (2006) The ghost map. Penguin Group, New York, New York
7. Kelsey RH, Scott GI, Porter DE, Thompson BC, Webster LF (2003) Using multiple antibiotic resistance and land use characteristics to determine sources of fecal coliform bacterial pollution. J Environ Monit Assess 81:337-348

Further reading

Longley PA, Goodchild MF, Maguire DJ, Rhind DW (2005) Geographical information systems: Principles, techniques, management and applications, 2nd edition. Wiley, New York, New York

Olea RA (1999) Geostatistics for engineers and earth scientists, 2nd edition. Springer, New York, New York

Tufte ER (2001) The visual display of quantitative information, 2nd edition. Graphics Press, Chesire, Connecticut

Analyzing environmental data

GATHERING RELEVANT DATA
FOR COASTAL ASSESSMENT

In the last section, the principles of analyzing data for incorporation into products that can be used to inform and engage the broader community was discussed. The challenge facing many existing or new assessment programs is collecting appropriate data for the subsequent stages of analysis, information building, and communication. Solving these challenges within an existing or newly established program needs to be conducted in partnership with experts from each of the stages, be it statisticians, modelers, science integrators, or communication specialists. With the ever-increasing diversity of instruments and platforms available for a monitoring program, this partnership becomes even more critical to avoid common pitfalls of collecting data that will not be used, or not used to the same extent that a well-considered program would use its data. In this next section, ways to avoid some of these pitfalls associated with designing a monitoring program and collecting data using *in situ* sensors and remote sensing will be discussed.

Program design: Effective monitoring depends on development of clear and achievable objectives that are defined within the context of the entire environmental campaign. With clear objectives set, the monitoring program can be designed to best meet these objectives. Questions such as what and where to monitor, sampling design, and data management are addressed.

In situ *measurements:* *In situ* instruments measure conditions of the immediate environment and, in many respects, are the more traditional instruments of a monitoring program. Technological advances in recent years have led to confusion over which sensor to use. This chapter reviews some of the reasons for using some of the more advanced *in situ* sensors and some of the challenges and realities to expect.

Remote sensing: Remote sensing that uses satellite or airborne sensors can provide spatial coverage and repeatable sampling that cannot be matched by *in situ* sensors. However, routine integration of remotely sensed data in coastal monitoring is relatively uncommon, reflecting some of the associated challenges. In this chapter, some of these challenges are demystified and guidance is provided for incorporating remotely sensed data into a monitoring program.

CHAPTER 11: PROGRAM DESIGN

DEVELOPING A COMPREHENSIVE DATA STRATEGY

Todd Lookingbill, Geoff Sanders, Shawn Carter,
Ben Best, Ben J. Longstaff, and Jane M. Hawkey

*In the field of observation,
chance favors only the prepared mind.*

—Louis Pasteur

In this chapter, we describe the logistics of *designing a monitoring program* to obtain data within an integrated coastal assessment framework. We begin with the challenge of explicitly defining program goals and objectives, and describe the role of conceptual models and diagrams in facilitating this process. We next describe the selection of a subset of physical and chemical indicators for monitoring ecosystem status and trends. We briefly provide some rules of thumb for sample designs, summarizing from other chapters within the handbook, and offer a more detailed exploration of the many data management issues frequently confronted by monitoring programs. The chapter concludes with discussions of data dissemination strategies and the benefits of collaborations and partnerships to leverage scarce data-collection resources.

Designing a monitoring strategy

*We are drowning in data
and starved for knowledge.*

—Anonymous

Over recent decades, society has witnessed a proliferation in the generation, storage, and transfer of information, leading to what is collectively referred to as the 'Information Age.' Coastal assessment has not been isolated from this information technology revolution, with many programs experiencing significant increases in data collection capacity.

One of the main technological reasons for the increase in data production is a rapid growth in the number and type of observing instruments (Figure 11.1), and in many cases the instruments are measuring more and more parameters. For example, in the 1980s, water quality probes typically measured just four parameters (i.e., temperature, salinity, dissolved oxygen, pH).

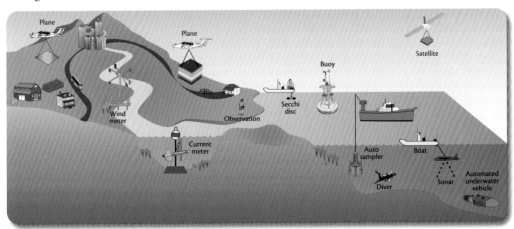

Figure 11.1. Monitoring observations can be taken along a continuum of platforms, ranging from dockside observers to *in situ* instrumentation that can be deployed directly in the environment being measured (e.g., the water column) to remote aerial and satellite sensors.

Obtaining environmental data

Today, they routinely measure six with chlorophyll fluorescence and turbidity sensors added to the common parameter set. In addition to the number of instruments being deployed, the manner in which the instruments are deployed is changing. Fixed network systems have been augmented with mobile and satellite observing systems (Figure 11.2). Instruments that were once just lowered over the side of the boat at a monitoring station are now being deployed in more and more imaginative ways, such as attached to autonomous vehicles, profiling systems, or boats underway. Chapters 12 and 13 address in detail the what, why, when, and how of selecting the most appropriate observation tool to meet specific monitoring objectives.

A second major reason for increased data production is improvements to data storage, transfer, and retrieval capacity. Instruments can now either store large amounts of data, or with what has become a relatively simple setup, transfer the data via wireless to a computer network. The advent of wireless technology in coastal research and assessment has led to an increased capacity to measure data at increased spatial and temporal frequency. Increased data production would not have been possible without rapid advancements in storage capacity and processing speed of personal computers (Figure 11.3). Data can now be stored and processed with greater ease than ever before.

Improvements to computer software such as environmental modeling packages, GIS systems, and databases, have also enhanced the processes of data analysis and interpretation. However, in many cases, there can be diminishing return on the value of each additional data point (Figure 11.4). A critical challenge for any assessment program, when considering what and how much data to acquire, is to determine how the vast amounts of data being collected will be used. Responding to this challenge requires finding a balance between: (a) the resources to generate, manage, and analyze the additional data, and (b) the added benefits the additional data provides to the decision-support process. The benefits gained from successfully striking this balance may include increased statistical power, reduced uncertainty of model runs, and increased temporal and spatial resolution of key indicators.

The broad-based, scientifically sound information obtained through monitoring will have multiple applications for management, decision-making, research, education, and promoting public understanding of environmental issues. We have found that consideration of these end goals in the initial stages of program design

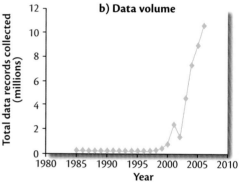

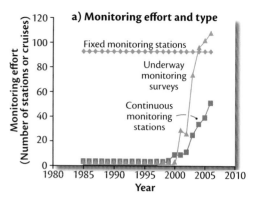

Figure 11.2. Rapid increase of volume of data records collected by Maryland Department of Natural Resources (not including remote sensing data) in the tidal regions of Chesapeake Bay during the 2000s.

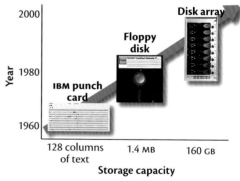

Figure 11.3. Changes in data storage technology over time.

greatly improves the probability of success of a coastal assessment program. Thus, this section builds on earlier sections and is presented at the end of the handbook rather than what may be a more conventional approach of beginning the book

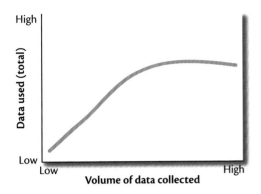

Figure 11.4. The relationship between the volume of data collected and that actually used for a poorly planned monitoring program. Increased data collection can lead to diminishing returns. In the extreme, additional data collection can draw resources away from analysis and interpretation, leading to a decrease in the total amount of data actually used in an assessment.

with a description of data collection strategies.

Establish monitoring goals and objectives: Asking the right questions

As illustrated by the Chesapeake Bay example on the following page, the need to institute a monitoring program may arise from a broad goal (e.g., to better manage the Bay), but effective monitoring depends upon the development of clear, achievable objectives (e.g., to understand the relationship between *Pfiesteria* and Bay fishes). The need to clearly articulate the goals and objectives of a monitoring program is emphasized in just about every "how to" guide that has ever been written about environmental monitoring, and yet good examples of specific, measurable objectives are hard to find.

The primary goals of a monitoring program may be investigative, operational, or surveillance oriented.[1] They may include the following:

- providing a basis for identifying and understanding the inherent variability of natural systems;
- providing an early warning of impending threats or changes in the state or dynamics of a system;
- evaluating the efficacy of management and restoration efforts; and/or
- responding to legislative mandates or legal obligations.

Objective statements provide additional focus about the purpose or desired outcome of the program. An effective set of monitoring objectives should meet the test of being SMART: Specific, Measurable, Attainable, Realistic, and Time-sensitive.

Four types of integration: ecological, spatial, temporal, and programmatic

A major challenge to designing a comprehensive assessment program is integrating the diverse types of measurements that are collected. Integration may involve ecological, spatial, temporal, and programmatic aspects:

- **Ecological**: Considers the linkages among ecosystem components. An effective ecosystem monitoring strategy will employ a suite of individual measurements that collectively monitor the integrity of the entire ecosystem. One approach for effective ecological integration is to select indicators at various hierarchical levels of ecological organization (e.g., community, population, genetic; see Chapter 5).
- **Spatial**: Establishes linkages of measurements made at different spatial scales, or between local monitoring efforts and broader, national programs. Effective spatial integration requires an understanding of scalar ecological processes, the co-location of measurements of comparably-scaled monitoring indicators, and the design of statistical sampling frameworks that permit the extrapolation and interpolation of spatially dependent data.
- **Temporal**: Establishes linkages between measurements made at various temporal scales. Different indicators are often measured at different frequencies. Temporal integration can be accomplished by nesting more frequently sampled indicators within the context of those indicators that are measured less frequently.
- **Programmatic**: Coordinates and communicates monitoring activities within and among other monitoring groups. Effective programmatic integration can promote broad participation in monitoring and broad use of the resulting data.

Obtaining environmental data

Case Study: The Chesapeake Bay

The evolution of Chesapeake Bay water quality monitoring programs has been driven, in part, by a failing ecosystem.[2] If resources were unlimited and commercial species abundant, it is unlikely that a robust monitoring program would exist today. Ecological tipping points frequently drive the need and funding for monitoring so that management actions can be formulated and subsequently evaluated for success. Ultimately, political will, public engagement, effective communication of monitoring results, and management successes maintain the program's integrity.

In the mid-1980s, faced with declining dissolved oxygen levels, increased phytoplankton abundance, concern about toxic materials, and depletion of commercially valuable species, a monitoring network of fixed stations was designed to 1) characterize the Chesapeake Bay's ambient water quality in time and space and 2) observe long-term trends and to answer questions about processes and causes relating to major management issues.

In 1997, an outbreak of the toxic algae *Pfiesteria piscicida* and a subsequent fish kill on the Pocomoke River, Maryland, raised environmental and human health concerns. The processes at work in the Pocomoke River were below the temporal and spatial scope of the existing fixed station monitoring programs and gave rise to a near and real-time continuous water quality monitoring program that now consists of over 50 sites statewide in Maryland. The concurrent development of surface water mapping hardware technologies provided unprecedented spatial characterization of water quality to investigate the expanse of algal blooms and impact of water clarity on submerged aquatic vegetation beds. The implementation of these technologies to investigate ecosystem events and weaknesses, led to the establishment of a regional (Maryland/Virginia) program of spatially- and temporally-intensive monitoring to investigate water quality criteria in shallow and open waters that were unable to be evaluated with the traditional fixed station network.

Moving ahead in 2008 and beyond, monitoring programs in the Chesapeake Bay will continue to be driven by management questions and needs, making use of vertical profilers, automated underwater and above-water vehicles, satellite and aerial remote sensing, automated 'wet chemistry' nutrient sensors, as well as new technologies that emerge.

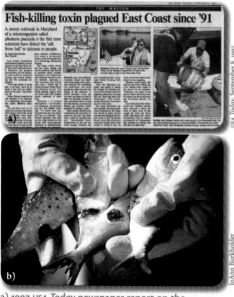

a) An algal bloom (mahoghany tide) in Chesapeake Bay. b) A nutrient sensor and c) a Chesapeake Bay Observing System buoy permit the acquisition of a range of data including nutrient concentrations before, during, and after algae blooms.

a) 1997 *USA Today* newspaper report on the harmful effects of *Pfiesteria* to fish and humans. b) *Pfiesteria*-caused lesions on young menhaden.

Case study written by Mark Trice

Conceptual framework as a first step

Common challenges confronted by long-term monitoring programs include poorly specified objectives, a piecemeal approach to selecting ecological indicators, and nebulous connections between the data being collected and management decisions. A strong conceptual framework can help to design synthetic monitoring strategies for responding to these challenges.

Development of a conceptual model helps in understanding how the diverse elements of a monitoring program interact. The process promotes communication between scientists and managers from different disciplines toward the establishment of common objectives. Conceptual models often take the form of "box and arrow" figures, whereby mutually exclusive components are shown in boxes and interactions among the components are shown with arrows. However, as has been discussed extensively in other chapters of this book, conceptual models have evolved to include conceptual diagrams that use symbols and legends to summarize and communicate understanding of the system (Figure 11.5).

Conceptual models can provide value throughout all phases of program design. Early in the process, simple conceptual models provide a framework for capturing and organizing information. The construction of models requires a prioritization of key resource features and threats, as well as the mechanisms by which the

> In representing multiple activities with varied direct and indirect linkages, models with modular components can provide a basis for organizing and conducting efficient environmental assessments.[4]

two interact. This information can be enormously useful in crafting specific monitoring objectives. Conceptual models also can be especially valuable for monitoring implementation by informing the details of sample design (e.g., addressing questions of variable selection, co-location, co-visitation, spatial and temporal scaling). Finally, they create a structure for interpreting data once they are collected and for translating the data into quantitative models and ultimately into management actions.

The process of constructing good conceptual models is an iterative one (Figure 11.6). It can be insightful to explore alternative ways to represent the system. These different representations can help articulate important, and often competing, hypotheses about how the system operates.[3] We encourage the formal statement of the hypotheses involved at each stage of model construction and the careful documentation and archival of alternative hypotheses that may arise during the construction process.

It may require multiple scoping meetings to obtain group consensus on model structure and content. There is a growing body of literature on how to integrate the outcomes of these meetings into models.[6,7,8] An excellent recommendation arising from this literature is the modularization of components around which there can be general group agreement. A hierarchically structured decision-making process, centered around the development of conceptual

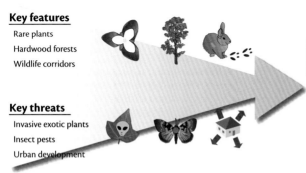

Key features
Rare plants
Hardwood forests
Wildlife corridors

Key threats
Invasive exotic plants
Insect pests
Urban development

The hickory forests 🌳 of the park protect a variety of forest-dwelling species and rare plant communities 🌿. But these natural resources are heavily impacted by development 🏠 along and within the park's boundaries, restricting wildife movement corridors 🐰 , and increasing the spread of insect infestations 🦋 and invasive exotic plants 🍃 .

Figure 11.5. The conceptual diagram process captures key natural resource elements as information-rich symbols, which are combined to tell visual stories of park resources in this example from the U.S. National Park Service National Capital Region Network's *A Conceptual Basis for Natural Resource Monitoring.*[5]

Obtaining environmental data

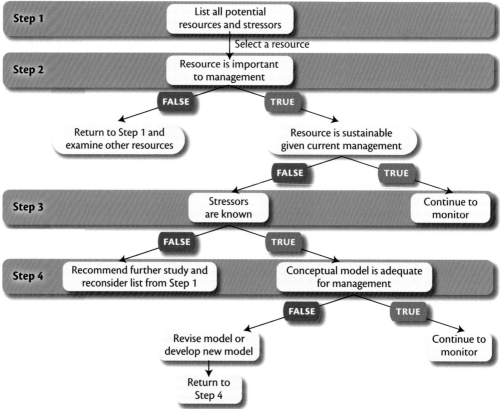

Figure 11.6. A hierarchical approach to conceptual model construction satisfies management needs to preserve valued resources, to anticipate the undesirable consequences of environmental change, and to advance scientific understanding of issues threatening ecosystem sustainability. A related set of questions can be used to guide model construction: Are resources sustainable given current management practices? If not, what stressors are inducing resource change? Is the modeled correspondence between resources and stressors sufficient for management purposes? This process is not linear but instead relies on continual iteration to ensure that critical processes are considered and the best management model is achieved.

models, has been adopted by a growing number of management agencies for the design of monitoring programs. The process relies upon the early and frequent collaboration between scientists and managers to ensure the efficient use of monitoring resources.

Select what and where to monitor

Deciding upon the details of what and where to sample usually involves a series of meetings, workshops, brainstorming sessions, questionnaires, literature reviews, and other information-gathering exercises to identify the data needed to respond to monitoring objectives (Figure 11.7). These activities are best focused on the key resources, stressors, and relationships depicted in the conceptual models.

The scoping and conceptual modeling efforts will result in a list of potential ecological indicators (Figure 11.8; Chapter 5), which must then be prioritized using some set of criteria agreed upon by the end users of the information. These criteria may include efficient use of personnel, cost and logistical feasibility, partnership opportunities with other programs, and a large dose of common sense. Ultimately, the indicators selected for monitoring will track only a small subset of the total physical, chemical, and biological features and processes of the studied ecosystem.[9]

Sampling design

Collecting data in a scientifically-credible manner is vital to the long-term success of any monitoring

Figure 11.7. Scoping workshops provide an important opportunity to explore alternative ways to compress a complex system into a small set of variables and functions.

program (Figure 11.8). Good sampling practices ensure that data meet the purpose for which they were collected and can withstand scrutiny by critics. A primary objective of many programs is to make inferences to larger areas from data collected at relatively few sampling locations. This topic was introduced in other chapters focused on spatial (see Chapter 10) and statistical (see Chapter 8) analyses. Here we gather together in one place some key recommendations for designing a defensible sampling scheme, keeping in mind that sample sizes will almost always be limited by shortages of funding and personnel.

The choice of measurement tool may be strongly linked to issues of sample design. For example, metrics used to quantify landscape pattern may differ by as much as a factor of 10 between different remote sensing platforms alone (e.g., SPOT and Landsat data).[10] Guidance is provided in

Recipe for Success

- Clearly articulated, achievable objectives
- Strong conceptual basis for all monitoring activities
- Effective integration between data gathering, management, analysis, and communication
- Adaptive strategy for dealing with changes in funding, leadership, and priorities
- Coordination with other local, regional, national, and international monitoring groups

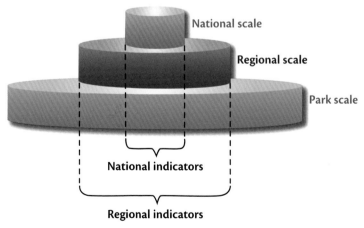

Figure 11.8. The list of ecological indicators monitored throughout the U.S. National Park System follows the 'wedding cake design,' adapted from the USDA Forest Service. The majority of indicators are selected to provide site-specific data needed by park managers for making decisions and working with other agencies and individuals for the benefit of park resources. Nationwide, or at the level of the park network or ecosystem, there is also a subset of indicators that are monitored in a standardized way to allow comparisons and synthesis of data across larger areas.

Chapters 12 and 13 for choosing among different sources for *in situ* and remotely sensed measurements. We focus here on the following three components of sample design: sample unit, arrangement, and intensity.[11]

The decision on what **sample unit** to use (e.g., resolution of pixels for remotely sensed imagery, plot size for field samples) will depend on the characteristic scale of the resource being monitored. For example, a smaller sample unit would be used to monitor processes that occur at the scale of an individual oyster bar rather than at the scale of an entire estuary. Schneider provides an excellent review of the concept of characteristic scale in ecology.[12]

The **sample intensity** strongly influences the certainty with which the status or trend of a resource can be determined. Taking too few samples may put resources at risk because important changes are missed or detected too late for management to be effective. Taking too many samples will waste time and money. The sample size that is needed to meet a monitoring objective is largely a function of the amount of change in the resource that the manager seeks to detect (i.e., the effect size), and the variability of the resource across space and time. Most statistical texts provide relatively simple procedures for calculating the sample size needed to produce a confidence interval of a specified width for a variable. For example, a rule of thumb minimum sample size to determine significant differences between two treatments is six measurements in each treatment.

Sample arrangement is often the component of sample design over which a practitioner can exert the most control. The size of individual units and the total amount of effort that can be invested (i.e., intensity) often have monetary and other constraints. In most cases, a probability sampling is desirable to avoid bias. Probability samples occur when each unit has a known, non-zero probability of being included in the sample. These designs always include a random component (such as a systematic sample with a random start). As a result, statistical estimates of population attributes can be produced with an estimate of their reliability.

Model-based inferences and professional

Sampling design is defined by three components:

- Sample unit

- Sample intensity

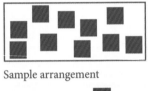

- Sample arrangement

judgment can be used to place samples in locations that had no probability of being included in the probability sample. However, data from judgment sampling of representative sites selected by experts can be difficult to interpret statistically (Bayesian methods can be useful here).[13] Because the accuracy of model-based inferences and the like is only as good as the decision-making process used to select the sites, models and judgment-based information can be an easy target for any potential critics of the program.

A few final considerations involve the spatial and temporal integrity of the sample. Monitoring data will be used for many purposes, and an initial view of the sample on a map will help to clarify the use and limitations of the sample. It is a good idea to display proposed samples on a GIS to ensure that adequate coverage occurs for areas of interest. Spatial co-location of samples is recommended to allow comparisons among indicators. For example, water quality, aquatic macroinvertebrates, and fish might all be sampled in the same sample locations.

When designing a monitoring program, it is not necessary to visit all of the selected sites every year. Sampling designs exist that allow for increased spatial coverage through rotating panel designs. For example, each site could be sampled every five years, allowing five times as many sites to be sampled because only 1/5 of them are visited each year. Data from a complex, rotating panel design with multiple strata can be difficult to interpret, so data analysis considerations need to be considered early in the design phase.

Fixed-point sampling stations are frequently used for monitoring and these have certain advantages, especially when the objective is to detect changes over time. Revisiting the same plots removes plot-to-plot variability from the change estimates. However, mobile sensing systems are becoming increasingly popular and allow greater flexibility in sampling design. The advantages of mobile sensor platforms are touched on in Chapter 12. Hybrid sample designs that combine the two approaches can be quite effective at capturing both spatial and temporal patterns (Figure 11.9).

Manage the data

Before committing to any new monitoring platform, a complete accounting should be taken of the long-term costs and benefits associated with attaining new data. These include the extra computer hardware and software needed to manage the data and the personnel time needed to maintain a quality-assured flow of data from point of collection to the final repository. The goal of any monitoring program is to produce high-quality data and data products that will be usable and informative to managers and decision-makers. To ensure that these goals are met, proper data management practices must be followed throughout the life cycle of the program. Otherwise the ever present risks of producing questionable, possibly unreliable data products are magnified and faith in the data is reduced.

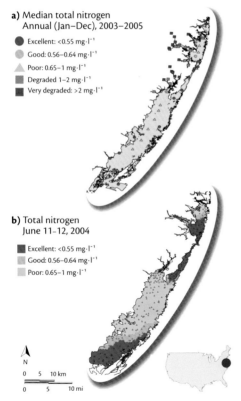

a) Median total nitrogen
Annual (Jan–Dec), 2003–2005

● Excellent: <0.55 mg·l⁻¹
● Good: 0.56–0.64 mg·l⁻¹
▲ Poor: 0.65–1 mg·l⁻¹
■ Degraded 1–2 mg·l⁻¹
■ Very degraded: >2 mg·l⁻¹

b) Total nitrogen
June 11–12, 2004

■ Excellent: <0.55 mg·l⁻¹
■ Good: 0.56–0.64 mg·l⁻¹
■ Poor: 0.65–1 mg·l⁻¹

N
0   5   10 km
0   5   10 mi

Figure 11.9 a) Sixty fixed monitoring stations indicate locations exceeding threshold concentrations in the Maryland Coastal Bays. b) These stations were supplemented with synoptic samples on June 11–12, 2004, to provide a more spatially-intensive estimate of nitrogen patterns in the Bays for a single point in time.[14]

It is important to realize that data management deals with more than just data. Data management strategies incorporate aspects from many different areas, including hardware (e.g., computers, file servers, and data collection devices), software (e.g., database applications and statistical packages), and physical files, both electronic and hardcopy. Good data management strategies also include policy and procedural documents that outline how and why certain things are done. Most importantly, effective data management strategies involve people who understand the importance and relevance of data management and take an active role in following all recommended or required procedures.

Incorporating sound data management strategies into the program is most easily accomplished at the beginning (Figure 11.10). These include program-specific policies related to sample design, roles and responsibilities, timelines, data collection procedures, data documentation standards, and storage routines. Developing data management strategies early in the process will allow for opportunities to refine and optimize the approach to data management, and help ensure that data are properly collected and processed once the monitoring program is implemented.

Software tools

Since the bulk of data management is handled electronically, it is important to consider the software stack which will satisfy a program's needs. A generalization of such a stack is represented by Figure 11.11. Specific choices of software should leverage existing expertise and in-house site licenses while being scalable to the size of the program. Technology is an ever-changing landscape, so function over any specific software package is emphasized. Realistic life spans of hardware and necessary maintenance of software should factor into the long-term budgeting.

At the most basic level of data management are files which could be data, information about the data (i.e., metadata), or other documents. In organizing the folder hierarchy, it is a good idea to consider file naming conventions, such as inclusion of a README.txt explanatory file of the folder contents, and a version-author scheme (e.g. somefile_2007-12-31a _JDoe.txt). Where possible, it is advisable to avoid proprietary binary formats which may be difficult to read later by software. In order to be both machine- and human-readable, XML formats are increasing in popularity as exemplified by the Microsoft Word 2007 *.docx default format. (The * indicates where the filename

Obtaining environmental data

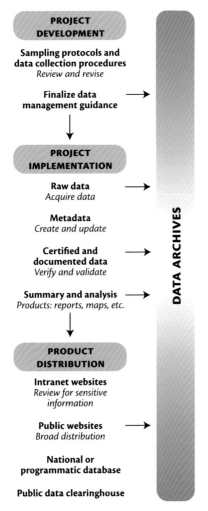

Figure 11.10. An overview of data management workflow from the onset of a program to product development.

reduces data entry (and the possibility for human error), as well as greatly enhancing the querying capability to extract desired information. By using relationships, data integrity is also preserved by cascading updates and deletions.

Lookup tables can enforce the use of controlled vocabularies. Such vocabularies could intelligently and consistently label data. For example, the Integrated Taxonomic Information System provides taxonomic serial numbers that relate to the full taxonomy, common names, and latest valid reference for the given taxa. The NASA Global Change Master Directory provides a set of scientific keywords for attributing data by realm, instrument, discipline, and so forth.

However data is stored, it is important that the analytical packages required for the program can operate on the data. Often, desktop analysis packages have direct read/write capabilities to common databases or through a database

would be inserted). The required technical sophistication will depend on the complexity of the data, i.e., interrelatedness and/or spatially explicit, and level of data-driven web content desired.

Relational databases

For most programs, a relational database can be greatly advantageous for organizing information, whether raw data or data about the data, i.e., metadata. Unlike a spreadsheet, validation rules can be strictly enforced for data entry, such as numeric formats. More importantly, data can be related in a one-to-many fashion between tables, also known as 'database normalization.' This relational aspect

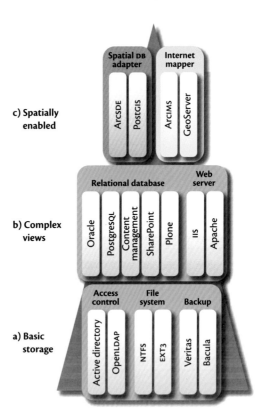

Figure 11.11 Hierarchical software stack for data management. 1) At the most basic level, files are securely accessed and backed up, 2) a database and web content management layer could be added, and 3) spatially enabled.

abstraction layer (e.g., Open Database Connectivity [ODBC]).

Simple mock-ups of a database can be accomplished with a file database (e.g., Microsoft Access) and migrated later to a true server-client enterprise system (e.g., open-source PostgreSQL or Microsoft SQL Server). Especially for enterprise systems, database administration skills for database design and maintenance should be accounted for within the program's personnel.

Who's who in data management?

Data management is a complex process characterized as much by attitudes and habits as it is by infrastructure, standards, and procedures. Although primary responsibility resides with the data management staff, good data management could not possibly be accomplished by the data management staff alone.

Data management staff typically develop standards and procedures and are ultimately responsible for ensuring the long-term integrity of data. Refining data management standards should be a coordinated process involving many people. Data management staff, monitoring program managers, and field crews work together to finalize procedures and guidelines with the goal of developing usable standards that meet the needs of the program and ensure a high degree of data quality. All those associated with a program have specific data management tasks that fall under the responsibilities of their position. These tasks should be clearly defined during the planning stages of the program. All personnel are responsible for providing data management staff with feedback on the effectiveness of data management procedures in an effort to improve the standards as a whole (Figure 11.12). This is especially important for field crews who serve as an invaluable resource for providing information on how well a protocol actually works once it has been implemented. If field crews fail to properly execute protocols at the ground level, the effects

> **Pitfalls to avoid**
>
> - Not accounting for personnel turnover
> - Failure to invest proportionally in both data collection and data analysis
> - Lack of stakeholder engagement
> - Infrequent and poor communication of results

> Successful data management relies on more than just the data managers—monitoring program managers and field crews ensure that tasks are conducted properly and in a timely manner.

will cascade through to the end products.

It is important not to allow staff to fall into the 'tunnel vision' trap. In other words, when people are hired for a position, such as working on a data collection field crew, they often lose sight of all of the other associated data management tasks. Investing time at the onset of a program or field season to impress upon field crews the importance of the associated data management tasks will pay dividends in the long run. Ensuring that field crews understand the rationale for workflows, methodologies, and guidelines will help them better appreciate the importance of their role.

Any successful long-term monitoring program must survive turnovers in personnel (as people change jobs or retire) and technology. In almost all cases measurements over time will be taken by different people. Several important conclusions follow from these facts: a) sampling protocols must be fully documented, with great enough detail that different people can take measurements in exactly the same way; b) protocols should not rely on the latest instrumentation or technology that may change in a few years, such that measurements cannot be repeated; and c) protocols should include training exercises, references, and quality control/quality assurance measures. Field crews should play an integral role in the quality assurance/quality control (QA/QC) process, as they are the most familiar with the data.

Quality assurance and quality control (QA/QC)

Data of poor quality can result in incorrect interpretations and improper management applications. Accordingly, all data analysis, reports, and publications require data of documented quality that minimizes errors and bias.

The initial steps of QA/QC start early on in the development stages when data management standards and procedures are established. These standards are put into practice during the collection of field data when careful and accurate

Obtaining environmental data

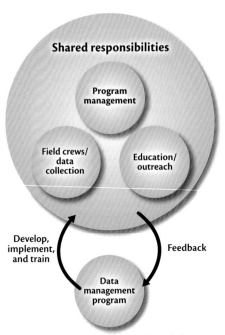

Figure 11.12. The collaborative efforts of good data management involves many individuals.

recording of field observations is essential. Unlike a typographical error that occurs after the data has been collected, an incorrect entry in the field cannot be easily corrected. Therefore, attention to detail during data collection is crucial to overall data quality. These types of errors can be greatly reduced by using customized data collection procedures. There are a number of options currently available to collect and store raw field data (Figure 11.13).

Paper field forms are probably the most common method of data collection. They are (for the most part) straightforward and easy to use but also are the most vulnerable for introducing errors. Sloppy data recording or handling can make interpreting data from data sheets very difficult. Also, no matter how well a data sheet is formatted, nothing exists that requires a user to enter data into all fields. Paper field forms must be formatted in a clear and organized fashion, and contain detailed instructions making it clear how to enter data.

Field computers are becoming more common place. These devices can be deployed with electronic data forms and databases that incorporate mechanisms, such as pick lists and validation rules to help reduce the chances of data entry errors. Additionally all of the data

entry occurs in the field at the time of data collection. This provides a much more efficient process by eliminating the additional step of manually entering the data into the database after returning from the field. Data are transferred electronically from the field machine to the main database application. This also eliminates the possibility of transcription errors that might occur when entering data from paper field forms. Certain situations exist where the use of paper in the field to record data is still necessary, such as when protocols require that field samples be collected for further analysis. In these cases, paper labels may be necessary to document where the sample came from, when it was collected, and by whom. Depending on the sampling protocol and programmatic requirements, additional information, such as geographic coordinates, may be required as well. These field samples are often archived and retained for long periods of time, and it is especially important that field crews take time to clearly document the required information.

Data verification and validation
Verification pertains mainly to data that are entered from paper data sheets but can apply to electronic collection methods as well. It involves ensuring that the information entered into the database is the same as that recorded in the field.

Data collected on paper data sheets should be entered into the program database as soon as possible. If data are entered quickly, details of that sampling event will still be fresh in the minds of the field crews, which will help if any questions arise about the data sheets. Once the data for a specific sampling event has been entered into the program database, the data must be verified. This

Quality assurance and quality control mechanisms are designed to prevent data contamination, which occurs when a process or event other than the one of interest affects the value of a variable and introduces two fundamental types of errors into a data set:

- Errors of commission include those caused by data entry and transcription errors or malfunctioning equipment
- Errors of omission often include insufficient documentation of legitimate data values which could affect the interpretation of those values.

Figure 11.13. a) Paper field forms have no data entry controls and require further data entry into a computer; b) field computers have data entry controls, such as pick lists, and data entry occurs at the time of data collection; and c) automatic data loggers collect and store data unattended.

involves the following:

- Someone other than the person(s) who entered the data should review the data that were entered.
- If errors are found, the record should be corrected and a notation made in the database as well as on the data sheet.
- The verifier should indicate in the database and as on the data sheets that he or she verified the data as well as the date.

If data are collected on field computers, the verification process is less laborious but still necessary. This usually involves the field crews reviewing the data at the site after data collection and confirming the integrity of the data transfer process to the program database.

Regardless of whether field data are collected on paper data sheets or on field computers, all data must be validated. Data validation involves making sure that the data collected make sense. For example, a temperature value of 300° C would be a fairly obvious error. Many of these checks can be automated either within the program database or on field computers. The benefit of having validation checks incorporated into databases in the field is that questionable data can be flagged immediately, checked, and corrected if needed. It is important to remember, however, that simply because data seem unusual or are identified as outliers does not necessarily mean that they are incorrect. Before deleting or changing any such errors, always double check to be sure that the information is indeed incorrect.

Field crews should indicate in the database and on field data sheets who entered and checked

the data as well as when each of these procedures occurred. Once data checking is complete, data sheets should be archived. In the case that errors were identified and corrections made, a record of these changes should also be maintained.

Data documentation

Data sets sometimes take on lives of their own. Some seem to have the ability to reproduce and evolve on multiple hard drives, servers, and other storage media. Others remain hidden in digital formats or in forgotten file drawers. In addition, once data are discovered, a potential data user is often left with little or no information regarding the quality, completeness, or manipulations performed on a particular "copy" of a data set. Such ambiguity results in lost productivity because the user must invest time tracking information down or, worst case scenario, renders the data set useless because this information cannot be found. Data documentation must include an upfront investment in planning and organization. It is a critical step toward ensuring that data sets are usable for their intended purposes well into the future.

Metadata
Metadata (i.e., data about data) provide the means to catalog data sets within intranet and internet systems, thus making the data available to a broad range of potential users. The information contained in metadata notifies potential users about the quality of data sets and helps to ensure that data sets are used properly.

Obtaining environmental data

179

The most commonly accepted format for metadata was designed by the Federal Geographic Data Committee (FGDC). The FGDC is a government interagency committee that promotes the coordinated development, use, sharing, and dissemination of geospatial data on a national basis. In the past, metadata were most commonly associated with spatial or geographic data sets. The importance of associating a data set with documentation has now been widely accepted, and the principles of metadata are relevant to all data, both spatial and non-spatial.

Metadata creation should begin at the onset of a program before data are finalized or even collected. The metadata record for each product should be updated as the program progresses by documenting data development and processing steps. Data products should not be considered final or complete until they are associated with a completed metadata record. Accordingly, no data should be distributed without being accompanied by a compliant metadata record. The metadata record should always be associated with the data file so that those working with the data sets have a clear understanding of how the data were collected, processed, and analyzed.

Data security and storage

Effective, long-term data maintenance is rooted in a comprehensive data storage and archiving plan. To guarantee a high degree of data integrity, it is essential that data are stored in a secure repository that is readily accessible to the assessment team. Network file servers provide a central repository for storing data. Servers consisting of multiple hard disks in a RAID (random array of independent disks) configuration provide a high degree of security for electronic data files by protecting against data loss in the case of hardware failure.

Simply storing data on a file server is not enough

> **Things to consider when creating a metadata record:**
>
> - What is the subject matter of the data set?
> - Where were the data collected?
> - Who collected the data?
> - When were the data collected?
> - How were the data processed?
> - What is the current state of the data?
> - Who are the appropriate contacts for the data set?
> - Does the data set contain sensitive or secure information?

to guarantee data security. A programmatic data back-up plan is essential to ensure that data are secure, especially in the case of unforeseen catastrophic events, such as fire, flood, user error, and hardware or software failure (Figure 11.14). Although these scenarios seem unlikely, the risks are very real and happen all too often. It is also important to remember that data back-ups should be stored off-site so that in the case of fire, for instance, the back-up media do not succumb to the same fate as the file server. Developing a regular back-up routine and arranging for off-site back-up storage is the best way to avoid the loss of data in the case of a major data loss event. The frequency of data back-ups often depends on how dynamic the data are. If data are not changing frequently, perhaps updated weekly or monthly, then weekly back-ups might suffice. Many data sets are very dynamic and should be backed-up. It is also important to determine an appropriate data recovery period. In other words, how long should data back-ups be maintained? If data are accidentally deleted, is a week enough time to notice the loss, or would a month be better? If back-ups are maintained for only a week and a data loss is not noticed until two weeks have passed, the likelihood of recovering that information is remote.

As electronic data progress through their life cycle, they evolve from a raw state when they are still developing, to a certified or final state, when the QA/QC and data documentation are complete.

> Metadata is defined by the FGDC as "information about the content, quality, condition, and other characteristics of data".

Figure 11.14. Fire damage to a server may be irreversible.

Data files should be stored in two locations. Working data files should remain in an accessible directory where data edits, reviews, and quality control procedures can be conducted by all those on the assessment team. These working data files should be periodically archived to preserve a copy in case of data corruption. If data were collected electronically in the field, the field data file should be archived before any changes in order to maintain a record of the truly raw data. Once data are certified and documented, the fully processed data file should be archived and stored in a separate directory—one where most users are granted 'read-only' access rights in order to reduce the chance of inadvertently altering the data.

Data archiving should occur based on milestones established during the program planning stage. It is important to establish benchmark dates for archival. The archival schedule for the raw data files might be weekly or monthly, whereas certified data sets may be archived semi-annually or annually.

One thing to keep in mind when planning for long-term archiving of data sets is to make sure to account for changes in hardware and software through time. A data set archived today in a specific file format may not be usable 10 years from now. Archived data sets should be updated to conform to the current file standard, and if possible, data files should be exported to a more universally accepted file format that could be interpreted by a number of software applications (e.g., ASCII files).

Storage and archival procedures apply to paper data products as well. If data are collected on paper in the field, the data sheets should be copied on returning to the office. The originals and copies should be stored in separate locations (different sites is ideal) with at least one copy being stored in fire-proof or archival cabinet.

Disseminate the data

Data and data products serve little purpose unless they are used and shared with peers, cooperators, or the public. To be most effective, monitoring data must be analyzed, interpreted, and provided at regular intervals to each of the key audiences in a format they can use, which means that the same information needs to be packaged and distributed in several different formats (Figure 11.15). Specific programmatic information may be distributed through internal e-mails, memos, or intranet. Other data may be published in widely distributed, peer-reviewed journals or distributed through national

Designing a program for real-time regional forecasting: LEO-15

Scott Glenn, professor

The Long-term Ecosystem Observatory at 15 meters (LEO-15) is an electro-optic-cabled underwater ocean observing system consisting of a suite of sophisticated marine instruments connected to a node on the seafloor.[15] Located in the coastal waters of New Jersey, the system provides real-time information for rapid environmental assessment and physical and biological forecasting. This observatory is one part of the expanding network of ocean observatories that will form the basis of a national observation network.

In 2005, a state-of-the-art observatory replacement was made for the system that enabled operators to monitor and control the underwater observatory securely and remotely, while providing real-time data to users worldwide through the Internet. LEO-15 "was a beginning", says Dr. Scott Glenn, professor at Rutgers University's Coastal Ocean Observation Lab. "It was the testbed for many of our new ideas on how to better observe a remote and sometimes hostile ocean environment. Along with the cabled bottom observatory, it is where we developed our ability to use satellites, aircraft, and shore-based radars to remotely observe the surface, and it is where we developed the robotic vehicles for sampling the full water column in between. Many of these new technologies are now being used by ourselves and others for scientific and applied programs worldwide."

LEO-15 research stations.[15]

data clearinghouses (see Further Reading at the end of the chapter).

The content and amount of detail included in the various data products differ depending on their intended purpose. At the local level, managers and collaborators need access to detailed scientific data relevant to natural resource issues and challenges. At the national level, however, a different scale of analysis and reporting is needed to be most effective. To report on the status and trends of the condition of environmental issues, ecological report cards that integrate and evaluate broad suites of indicators can be valuable tools. The communication of integrated results in report cards and other products is covered in earlier chapters or Section 1 of this book. Here, we focus on the dissemination of the raw data itself to varied user communities.

Data feedback

Regardless of the scope of dissemination, the target audience should be provided with the ability to comment and provide feedback on the product. Whether feedback is received through e-mail, phone, or a website, comments from a larger group often help to improve products and provide guidance for future work. It is also a good idea to track feedback and error notifications because

these help to improve the quality of future data products.

Sensitive information

Program staff should be wary of sensitive information that if released to a large audience, could threaten the resource. For example, data and data products may deal with endangered species or other sensitive resources. Information that could jeopardize resources should be classified as sensitive and withheld from release to the general public. It is possible to provide a certain level of information without jeopardizing a resource by withholding key information, such as specific locations. It is up to program staff to determine the level of information that should be released and the time frame for releasing information. In addition, appropriate time should be allotted for researchers to publish their results before their data are made publicly available.

Spatial aspects

Monitoring for ecosystem assessment and management, as with any environmental resources monitoring program, is very place specific. Whether making maps, performing spatial statistics, or analyzing remotely sensed imagery, a

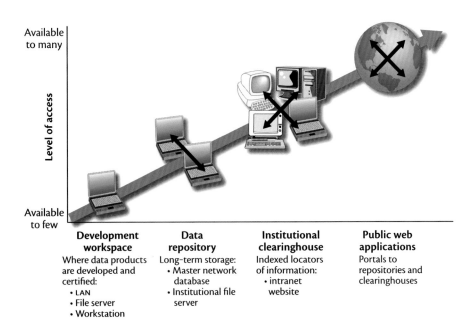

Figure 11.15. The most appropriate level of disseminating information is determined by program staff.

GIS will likely be required. The simplest, traditional approach to a GIS is management of a loose collection of vector files (e.g., point, line, polygon shape files) and/or raster imagery (e.g., GEOTIFF). As long as features are considered static, this simple file system framework for managing and distributing spatial data makes sense.

As recorded features are associated with measurements that change in space and time, a more relational framework may be needed. Spatial data are being managed more frequently within the context of a relational database. This maximizes the querying and validation of the spatial and attribute data. The GIS industry software leader, Environmental Systems Research Institute (ESRI), Inc., now provides community-developed "geodatabase" templates for use with ESRI ArcGIS. The Marine Data Model is one such template that provides relational data structures for data types more dynamic in space and time (Figure 11.16). By defining common relational structures, tools can be built to exploit complex information, and data can be shared more easily.

Web publishing

Websites can be static entities manually updated with text and graphics, or they can be dynamically driven with data and maps by a (spatially-enabled) database. Naturally, the latter is more complicated.

Even static websites are becoming easier to manage now, with the accessibility of content management systems CMS (e.g., open-source Plone or Microsoft Sharepoint). Different types of content can typically be added through the web using formatting menus similar to those found in word processors. By handling content through a web browser, HTML coding and web editing software are unnecessary, making it easy for end users to update the site. Web hosting solutions are also commercially available if the ability to host a website on the program's server is limited.

Presenting dynamic content from a database requires some level of customized application building (Figure 11.17). Working with query-able tables is more straightforward than interactive maps. Commercial (e.g., ESRI ArcIMS) and open-source (e.g., GeoServer) internet mapping software is available along with spatial database adapters (e.g., ESRI ArcSDE or PostGIS) for the task. Another option is the use of mapping web services (e.g., Google Maps; Figure 11.18) which typically only require some JavaScript coding to fetch spatial layers rendered from remote servers. Some server-side scripting (e.g., PHP, Python, or ASP) may still

be needed if it is desirable to access data residing locally to the file system or database.

Leverage partnerships and collaborations

Monitoring is inherently a collaborative effort. The size and scale of monitoring activities often dictate coordination between and within governmental, academic, and non-profit organizations.

Most large-scale monitoring programs are organized by a state or regional entity but require participation at many levels. For example, federal government agencies may provide partial support for new technology implementation and program operation and can serve as arbiters of regional efforts. Partnerships with universities can provide much-needed laboratory services, new technology testing and deployment, and analytical support.

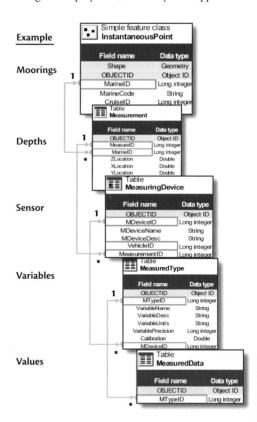

Figure 11.16. Example of a spatio-temporal relational database structure from the instantaneous point containing measurement data in the ArcGIS Marine Data Model. Metadata about the sensor and variable are also captured with this type of one-to-many table separation.

Obtaining environmental data

Local jurisdictions, through economies of scale, can often benefit from the regional monitoring program's existing network by paying for monitoring services. Non-profit organizations, such as watershed groups, can use existing monitoring information to further their activism and help to pinpoint areas in need of more localized citizen monitoring. Citizen monitoring is often difficult to incorporate into a regulatory framework, but the important contributions that citizen scientists can bring to monitoring have been increasingly acknowledged.[16] These contributions include providing supplemental information and insights to the assessment process, engaging the local population in environmental matters, and stimulating the necessary media attention that guides local policy. Teaming with other agencies both inside and outside the jurisdiction can prevent duplication of effort, promote adherence to standardized collection and analysis methods, and create potential cost savings.

Finally, working closely with technology vendors is essential for proper hardware operation and maintenance. Nurturing these relationships can provide opportunities to test new equipment and receive product discounts.

Front-end investments in partnerships at the program design phase ensure that any new data collection will build upon existing information and maximize leverage with other agencies, academia, and the public. These relationships will be critical throughout program implementation to achieve the following:

- establish and maintain public trust and credibility;
- build upon and improve existing knowledge; and,
- effect change through improved resource management.

Figure 11.18. The use of Google Maps to show water quality sampling locations at Rock Creek Park, Washington, DC, U.S. National Park Service National Capital Region Network website.

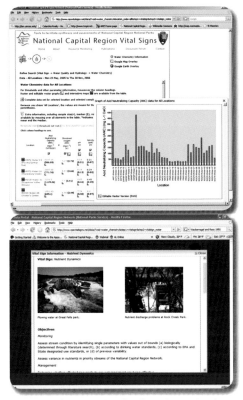

Figure 11.17. The U.S. National Park Service National Capital Region Network natural resource inventory and monitoring website provides dynamic features to upload and download raw or synthesized data.

References

1. Chave PA (2001) The EU water framework directive: An introduction. IWA Publishing, London, United Kingdom
2. Trice M (2009) Maryland Department of Natural Resources' Tidewater Ecosystem Assessment Division. Accessed 30 Jun. www.eyesnnthebay.net
3. Lookingbill T, Gardner R, Townsend P, Carter S (2007) Conceptual models as hypotheses in monitoring urban landscapes. Environ Manage 40:171-182
4. Sutter II GW (1999) Developing conceptual models for complex ecological risk assessments. Hum Ecol Risk Assess 5:375-396
5. National Park Service (2006) A conceptual basis for natural resource monitoring. National Capital Region Network, U.S. National Park Service, Washington, District of Columbia

Case study: *worldwide seagrass monitoring*

Seagrass-Watch (*www.SeagrassWatch.org*)[17] is a nearshore seagrass monitoring program that began in 1998. It consists of scientists and community members interested in conservation-related activities. Primarily in the Asia–Pacific region, the major objective of the program is to provide rapidly available data on overall seagrass meadow health and condition. Locations in USA, Caribbean, Mediterranean, and northeastern Africa have recently expressed interest and are currently building their capacity to participate.

Seagrasses are often at the downstream end of catchments, receiving runoff from a range of agricultural, urban, and industrial land uses. Their ecological values and location in areas likely to be developed for harbors and ports have made seagrasses a likely target for assessing environmental health and impacts on coastal systems. Data are obtained on seagrass abundance, seagrass composition, canopy height, macroalgae abundance, epiphyte abundance, substrate composition, associated fish and invertebrates, and obvious signs of impacts (natural and human).

The range of *Seagrass-Watch* monitoring is primarily in the Asia-Pacific region but is expanding.

Scientists train local community members in the methodology, and supervise data collection and transcription. Because the methods are straightforward and easy to learn, they are less intimidating to non-scientists. *Seagrass-Watch*, therefore, serves a dual purpose: It is an invaluable source of scientific information comparable on a global scale and a highly effective mechanism for promoting conservation and community activism through a cost-effective approach.,

Field crews use a data entry chart that, along with photographs and collected specimens, is submitted to *Seagrass-Watch*. The data are integrated into a report card. Photo credits: *www.SeagrassWatch.org*.

a) There are 13 species of seagrass found in the Philippines and mixed meadows are common. b) In April 2007, a *Seagrass-Watch* training workshop was held in Bolinao, Philippines. Approximately 30 local participants attended. Photo credits: *www. SeagrassWatch.org*.

Obtaining environmental data

6. van den Belt M (2004) Mediated modeling: A system dynamics approach to environmental consensus building. Island Press, Washington, District of Columbia

7. Hagan JM, Whitman AA (2006) Biodiversity indicators for sustainable forestry: Simplifying complexity. J For 104:203-210

8. Nichols JD, Williams BK (2006) Monitoring for conservation. Trends Ecol Evol 21:668-673

9. Fancy SG, Gross JE, Carter SL (2009) Monitoring the condition of natural resources in U.S. National Parks. Environ Monitor Assess 151:161-174

10. Townsend PA, Lookingbill TR, Kingdon CC, Gardner RH (2009) Spatial pattern analysis for monitoring protected areas. Remote Sens Environ 113:1410-1420

11. Urban DL (2002) Tactical monitoring of landscapes. In: Liu J, Taylor WW (eds) Integrating landscape ecology into natural resource management. Cambridge University Press, Cambridge, MA. p 294-311

12. Schneider DC (2001) The rise of the concept of scale in ecology. Bioscience 51:545-553

13. Pourret O, Naïm P, Marcot B (2008) Bayesian networks: a practical guide to applications. Wiley, Hoboken, New Jersey

14. Fertig B, Carruthers TJB, Dennison WC, Jones AB, Pantus F, Longstaff B (2009) Oyster and macroalgae bioindicators detect elevated $\delta^{15}N$ in Maryland's Coastal Bays. Estuaries Coasts 32:773-786

15. Coastal Ocean Observation Lab (2009) Coastal Ocean Observation Lab-Rutgers University. Accessed 30 Jun. www.marine.rutgers.edu/cool/leo15.htm

16. Danielsen F, Burgess ND, Balmford A (2005) Monitoring matters: Examining the potential of locally-based approaches. Biodiversity Conserv 14:2507-2542

17. Seagrass-Watch (2009) Seagrass-Watch: Local eyes global wise. Accessed 30 Jun. www.SeagrassWatch.org

Further reading

du Toit JT, Rogers KH, Biggs HC (2003) The Kruger experience: Ecology and management of savanna heterogeneity. Island Press, Washington, District of Columbia

Federal Geographic Data Committee (2009) The federal geographic data committee. Accessed 30 Jun. www.fgdc.gov

Jones MB, Schildhauer MP, Reichman OJ, Bowers S (2006) The new bioinformatics: Integrating ecological data from the gene to the biosphere. Annu Rev Ecol Evol Syst 37:519-544

Limoncelli T, Hogan CJ, Chalup SR (2007) The practice of system and network administration. 2nd edition. Addison-Wesley, Upper Saddle River, New Jersey

Michener WK, Brunt JW, Helly JJ, Kirchner TB, Stafford SG (1997) Nongeospatial metadata for the ecological sciences. Ecol Appl 7:330-342

National Park Service (2005) Data management plan for natural resources in the National Capital Region Network. Inventory and Monitoring Program, Center for Urban Ecology, U.S. National Park Service, Washington, District of Columbia

Noss RF (1990) Indicators for monitoring biodiversity: A hierarchical approach. Conserv Biol 4(4):355-364

Examples of data clearinghouses:
EPA STORET
USGS NWIS
Data Basin (Conservation Biology Institute)
LandScope America
USGS Seamless Server
GeoSpatial OneStop
National Map
NPS Data Store
NRCS Data Gateway

CHAPTER 12: *IN SITU* MEASUREMENTS

UTILIZING THE EVER-GROWING TOOLBOX OF SENSORS AND PLATFORMS

Mario N. Tamburri and Ben J. Longstaff

The machine does not isolate man from the great problems of nature but plunges him more deeply into them.

—Saint-Exupéry

The previous chapter described how to design an effective monitoring program within a coastal assessment framework. That monitoring program is supported by data measurements. A data gathering strategy needs to ensure that the monitoring program design and the data management protocols will lead to the program's objectives being met. Additionally, there are three main approaches to data collection: using instruments to measure the parameters *in situ* (this chapter); data being collected remotely such as by satellites (Chapter 13); or samples collected for analysis at a later date in a laboratory.

As highlighted in the title of this chapter, the array of *in situ* instruments available for coastal monitoring is increasing rapidly—"the ever-growing toolbox," (Figure 12.1). This growth is driven in part by research and development into new or existing sensors, sensor platforms, data logging, and data telemetry. Because there are such rapid changes in the field of *in situ* monitoring, this chapter gives specific focus to many emerging technologies, such as nutrient analyzers and pathogen detectors. Although these examples have been included to illustrate the cutting edge of *in situ* monitoring, there are often inherent challenges of new instruments do not have a long history of use and application. Therefore, it must not be forgotten that there are many well established *in situ* instruments to consider ranging from the classic and very simple Secchi disc to more complex water quality probes.

In situ monitoring in itself is a very large topic and is covered in more detail by many books.[1] The purpose of this chapter, therefore, is to provide a brief discussion on why to use *in situ* monitoring, to identify what the most suitable situations and tools to use for *in situ* monitoring are, and to identify some of the associated challenges with *in situ* monitoring.

Figure 12.1. Examples of *in situ* instrument packages that take measurements of different environmental parameters directly in the field: a) oceanographic buoy system, b) a sensor for conductivity, temperature, and depth (CTD) being deployed from a research vessel, and c) a dock-side tide station.

Obtaining environmental data

What is *in situ* sensing?

In situ is a Latin phrase meaning *in the place*. In the environmental and biological sciences, *in situ* often means to examine a phenomenon or measure a parameter exactly in the place where it occurs (i.e., without moving it to some special medium or back to the laboratory). Although different disciplines might categorize instruments that collect field data in different ways, for the purpose of this chapter, we will refer to *in situ* instruments or sensors as technologies that collect information (physical, chemical, biological) from the location or environment where it is directly located (e.g., sensors that measure dissolved oxygen at the end of an electrode or optode).

Why use *in situ* measurements?

Sensors are an essential part of scientific inquiry and environmental monitoring. The fundamental purpose for *in situ* measurements is to understand and interpret the environment without having to collect samples from the field and then analyze them in the laboratory. The main advantages of *in situ* instruments vs. sample collection and remote analysis are:

- The detectors are at the site, thus the measurements are made at the site, allowing for data evaluations in real or near-real time for rapid response, adaptive monitoring and management, and identification and tracking of pollution or contaminants to their source (Figure 12.2).
- Measurements are not subject to sources of error associated with remote sensing (e.g., atmospheric interference) and sample collection (e.g., sample deterioration).
- *In situ* sensors can provide high spatial (many locations) and temporal (sampling frequency) resolution for better understanding of changing variables and dynamic processes (see Chapter 11 for discussion of sampling approaches).

Recipe for success

- Take advantage of *in situ* instruments to understand spatially and temporally dynamic processes
- Understand the parameter you want to measure and how different sensors quantify or estimate that value
- Understand the trade-off among instrument accuracy, precision, and cost
- Understand the limitations and realities of sensor deployment in the field
- Always set up and calibrate instruments as recommended by the manufacturer
- Collect and analyze occasional reference samples to identify problems or to correct data

- *In situ* sensors are a means for field ground-truthing of remote sensing (e.g., satellites) and predictions (e.g., forecast modeling).

Because of these advantages, *in situ* instrumentation is becoming the foundation of coastal assessment and environmental observing systems.

When to use *in situ* measurements

For rapid response such as beach monitoring and human health

In situ instruments are most suited for applications where rapid responses based on real-time or near-real time data acquisition are required. In these applications, data processing and interpretation (e.g., automated flagging of values exceeding a defined threshold) protocols have to be established to trigger responses in a timely manner. Although responding to traditional *in situ* water quality measures, such as high chlorophyll *a* and low dissolved oxygen, is currently operational in many programs, methods of measuring bacteria *in situ* are currently being developed, and will likely have many important applications.

Figure 12.2. Public beaches may be closed due to urban runoff and sewage contamination.

Considerable resources are expended each year to measure bacterial levels at recreational beaches and assess whether these beaches are safe for people to use. However, these monitoring programs are of limited value because accepted methods of sample collection and bacteria enumeration are too slow to provide full protection from exposure to waterborne pathogens. The current u.s. Environmental Protection Agency (EPA)-approved methods to evaluate recreational waters are culture based and require an 18 to 96 hour incubation period.[2] However, changes in bacteria levels in beach water occur in much shorter time frames. Thus, contaminated beaches remain open during laboratory sample analysis and are often clean by the time warnings are posted. This slow processing time also makes tracking the source of contaminations extremely difficult because contamination signals can quickly dissipate or disperse.

The effective management of recreational waters requires rapid results that can be provided by *in situ* sensors. Although not yet validated and approved, new molecular methods and technologies that allow direct measurement of cellular properties without incubation are becoming available (similar to those in the medical and food service industries) and have the potential to reduce the measurement period to less than an hour.[3]

For increased temporal resolution such as nutrient monitoring

Monitoring of waters affected by excessive nutrient additions has become more and more widespread and intensive as the magnitude of the over-enrichment impacts has become clearer and more pervasive. Much of the water quality monitoring done to date uses traditional methods

of sample collection, processing, and laboratory-based analytical determinations of nutrient concentrations. Sampling using this approach is generally labor intensive, so sample collection rates are generally low—often on a seasonal or monthly basis—even if there are indications that field concentrations are responsive to short-lived but intense climate- or human-induced events.[4] A better understanding of nutrient conditions could be achieved if sampling frequencies could be more readily adapted to individual situations (Figure 12.3).

In recent years, a variety of nutrient measurement instruments has become available. *In situ* nutrient analyzers that are capable of measuring concentrations of a number of different nutrients in coastal waters are now in production by at least six companies (Table 12.1). Some of these

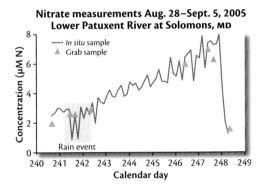

Figure 12.3. The importance of high temporal frequency sampling to understand changes in nitrate levels is demonstrated by comparing grab sample data and continuous monitoring data.[5] Periodic grab samples track the general increase (and rapid decrease) in nitrate levels through time but completely miss the daily fluctuations and a rain event.

Table 12.1. *In situ* sensors and analyzers can now monitor a variety of different nutrients.[6]

In situ nutrient measurement instrument systems

Nutrients measured	SubChem SubChemPak	Trios Props	Envirotech ECOLAB	YSI 9600	Satlantic ISUS	EcoTech 1000	WET Labs CYCLE-P	Systea DPA
NO₃	X	X	X	X	X			X
PO₄	X		X			X	X	X
NH₄	X		X					X
NO₂	X		X	X				X
SI	X		X					X
Fe	X		X					X

Obtaining environmental data

systems are automated analyzers that perform colorimetric chemical analyses based on standard "wet-chemical" methods used in the laboratory. Such systems are often adaptable to monitor a variety of different chemicals by changing the chemical reagents that are used in the analysis. Others are sensors based on direct optical measurements of the nitrate ultraviolet (UV) absorption spectrum. Ion-sensitive electrodes are also available for *in situ* measurements of nutrient concentrations.

How to use *in situ* instruments

Selecting from the ever-growing toolbox

With the abundance of tools that are currently available and emerging technologies coming online, it can be difficult to identify the instrument that best meets your needs. In addition to novel technologies continuously coming online to measure critical environmental variables (e.g., sensors specific for harmful algae or their toxins), existing instrumentation is constantly being improved. For fundamental parameters of interest, such as salinity, there are well over 40 different sensor packages or models currently available.

There are, however, resources that can help you to make an informed selection. Online databases, such as the one developed and maintained by the Alliance for Coastal Technologies (ACT), have been established to provide the information required to select the most appropriate tools for studying and monitoring coastal environments. This is a living database that is continuously updated and allows visitors to search approximately 5,000 instrument listings by environmental parameter of interest, sensor types, associated equipment, and technology provider. ACT also conducts third-party technology evaluations and releases public reports on instrument performance under diverse environmental conditions and applications.

Knowing what tools are available is only half the challenge. You need to have a clear understanding of what you need to measure and why you need to measure it (see Chapter 11 for more details). Choosing the most appropriate instrument also needs to acknowledge whether the data will be used to answer an academic question or for regulatory requirements. For example, monitoring environmental parameters (e.g., turbidity, dissolved oxygen) for U.S. EPA water quality criteria will often have requirements for how measurements are collected.

Depending on the parameter or process of interest and its variance over space and time, it is important to consider sensor performance specifications to select the most appropriate tool. Table 12.2 lists some basic sensor specification categories and questions to ask yourself.

Deploying in situ instruments

Another variable to consider is how the *in situ* sensor(s) will be used or deployed. Common instrument deployments include handheld spot measurements; vertical profiling or surface mapping from a vessel; or deployment of a fixed platform, such as a buoy. However, the ability to monitor various environmental parameters at multiple locations is often as important as high-frequency sampling at a single location. The deployment of multiple instruments in multiple locations or use of research and agency vessels to cover large areas through time is typically cost prohibitive. Therefore, new technological approaches are being adapted to provide increased spatial resolution. A recent development, driven by the ability to create very small sensors and

Table 12.2. Basic sensor specification categories and considerations.

Categories	Considerations
Range and detection limits	What is already known about the range of values for the parameter you want to measure for the location(s) of interests or similar environments?
Accuracy	Accuracy reflects the closeness of the sensor-measured value to the true value. How much are you willing to spend on the most accurate instrument possible and does that added accuracy truly provide a better answer to your question?
Precision	Precision is 1) the ability of a measurement to be consistently reproduced and 2) the number of significant digits to which a value has been reliably measured. How many decimal places do you need to answer your question?
Reliability	Reliability is the measure of the ability to maintain integrity of the instrument and data collection over time. New technologies are often less reliable than well-established sensors and typically require more care (e.g., maintenance and calibration). How important are the data that only a new technology can provide? Can a more mature instrument provide a reliable proxy?

Table 12.2. (continued) Basic sensor-specification categories and considerations.

Other specifications to consider when selecting an instrument	
Sampling interval and frequency	How fast or slow can the sensor package sample?
Operating life	How long do you need the instrument to last?
Fouling prevention	Does the instrument package include an anti-fouling system?
Operating pressure and depth range	How deep will the sensor go?
Calibration life and automatic calibration	How often will you be able to recalibrate the instrument?
Ease of calibration	Is extensive laboratory work required to calibrate it?
Real-time sensor data display and analysis	Do you need to see the data as they are being collected?
Off-sensor telemetry	Do you need to receive the data from a remote location?
Packaging and input and output interfaces	How easy is the sensor package to use for your application?
Quality of product handbook/ documentation/ support	How easy is it to learn to use, and is it helpful?
Cost	How much are you willing to spend on both the instrument and its operation and maintenance?

transmitters, is attaching instruments to animals such as fish and marine mammals (Figure 12.4).[7] Data, such as temperature and salinity, are collected as these animals dive in search of food, and then is transmitted to a receiving station once the animal surfaces (Figure 12.5). A variety of mobile platforms, such as autonomous underwater vehicles, drifters, gliders, and vertical profilers that carry a full suite of *in situ* sensors, are now being used as research tools and have great potential for coastal monitoring (Figure 12.6).

Perhaps the most cost-effective approach for increased spatial resolution is to take advantage of vessels of opportunity. The use of self-contained, low-maintenance sensor packages installed on commercial vessels (e.g., as ferries) is becoming an important monitoring and scientific tool in many regions around the world (Figure 12.7).[9] These systems integrate data from meteorological and water quality sensors with Global Positioning

Pitfalls to avoid

- Not planning or accounting for long-term resources needed to maintain and deploy an instrument
- Purchasing unproven instruments that may promise a lot, but may be unreliable and require significant investment in time to obtain usable data
- Not calibrating the instrument at routine intervals
- Purchasing instruments that do not meet the data quality needed (precision and accuracy) or are overspecified for the intended application
- Collecting by instruments that have no or little application to the program needs

Figure 12.4. A seal with an electronic tag that can measure environmental conditions.

Martin Biuw

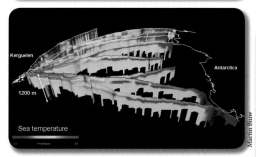

Kerguelen

Antarctica

1200 m

Sea temperature

Martin Biuw

Figure 12.5. Data showing dive patterns and water temperature from a marine mammal tag.

Obtaining environmental data

Case study: The Venice Lagoon

Venice Lagoon is an enclosed, shallow, brackish embayment adjoining the Adriatic Sea in which the city of Venice, Italy, is situated. The lagoon provides an important seaport, large tourism industry, and commercial fishing and fish farming. Like many coastal regions, Venice Lagoon is a fragile ecosystem highly influenced by industrial and anthropogenic emissions as well as continuing land subsidence and acceleration in the rate of sea-level rise.

To address some of these issues, the Venice Water Authority (*www.magisacque.it*) is taking a series of measures to counteract the degradation of the lagoon, including dredging of contaminated sediments, clean-up of contaminated sites inside the lagoon, pollution prevention from industrial discharges, and wetland reconstruction. To control the status of the ecosystem and to verify both the short- and long-term effects of such initiatives, the Venice Water Authority has set up a real-time monitoring network of the water quality parameters of the lagoon.[8]

Satellite photo of Venice Lagoon.

The monitoring system is composed of 10 stations placed in different parts of the lagoon, to cover the most significant areas of the lagoon: the area surrounding the city of Venice; the part of the lagoon directly influenced by the industrial area of Porto Marghera; the area of the southern lagoon close to the city of Chioggia, an important economical center for fishing activities; and various areas close to the outlet of the main rivers that flow into the lagoon. Each station is solar-powered and encased in a plastic housing to avoid any possible interference of trace metal measurements. They are equipped with multiparameter probes measuring the depth of the water column, temperature, pH, salinity, dissolved oxygen, redox potential, turbidity, and chlorophyll *a*. Each station is also equipped with static sampling systems for the collection of both wet and dry atmospheric deposition, which are analyzed periodically for the evaluation of inorganic (e.g., metals) and organic (e.g., dioxins) pollution due to atmospheric fallout. Using telemetry, the stations transmit the collected data to a remote laboratory station. The different operations of the probes are controlled by a device called a "buoy controller." The probes are calibrated in the laboratory using certified reference materials and standards, and every one to two weeks, depending on the season or when anomalous data are measured, the field probes are changed so that all parameters can be continuously monitored with limited risk of drifts of the signals and unreliable data due to biofouling.[8]

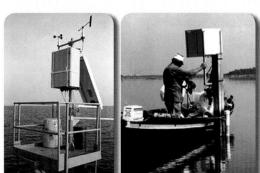 

A variety of *in situ* monitoring stations are deployed in the Venice Lagoon.

Figure 12.6. A glider being deployed by a researcher at Mote Marine Laboratory, Florida.

System (GPS) data into a data stream that is automatically transferred from ship to shore (Figure 12.8). Although limited to predetermined vessel routes, these sensor packages provide high spatial and temporal resolution, have no power restrictions, are easy to maintain, are protected from harsh environments and biofouling, and provide public outreach opportunities.

The realities of in situ *instrumentation—biofouling*

Biofouling is one of the biggest factors affecting the operation, maintenance, and data quality of *in situ* sensors deployed for any length of time.[9] This is especially true for instrumentation deployments in shallow coastal zones. Biofouling inhibits sensor operations and diminishes performance by interfering with optical, membrane, and electrode sensors, interfering with water flow through orifices and hoses, adding weight to the instrument, adding hydrodynamic drag to the instrumentation, and inhibiting the mechanical movement of some sensor types (Figures 12.9 and 12.10). Platform performance is diminished through increased weight, increased hydrodynamic drag, and interference with mounted sensors. Although the cost of biofouling to instruments and platforms has not been completely quantified, it is

Figure 12.7. A water quality monitoring program, FerryMon, has equipped three North Carolina state ferry vessels to monitor the waters of Pamilico Sound and its tributary rivers using onboard instruments (*www.ferrymon.org*).

Crittercam, *a unique perspective*

Greg Marshall, marine biologist and inventor

Greg Marshall is a scientist, inventor, and filmmaker who has dedicated more than 20 years to studying, exploring, and documenting life in the oceans.

In 1986, while diving on the reefs off Belize, Greg encountered a shark, and was struck by the sight of a remora fish clinging to the shark's side. Imagining the unique perspective the remora must have when hitchhiking with its host, Greg conceived a remote camera that would mimic the remora's behavior.

Recognizing the scientific potential of such a tool, Greg decided to make it a reality. In early 1992, he successfully deployed vastly improved prototypes on free-swimming sharks and sea turtles, and *Crittercam* was born.[10]

More than a decade later, this revolutionary tool is deployed on approximately 50 aquatic species to record images, sound, and data, such as depth, temperature, light, and speed, from an animal's perspective. Collaborating with scientists worldwide, Greg and his team have used *Crittercam* to capture information that was previously inaccessible to humans.

For whales, dolphins, and leatherback turtles, special suction cups have been developed. With seals and hard-shelled turtles, a small adhesive patch is used. Custom-tailored, backpack-like harnesses do the job for penguins, and a passive fin clamp keeps *Crittercam* swimming with sharks.

Obtaining environmental data

JENA engineering GmbH

Figure 12.8. An example of an integrated sensor system deployed on ferries and other commercial vessels around the world.

not unusual for the majority of the long-term cost of instrumentation deployment to be dominated by biofouling control and maintenance.

Current biofouling prevention approaches include anti-fouling paints (copper and peroxide based), silicone greases, peel-away plastic wraps, copper screens, mechanical shutters, and mechanical wipers. Although many instruments are equipped with biofouling removal and prevention systems, it is not uncommon for the

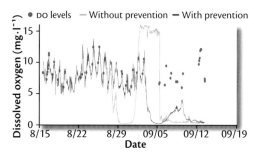

Figure 12.9. Comparison of two dissolved oxygen sensors—one with a biofouling prevention system and one without. The red dots represent dissolved oxygen levels measured by Winkler titration of collected water samples as a standard against which performance was measured. Without biofouling prevention, the sensor was compromised after 10 to 14 days and prevention, data were compromised after 21 days. Data source: ACT.

NOAA

ACT

Figure 12.10. Accumulated biofouling can form enormous masses that diminish instrument operations.

user to have to develop his or her own system that is applicable to the specific environment the instrument will be deployed in.

The realities of in situ sensor use—indirect measures

It is often the case that the exact parameter of interest cannot be measured directly with an *in situ* sensor, but other related variables can be quantified and converted to an estimate of the parameter. While the sensor output values may claim, and use units of, the parameter you are trying to measure, it is important to keep in mind that these estimates come from algorithms and conversions that are based on known relationships but are not absolute values. Following are two examples of commonly used indirect measures of water quality.

In situ fluorometers

Chlorophyll measurements are widely used by resource managers and researchers to estimate phytoplankton abundance and distribution and can be used as a tool in assessing eutrophication status. Chlorophyll is also the most important light-capturing molecule for photosynthesis and is an important parameter in modeling primary production. These data are used for numerous industrial applications as well, including water quality management, water treatment, ecosystem health studies, and aquaculture. There are various techniques available for chlorophyll determinations, including spectrophotometry, bench-top fluorometry, and high performance liquid chromatography using samples collected on filters and extracted in solvents. However, chlorophyll measurement by *in situ* fluorescence is widely accepted for its simplicity, sensitivity, versatility, and economic advantages.

In situ fluorometers are designed to detect chlorophyll in living algal and cyanobacterial cells in aquatic environments (Figure 12.11). The excitation light from the fluorometer passes through the water and excites chlorophyll within the living cells of the algae present. Because light absorption by chlorophyll and its accessory pigments is the initial biophysical event driving photosynthesis, several factors make *in situ* fluorescence monitoring of chlorophyll more of a semi-quantitative measure. Environmental conditions, phytoplankton community composition, physiological status, cell morphology, irradiance history, and the presence of interfering compounds all play a role in altering the relationship between fluorescence and the concentrations of chlorophyll. Interfering materials can compete with light absorption or change the optical path of fluoresced light and include other plant pigments, degradation products, and dissolved organic matter. Even with these diverse natural constraints, *in situ* fluorescence in a variety of deployment modes supplies valuable information on the relative temporal and spatial distribution of chlorophyll concentrations in

Figure 12.11. Deployment of an *in situ* nutrient sensor as part of an ACT technology demonstration.

ISUS, *an* in situ *chemical sensor*

Ken Johnson, chemical oceanographer

Ken Johnson is a senior scientist at the Monterey Bay Aquarium Research Institute (MBARI), where he has been developing new analytical methods for chemicals in seawater and then applying these tools to studies of chemical cycling throughout the ocean. Perhaps his largest contribution to coastal assessment has been the invention of a novel nutrient analyzer, the *In Situ* Ultraviolet Spectrophotometer (ISUS). Working with Luke Coletti in 2000, Johnson developed a unique submersible chemical analysis system that optically detects nitrate concentrations without reagents or laboratory testing. Nitrate detection is especially critical to the understanding of primary production and carbon dioxide uptake. ISUS is effective for long-term monitoring of remote marine environments as well as for nitrate pollution and salinity measurements.[11]

MBARI and Satlantic, Inc., of Halifax, Nova Scotia, have collaborated to commercialize and market ISUS, which can be deployed on towed, undulating vehicles; water column profilers; remotely operated vehicles; and moorings for long-term deployments. ISUS has been successfully used in a number of oceanographic studies (e.g., 2002 Southern Ocean Iron Experiment) and is now being considered for routine coastal and estuarine monitoring applications.

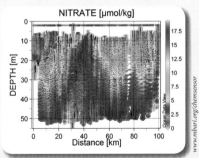

Nitrate concentrations measured with an ISUS mounted on a SeaSciences Acrobat undulating, towed vehicle.[11]

Obtaining environmental data

Case study: the Argo *ocean observing array*

Argo (*www.argo.net*) is a global array of more than 3,000 free-drifting profiling floats that measure the temperature and salinity of the upper 2,000 m of the ocean. In 1998, an international consortium presented plans for an array of 3,000 autonomous instruments that would revolutionize the collection of critical information from the climatically important upper layers of the worlds' oceans. That vision is now a reality because the *Argo* array of profiling floats has reached its target, and each year provides more than 100,000 high-quality temperature and salinity profiles and global-scale data on ocean currents. This is a factor of 20 greater than the rate of collection of comparable ship-based profile measurements and provides immediate access to high-quality data throughout the oceans without seasonal bias. (Most ship measurements, particularly in high latitude regions, are made in the summer season.)[12]

An *Argo* float just before recovery by the Japanese Coast Guard vessel *Takuyo*.

One benefit from *Argo* has been a marked reduction in the uncertainty of ocean heat storage calculations. These are a key factor in determining the rate of global climate warming and sea-level rise and in projecting their future progression. The steady stream of *Argo* data coupled with global-scale satellite measurements from radar altimeters has also made possible huge advances in the representation of the oceans in coupled ocean–atmosphere models, leading to seasonal climate forecasts and routine analysis and forecasting of the state of the subsurface ocean.

Argo data are being used in an ever-widening range of research applications that have led to new insights into how the ocean and atmosphere interact in extreme as well as normal conditions. Two examples are the processes in polar winters when the deep waters that fill most of the ocean basins are formed and, at the other temperature extreme, the transfer of heat and water to the atmosphere beneath tropical cyclones. Both conditions are crucial to global weather and climate and could not be observed by ships.[12]

Having deployed the array and built an effective data delivery system, the next challenge is to maintain the full array for a decade in a preoperational, sustained maintenance phase. This will allow the array's design to be optimized and its value fully demonstrated and exploited.

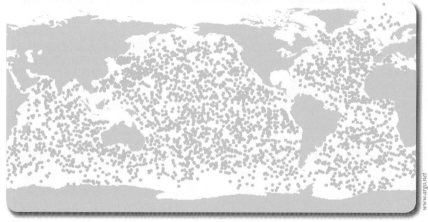

The *Argo* ocean observing array has now exceeded its initial target of operating more than 3,000 robotic floats worldwide. This map shows the locations (green dots) of the various measurements that are being monitored globally by *Argo* floats as of June 2009.

the water column and under similar conditions correlates well with extracted chlorophyll samples.[13,14]

In situ turbidity sensors

Turbidity is a property commonly used to describe water clarity in both marine and freshwater environments and provides a gross assessment of the amount of suspended material and dissolved substances. However, turbidity is often not a direct measure of the quantity of interest, such as suspended sediment or living particles, but rather a measure of the effect of the desired quantity on a specific optical property of the water. At present, there are numerous methods for quantifying turbidity (e.g., light attenuation, optical scatter, acoustic back-scatter). Differences in methods of measurement and their individual responses to varying types of suspended material have made the measurement of turbidity difficult to perform in a consistent and standardized way.[15] This has necessitated many public-service agencies (e.g., USGS, U.S. EPA) to define turbidity in very specific terms based on optical methods of measurement, because optically based approaches have conventionally been the most used. Although such standards and definitions were created to be both technically and legally specific (thereby minimizing the ambiguity in interpreting what turbidity is and how it is measured), it is still not possible to create an absolute standard that is applicable for different natural water types and different instrument designs that are the exact same principles of measurement. Despite these limitations, a variety of *in situ* instruments that provide some measure of turbidity are commonly and successfully used in many research and monitoring settings as at least a relative measure of water clarity.

A comprehensive in situ *water quality monitoring program*

The full utility and benefit of *in situ* sensors has been harnessed by the Maryland Department of Natural Resources (MD DNR) to monitor Chesapeake Bay water quality. MD DNR, like many other programs, uses *in situ* water quality probes to monitor parameters such as salinity, dissolved oxygen, and turbidity. However, what makes this program stand out from others is the scale of the program (large numbers of instruments and measures taken), the variety of monitoring approaches, and the manner in which data is presented and made available on the web (Figures

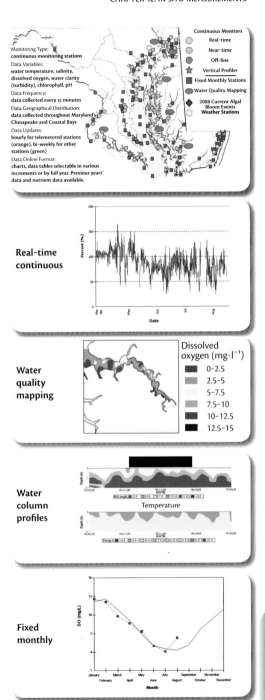

Figure 12.12. Extracts from the MDNR, "Eyes on the Bay" website (*www.eyesonthebay.net*), showing a diversity of *in situ* products available and the types of graphical outputs provided.

Obtaining environmental data

197

12.12, 12.13). Applications of the *in situ* probes include 1) continually measuring water quality at fixed stations, with real- or near-time data telemetry and web access; 2) mapping water quality by collecting data from a boat while underway; 3) conducting profiles of the water column; and 4) collecting data at fixed long-term routine monitoring stations.

As discussed at the beginning of this chapter, rapid expansion in monitoring has led to an exponential increase in data collection, requiring significant investment in database development. Although the data collected by MD DNR is used for specific products, such as report cards and assessing impaired water status, it is the ease at which data can be viewed and accessed on it's website (*www.eyesonthebay.net*) that has probably been most beneficial to the scientific, management, and public communities (Figure 12.12). Eyes on the Bay enables users to select the monitoring stations and parameters of interest and then display and download the data. Of course, this scale of monitoring requires a major investment to not only maintain the *in situ* instruments (i.e., deploy, calibrate, clean) but also to continually manage the data. Funding for this type of program requires multiple sources, such as state and federal agencies. Additionally, the program needs to be staffed by people with a variety of technical, analytical, information technology, and data management skills.

In summary, this chapter provided an overview of *in situ* data collection. Although collecting data *in situ* has many benefits, such as immediate data

availability, there are many issues that need to be considered before using *in situ* sensors. Chapter 13 continues the theme of data collection by discussing the application of remotely sensed data collection for coastal assessment.

References

1. Buffle J, Horvai G (2000) *In situ* monitoring of aquatic systems: Chemical analysis and speciation. Wiley, Chichester, New York
2. U.S. Environmental Protection Agency (2000) Improved enumeration methods for the recreational water quality indicators: *Enterococci* and *Escherichia coli*. U.S. Environmental Protection Agency, Office of Science and Technology EPA-821-R-97-004, Washington, District of Columbia
3. Noble RT, Weisberg SB (2005) A review of technologies for rapid detection of bacteria in recreational waters. Water Health 03.4:381-392
4. Castro MS, Driscoll CT, Jordan TE, Reay WG, Boynton WR (2003) Sources of nitrogen to estuaries in the United States. Estuaries 26:803-814
5. Boynton WR (2009) University of Maryland Center for Environmental Science, Chesapeake Biological Laboratory, Solomons, MD. pers. comm.
6. Alliance for Coastal Technologies (2007) Recent developments in *in situ* nutrient sensors: Applications and future directions. Alliance for Coastal Technologies, Solomons, Maryland
7. Charrassin JB, Hindell M, Rintoul SR, Roquet F, Sokolov S, Biuw M,Costa D, Boehme L, Lovell P, Coleman R, Timmermann R, Meijers A,Meredith M, Park YH, Bailleul F, Goebel M, Tremblay Y, Bost CA,McMahon CR, Field IC, Fedak MA, Guinet C (2008) Southern Oceanfrontal structure and sea-ice formation rates revealed by elephant seals. Proc Nat Acad Sci 33:11634-11639
8. www.magisacque.it
9. Holley S, Hydes DJ (2002) "Ferry-Boxes" and data stations for improved monitoring and resolution of eutrophication related processes: application in Southampton Water UK, a temperate latitude hypernutrified estuary. Hydrobiologia 475/476:99-110
10. National Geographic (2009) Crittercam. Accessed 30 Jun. www.nationalgeographic.com/crittercam
11. Monterey Bay Aquarium Research Institute (2009) Chemical Sensor Program. Accessed 30 Jun. www.mbari.org/chemsensor
12. www.argo.net
13. Alliance for Coastal Technologies (2003) Biofouling prevention technologies for coastal sensors/sensor platforms. Alliance for Coastal Technologies, Solomons, Maryland
14. Beutler M, Wiltshire KH, Meyer B, Moldaenke C, Lüring C, Meyerhöfer M, Hansen UP, Dau H (2002) A fluorometric method for the differentiation of algal populations in vivo and *in situ*. Photosynth Res 72:39-53
15. Cullen JJ, Lewis MR (1995) Biological processes and optical measurements near the sea-surface: Some issues relevant to remote sensing. J Geophys Res 100:13,255-213,266

Further reading

Downing J (2005) Turbidity monitoring. Down RD, Lehr JH (eds) Wiley, New York, NY. In: Environmental instrumentation and analysis handbook. p 511-546

Figure 12.13. a) The instrumentation used for MDNR's Continuous Monitoring project are YSI 6600 data loggers. Each YSI 6600 data logger is programmed to record seven environmental parameters: water temperature, salinity, dissolved oxygen (DO) saturation, DO concentration, pH, turbidity, and fluorescence (a measure of chlorophyll *a* present in the water column). b) Periodically, the stored data are downloaded, or telemetered, to provide real-time data on the website.

Environmental Technology Verification (ETV) Program. www.
epa.gov/etv/

Interagency Methods and Data Comparability Board. wi.water.
usgs.gov/methodsboard/workgroups/sensors/index.htm

Integrated Ocean Observing System. ioos.noaa.gov/

Ocean Observatories Initiative. www.oceanleadership.org/
programs-and-partnerships/ocean-observing/

National Ecological Observatory Network. www.neoninc.org/

Obtaining environmental data

Chapter 13: Remote sensing

Discerning the promise from the reality

Stuart Phinn, Chris Roelfsema, and Richard P. Stumpf

Man must rise above the Earth—to the top of the atmosphere and beyond—for only thus will he fully understand the world in which he lives.
—Socrates

Now that *in situ* measurements have been discussed in the previous chapter, we will now consider data measurements that are collected by remote sensing. Collecting data remotely from platforms such as satellites and airplanes has some major benefits, most notably, the continuous spatial coverage of an area on a repeatable basis. Of course, with the benefits, there are challenges, one of which being to discern some of the promises or potentials of remote sensing from the current reality. This chapter explores questions such as why and when to use remote sensing and then gives some guidance on how to build remote sensing into a coastal assessment program.

What is remote sensing?

Remote sensing is the acquisition of information about an object while not being in direct contact with it. For earth observations, remote sensing is usually is considered to involve the creation of spatial data in the form of an image and a subsequent map (e.g., ocean chlorophyll image), whereas time series data (e.g., sea surface temperature (SST) over time) can be extracted from image points. Ultimately, a remote sensing project is not just the collection of a satellite image of the coastal zone; but also a collection of activities that delivers validated information about the current state or changes of an environmental variable. Numerous instructional resources exist for exploring this topic further.[1,2]

The remote sensing process includes using knowledge of how a feature interacts with light and energy, acquisition of image data from any remote platform, applying algorithms to transform the image data into single or multiple data maps of a biophysical variable, assessing the accuracy of the biophysical variable map, and disseminating the information to users so that they can use them appropriately (Figure 13.1). If you are going to use remotely sensed information, you may enter the process at any stage, depending on

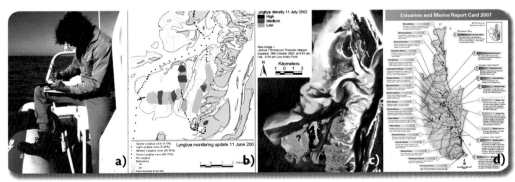

Figure 13.1. The step-by-step process of creating a product from remote-sensing data: a) collecting field data; b) creating an image from field work;[3] c) using field data as training data in image classification to measure the regional extent of environmental variables measured at specific locations;[3] and d) using remote-sensed data in a product such as an ecosystem health report card. Source: University of Queensland and Healthy Waterways Campaign.

Obtaining environmental data

your information needs and available skills. This may mean using image-based products that are widely distributed on websites (e.g., ocean color parameters, SST, coastal bathymetry) or running a project to acquire your own images and process them using an image processing software system to derive image-based maps of a coastal ecosystem heath indicator.

Remote sensing data are categorized by the type of sensor and the platform housing the sensor. These attributes also control the type and scale of information to be collected, enabling the full range of environmental features to be measured from site or patches to global scales (Figure 13.2). There are two primary types of data collection: passive and active. Passive systems record the ambient energy from an object, including ultraviolet, visible, near-infrared, and thermal infrared radiation. These are the most familiar and include film and digital camera systems, non-imaging spectrometers and fluorometers, and thermal sensors. Active systems emit and record their own source of energy (flash photography at night could be considered an active system). They include radar, LIDAR (laser),

scatterometers, and acoustic systems. These systems do not depend on sunlight, and some, like microwave, radar can "see" through clouds. Active systems are used primarily to determine the vertical and horizontal position of the feature, but the characteristics of the return can be used to identify feature properties. Passive systems are normally used to identify properties but can be used to identify position, such as through photogrammetric image processing. Each of these sensors can be operated from a variety of platforms, including hand-held or fixed points of observation, boats, remotely piloted vehicles in the air or underwater, aircraft, and satellites.

Why use remote sensing

A fundamental requirement for coastal ecosystem management is understanding what the environment is made up of and how these features are changing over time. Field surveys can only cover limited areas in both space and time and can require substantial resources to perform regular or spatially extensive surveys. Remote sensing

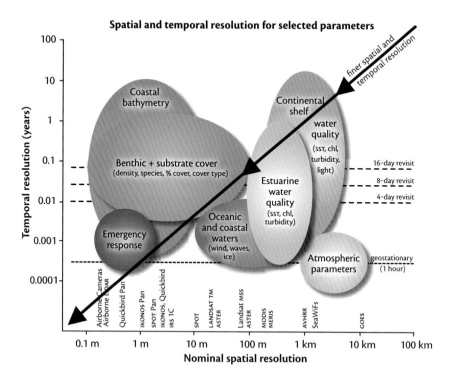

Figure 13.2. Spatial and temporal scales of coastal monitoring applications in relation to the pixel size of commercially available airborne and satellite image data sets.[4]

provides spatial and temporal information that would be impractical to obtain with field surveys. Detailed consideration of information needs and possible integration of image-and field-based approaches provide the means to address the fundamental trade-off in the use of field and/or image-based approaches (Figure 13.3).

Remote sensing data cannot be used to accurately measure all biophysical properties and processes in coastal environments; however, sufficient work has been completed where information is available to define which biophysical properties and processes can be determined, under

what environmental conditions (e.g., depth and suspended sediment concentration; Figure 13.4, Table 13.1), and with what types of image data sets or image-based map products. An extensive outline of where remote sensing does and does not work for mapping seagrass, coral reefs, and water quality parameters can be found on the Coastal Remote Sensing Toolkit website[5] and in various reviews.[1,6,7]

Remote sensing applications are not restricted to single images and photographs, and often the most effective use of these approaches is when they have been used in combination with other

Field data (individual stations):
0.5% area coverage with 95% accuracy

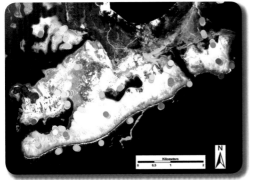

Remote sensing data (Quickbird 2):
100% area coverage with 70% accuracy

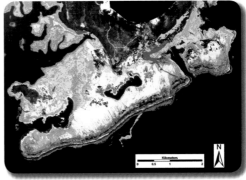

Figure 13.3. An example of the fundamental trade-off to be considered when using remotely sensed information for environmental monitoring (colors on maps represent benthic communities categories).[4] How much of an area do you want to cover and at what level of accuracy?

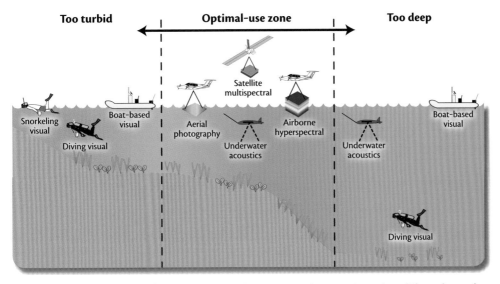

Figure 13.4. A conceptual diagram for seagrass mapping in a near-coastal zone to show where different forms of remote sensing data acquisition (depth and turbidity limitations) can and cannot be used.

Obtaining environmental data

Table 13.1. The conditions under which remote sensing should be used.

Questions	Answers indicating that you need to use remote sensing
What size area do you need to cover and to what level of spatial detail?	Area larger than field sampling capacity. Complete spatial coverage required. Cannot use representative sampling.
What type of information (e.g., biophysical variable) do you need?	Biophysical variable that cannot be measured repeatedly over large areas using *in situ* point-based approaches.
When and how often do you need the information?	Repetitive sampling, especially over a large area. Information required at a higher sampling frequency than can be achieved with field surveys. Data pre-dating current monitoring programs.
What is the precision and accuracy required for your information?	Precision and accuracy considered in relation to the area and frequency of sampling. Spatial accuracy and repeatability more critical than sample accuracy.
What are the environmental conditions in the area to be mapped?	Conditions do not allow (easy) access to the area to be monitored.
In what form is the monitoring information required and how will it be used?	Spatial information in a digital format for integration in a GIS with other spatial data for the area to be monitored.
What capacity do you have to acquire, process, validate, and distribute image-based map products?	GIS capable. Resources and training for collection and processing of imagery as appropriate. Necessary equipment for collection of imagery and field data.

spatial information, historic image archives, and field surveys. Image-based approaches can only be used under certain conditions, so developing complementary image and field-based approaches maximizes the coverage of the monitoring approach and introduces redundancy.

When to use remote sensing

The decision on when to use remote sensing for your coastal monitoring application can only be reached once you have answered the specific questions outlined in Table 13.1 and considered what existing field survey data and ongoing field programs are in place, along with existing images and image-based map products. Having answered these questions, the fundamental decision depends on whether remote sensing approaches can and have been demonstrated as an accurate and cost-effective method to map and monitor the coastal ecosystem health metric that you require in the environment you are working in.

The promise of an ideal monitoring instrument

For many satellite-based systems, archives of previously collected images mean that data can be available even before to the development of a field program.[8] When trying to decide whether and then how you would use remotely sensed data to monitor your coastal environment or a specific process or structure within that, it is instructive to consider what system would be ideal for your purpose.[9,10] This requires consideration of the capabilities and costs involved with acquiring data and making map products.

The ideal remote sensing approach would provide a suitable sensor, data, and algorithms able to create maps of the area needed at the level of detail and accuracy required, and at an appropriate price. The output map products, or series of map products indicating changes or trends, would be in a format that could be used by all resource managers and scientists in their geographic information system (GIS) or desktop graphics environments. The algorithm used to derive the map product would be fully documented, and the products would be validated against suitable field data, demonstrating the positional and attribute accuracy of the products. The process required to deliver this information would be fully funded and would deliver regularly to all interested parties.

It is impossible to have a mapping program that would meet all of these requirements. Trade-offs are required in terms of the spatial and temporal

> *The conditions under which the use of remotely sensed information, in the form of existing products or processing of image data, would be an appropriate solution:*
>
> - Appropriate spatial resolution and temporal frequency;
> - Appropriate area coverage, from site specific (<1 ha) to regional, national, and global scales;
> - Measurement of suitable spectral bandwidths, allowing the coastal ecosystem health indicator of interest to be mapped accurately and precisely;
> - An established and validated method to convert the remotely sensed image to a map of an accepted coastal ecosystem health indicator;
> - A cost-efficient and robust validation program for assessing the accuracy and precision of the image-based coastal ecosystem health indicator map;
> - An effective system for disseminating the map products and associated metadata;
> - A cost-efficient system for acquisition, processing, and dissemination; and,
> - A long-term commitment.

scales of images and map products along with the level of detail and accuracy in the information provided. Figure 13.2 illustrates the range of spatial and temporal scales at which image data currently can be accessed. The major trade-offs to be aware of are in the level of spatial detail required in your map (i.e., what is the smallest feature you need to be able to see and how often you require the information to be mapped). Trade-offs also exist between desired resolution (what you would like to get) and practical resolution (what you ultimately will use to answer the management question). The remainder of this chapter takes you through an established sequence for assessing your monitoring needs and then selecting an optimum combination of image data, processing techniques, validation activities, and data distribution systems.

Link between remote sensing and specific coastal ecosystem metrics (biophysical properties and processes)

To answer the question of what we can accurately and reliably map and monitor in the coastal zone using remote sensing, we must first understand how remotely sensed images are converted into maps of biophysical properties or processes (Figure 13.5). Figure 13.6 shows the fundamental link between environmental properties and remotely sensed data. When you look at a remotely sensed image of a coastal environment, each image pixel is a quantitative record of how light has been absorbed, scattered, or transmitted by specific environmental features. For water bodies, the controlling features include surface roughness, depth, and concentration of organic and inorganic material in suspension and solution. The controls on absorption, scattering,

and transmission are understood for chemicals, structures, and processes down to molecular levels, which means we can estimate the quantity of some chemicals, size of a structure, or rate of a process, based on how much light has been absorbed, scattered, or transmitted. These radiative transfers are used to define algorithms that convert the values in each pixel in an image, from a measure of reflected light to a measure of a biophysical property (e.g., water depth, sea surface temperature, suspended sediment concentration, or vegetation cover). Research on radiative transfer has been used to design imaging sensors for use in the coastal zone along with algorithms for delivering maps of biophysical properties in coastal environments. Table 13.2 lists the range of biophysical properties relevant to the coastal zone that could be mapped and monitored using remote sensing.

Figure 13.5. Collecting spectral reflectance signatures of features to be mapped from airborne and satellite imaging systems using a specialized underwater spectrometer system.

Diana Kleine

Obtaining environmental data

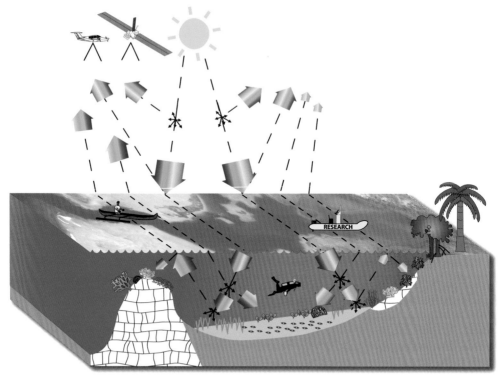

Figure 13.6. Light interactions in the remote sensing process of a coastal coral reef area in Viti Levu, Fiji. The colored arrows represent solar radiation, initially incident from the sun, and then interaction with the atmosphere, ocean surface, water column, and benthos. Changes in the size of the arrow indicate the relative amount of radiation being transmitted.

How to use remote sensing

Once you have decided that remotely sensed data would be suitable for your coastal monitoring application, the approach that you take will depend on the answers you gave to the information assessment exercise outlined in Table 13.1. There are four possible options for use of remotely sensed data, and the approach to take in each is outlined next.

Select an existing image and use it as it is

This is the simplest option where an image of an area can be used without any quantitative analysis or subsequent processing. Images are often in graphics formats or able to be viewed through web browsers and Internet map servers (including Google Earth™, Microsoft® Virtual Earth™, Millennium Coral Reef mapping project), which let you see the environment at a specific point in time.

Select an existing image-based map product and use it as is

This option applies if you are able to locate an existing image-based map product that matches your coastal ecosystem health metric requirements in terms of spatial and temporal scales, information content, accuracy and precision, and delivery format. These data sets can be accessed through local, state, and national government agencies (e.g., U.S. Coastal Change Analysis Program, NASA Rapidfire site for MODIS, NOAA CoastWatch), as well as through international agencies, and some Web and Google Earth/maps interfaces, and cover products from bathymetry, land-cover, sea surface temperature, and water quality (Figure 13.7). Some data may require purchase (e.g., IKONOS and Quickbird), and some, while available, may involve use restrictions (Google Earth™ real-time SeaWiFS). This means you will have to select the most appropriate that image data, order the data, and then apply appropriate corrections and algorithms to generate maps of the required biophysical variable, such as chlorophyll concentration (e.g., NASA ocean color data sets, standard Landsat product set). Always ensure that you can access the metadata associated with these products to check on how they were derived and their accuracy. These data can then be integrated into your own image processing system or GIS.

Acquire new image data and process the image to produce a map

In the case that existing spatial information does not exist for your application or is not in a suitable form or current enough, you will need to acquire new image data and process it to the level required for your mapping and monitoring needs. This means that you will have to select the most appropriate image data, order the data, map the data, and potentially apply appropriate corrections and algorithms to generate mapped biophysical variables. This requires a quantitative measure of geometric accuracy (e.g., NASA ocean color data sets, standard Landsat product set).

Acquire new image data and integrate with field survey data to produce a map and validate

This is a similar approach to the situation outlined above, with the exception that you have access to an existing field data set, that covers parts of the area to be mapped and monitored. The design of the mapping and validation program should integrate both data sets so that the field data are used to drive and validate the image mapping.

Image acquisition: can existing image-based products be used?

Answering this question requires that you have first clearly defined your information needs based on the questions in Table 13.1. These mapping requirements become the criteria for evaluating the suitability of existing image-based products to meet your monitoring program needs. The next stage is to compare your needs to relevant existing image-based map products. Table 13.3 is a source of existing image-based map products that may be used for monitoring coastal environments. This listing is by no means exhaustive, and you

Using remote sensing for algal bloom monitoring and assessment

Karen Steidinger, scientist, and Ken Haddad, executive director

The Coastal Zone Color Scanner (CZCS) launched October 24, 1978.[12] On November 14, 1978, it captured an image of Florida that proved to be a classic (see figure below). This was the first published account of using a satellite image to study a harmful algal bloom. Sampling by the state of Florida confirmed high concentrations of "Florida red tide" algae, *Gymnodinium breve*. The bloom was analyzed by Karen Steidinger (and was renamed *Karenia brevis* for her in 2001) and Ken Haddad of the Florida Marine Research Institute.[13] This CZCS image and the analysis completed by Steidinger and Haddad showed the potential value of applying satellite data to real monitoring problems, was a critical justification for the ocean color component of NOAA's CoastWatch program, and resulted in the operational NOAA harmful algal forecasts. Although the CZCS was an experimental mission and could not be processed and analyzed in real time, the SeaWIFS sensor, launched in 1997, does have such a capability, and it is being used to monitor for red tide, specifically in the eastern Gulf of Mexico.[14] Subsequently, other real-time research and monitoring programs have been developed.

This 1978 CZCS image shows an area of high productivity. Concentration measurements of *G. breve* taken at the shore indicated a red tide was occurring in southwestern Florida.

Obtaining environmental data

Table 13.2 Listing of biophysical properties that could be used as coastal ecosystem health indicators and an assessment of remote sensing for mapping and monitoring.[11,15]

Coastal ecosystem metric indicator	Can remote sensing be used?	Environmental constraints on application (e.g., depth, clarity)	Sensor
Land-cover types	Operational	Ecotone resolution; Confusion of usage and cover (e.g., pasture vs. grassland)	MODIS LANDSAT TM/ETM SPOT IKONOS/Quickbird RADARSAT Aerial photography
Terrestrial vegetation • Community/species	Operational	Number of classes required	LANDSAT TM/ETM SPOT IKONOS/Quickbird RADARSAT Aerial photography
Topography	Operational	None	Airborne laser scanner Stereo-aerial photography
Depth	Operational	Depth Water clarity Optical properties for passive systems	MODIS MERIS Hyperion LANDSAT TM/ETM CASI/HyMap Airborne Laser Scanner
Terrestrial vegetation • Condition	Operational	None Water level in marshes	MODIS LANDSAT TM/ETM SPOT IKONOS/Quickbird Aerial photography AVHRR
Terrestrial vegetation • Structure	Feasible	Topographic effects	LANDSAT TM/ETM SPOT IKONOS/Quickbird RADARSAT Stereo-aerial photography
Water quality • TSM/Tripton • Chl *a* • CDOM • Algal blooms	Operational only in coastal waters to a limited extent Feasible Feasible Feasible (clear/turbid water) Operational (clear water)	Inherent optical properties Depth Water clarity	MODIS SeaWiFS MERIS Hyperion LANDSAT TM/ETM CASI/HyMap
Toxic chemical spills	Feasible	Ocean surface roughness	Hyperion CASI/HyMap RADARSAT
Coral live/dead	Feasible (clear and optically shallow water)	Inherent optical properties Depth Water clarity	MERIS Hyperion IKONOS/Quickbird CASI/HyMap Aerial photography
Sea-surface temperature	Operational	Roughness of the water surface from wind and waves	NOAA-AVHRR MODIS

Table 13.2 (continued) Listing of biophysical properties that could be used as coastal ecosystem health indicators and an assessment of remote sensing for mapping and monitoring.[11,15]

Coastal ecosystem metric coindicator	Can remote sensing be used?	Environmental constraints on application (e.g., depth, clarity)	Sensor
Substrate cover type: estuary, coral reefs	Operational (clear and optically shallow water)		
Substrate cover type: rock platforms	Feasible (exposed areas, clear and optically shallow water)	Inherent optical properties Depth Water clarity	Hyperion LANDSAT TM/ETM SPOT IKONOS/Quickbird CASI/HyMap Aerial photography
Submerged aquatic vegetation: type	Feasible (clear and optically shallow water)		
Submerged aquatic vegetation: density	Operational (clear and optically shallow water)		
Submerged aquatic vegetation: biomass	Feasible (clear and optically shallow water)	Inherent optical properties Depth Water clarity	SPOT IKONOS/Quickbird CASI/HyMap Aerial photography

TSM: Total (organic + inorganic) Suspended Matter concentration in the water column

CDOM: Colored Dissolved Organic Matter in the water column

Chl *a*: Chlorophyll *a* concentration in the water column

RS: Remote Sensing

Obtaining environmental data

Case Study: Monterey Bay Sanctuary

Low or coarse spatial resolution satellite imaging systems with high temporal repeat frequency provide insight into the response of ecosystems to various events. Sea surface temperature (SST) from the NOAA Advanced Very High Resolution Radiometer (AVHRR) provides data on these conditions, with global high-quality data since 1985. The Monterey Bay Sanctuary is within the upwelling region of the California coast. The upwelling brings nutrients from deep water to the surface. These nutrients cause phytoplankton to grow, which leads to the great productivity of the region. The productivity influences a variety of sealife, including fish that thrive in the area, birds, and mammals. This area is influenced by the wind patterns driven by the El Niño-Southern Oscillation. During a strong El Niño, the winds shift, weakening the upwelling. In 1997 to 1998, one of the strongest El Niños of the century occurred. The upwelled water is cold during an event, allowing it to be identified by satellite. A time series from NOAA shows that the temperatures were much warmer than the 20-year average in 1997 to 1998. The result was much lower than normal chlorophyll concentrations through 1997 and 1998 in the shallow sanctuary. (Although shallow areas are shown in the figure, the same conditions occurred in the deep water of the Sanctuary.) By contrast, the water temperature was much cooler in 2000 and 2001, suggesting much stronger upwelling. During these years, higher than normal chlorophyll concentrations occurred. In 1998, the number of dead seabirds found on the coast was much higher than other recent years, implying that the lower productivity may lead to greater mortality in these birds.[16]

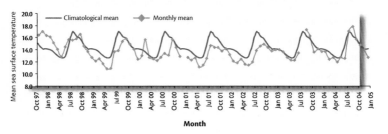

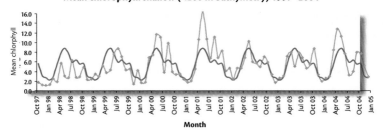

The graphs show the mean SST and chlorophyll in the Monterey Bay Sanctuary in water less than 200 m.[16] The 1998 *El Niño* led to low chlorophyll. A nutrient pulse from offshore water caused more intense blooms during the upwelling in 2001.

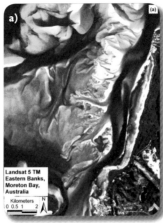

Figure 13.7. Examples of products derived from Landsat TM5 data in Moreton Bay, Australia. a) a true color image; b) a 30x30-m pixel image of seagrass cover; and c) an image of the same area, but different time, showing the distribution of a filamentous cyanobacterium bloom (*Lyngbya*) that periodically smothers the seagrass beds.

Table 13.3 Existing image-based products of environmental variables able to be used for coastal zone mapping and monitoring.

Image-based map product	Example sources
Atmosphere	
Aerosols/dust surface winds	*gacp.giss.nasa.gov/data_sets, manati.orbit.nesdis.noaa.gov, podaac-www.jpl.nasa.gov*
Cyclone/hurricane tracks	Various national weather services
Ocean surface	
Waves	*gs.mdacorporation.com* (RADARSAT), *earth.esa.int/ers* (ERS-2)
Sea-surface temperature (SST)	*Coastwatch.noaa.gov*
SST climatologies and products	*Oceancolor.gsfc.nasa.gov*
Ocean/water column	
Depth/bathymetry Optical properties: Clarity Suspended sediment Chlorophyll content	*www.ngdc.noaa.gov Oceancolor.gsfc.nasa.gov*
Algal blooms	
Coral reefs	*Coastwatch.noaa.gov*
	eol.jsc.nasa.gov/reefs, ccma.nos.noaa.gov
Seagrass	
	Various
Terrestrial	
Land cover/ Land use	*Csc.noaa.gov* (C-CAP program), *landcover.usgs.gov, glcf.umiacs.umd.edu*
Elevation/terrain	
	Csc.noaa.gov, various national, state, local
Wetlands	
	wetlandsfws.er.usgs.gov
Vegetation communities	(see wetlands and land cover)

should check with your relevant local, state, and national government agencies on the spatial data products they provide for the coastal environment. In particular, many sources exist for unmapped or unreferenced photographic type images.

There are three possible outcomes from your assessment of available image-based map products, each with its subsequent actions outlined in the following paragraphs.

Case Study: marine sanctuaries on the California coast

One of the challenges of managing marine sanctuaries and protected areas is understanding the habitat. Although benthic habitat stays in one place (but may change over time), the ocean is constantly moving and changing. Satellite imagery offers the means to understand conditions in the larger area, and how different areas may be coupled. In the example maps, three sanctuaries on the California coast are outlined. In the north are Cordell Bank (offshore) and Gulf of the Farallones (closer to the coast), and to the south is the much larger Monterey Bay Sanctuary. The imagery shows turbidity, which indicates particulates, including sediment. The area potentially influenced by San Francisco Bay crosses sanctuaries. In contrast, the high productivity areas produced by upwelling can extend well offshore. Although upwelling promotes the growth of chlorophyll, the temperature and chlorophyll patterns do not align as well as one would expect. The coldest water at the coast is farthest to the north, yet the most productive water is in the Monterey Bay Sanctuary.[16]

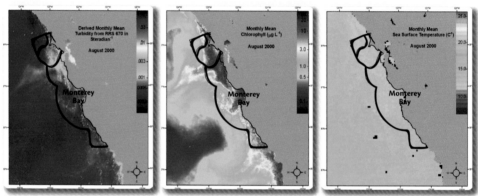

The maps show turbidity and chlorophyll from SeaWiFS and temperature from the Pathfinder SST within boundaries of sanctuaries on the California coast.[16] Pathfinder SST is a climatologic data set at 4 km, which takes several months to update.

An exact match of an existing product to your needs and processing capacity

Acquire the data sets and metadata and check that you are able to use the information within your image processing or GIS environment and for subsequent decision making.

A not-perfect but close match to your needs and processing capacity

In this situation, you now need to critically assess what your most important information requirements are, (e.g., Is the timing or spatial scale of the image-based map suitable?) and whether you can still use the information, even if it does not match your needs exactly. The alternative of additional collection,

processing, and validation may (or may not) greatly exceed the value of a perfect match. Do you have the resources (financial, personnel, hardware, software) and time to acquire and process your own data, or can you live with slightly imperfect data?

No match of existing products to your needs and processing capacity

You now need to work out which image data set is required to produce the information needed and how you will acquire, correct, process, and validate the output image-based map so that it can be used in your image processing or GIS environment and for subsequent decision making.

New data acquisition: what to do when existing products and archives are not enough

If you have established that there are no existing image-based map products to meet your coastal monitoring requirements, you have two options to produce an image-based map: 1) acquire, process, and validate the image data inhouse if you have the capacity or 2) contract out the acquisition, processing, and validation. In each case, it is critical that the acquisition, processing, and validation are done to a clearly established set of standards for all stages of the process. If you are not an image processing expert, you will need to carefully work out exactly what you need and use that to draft the specifications for the contract or tender to produce the information. In either case, the process to use draws directly on your monitoring information requirements (Table 13.1). These data are used as the criteria to select a suitable image data source, image processing approach, and validation approach.[5,9]

Deciding to complete this process in-house means that you have suitably skilled personnel, hardware, software, and operating protocols for acquiring images and processing them into maps of biophysical variables. These requirements are described in the next section. In this situation, answering the questions in Table 13.1 will define the spatial and temporal scales of the required image data along with the type of map to be produced and the required level of accuracy. The spatial (extent and pixel) and temporal scale of the required information are the primary criteria used to select a suitable image data set (Figure 13.8). Table 13.4 lists the major international providers and the scales of the satellite image data. In addition, local providers of airborne and other image data should be consulted. Once you have located a suitable type of sensor, an order will need to be placed to capture new data or use an archive. In each case, you should specify exactly what type and format of data is required and what data are not suitable. This latter point refers to the amount of cloud cover, smoke, surface wind and whitecaps on the water in your image, and the look-angle of a sensor. The look angle of a sensor describes how far from vertical the sensor's perspective was when your image was acquired. In some cases, you may do all of this online through a website, and in other cases, you may work with a consultant.

Once you have the data, the next stage is to design the process for converting the image into a map of the required biophysical variable and for assessing the accuracy of the output product. This process is described in detail in the following section and for an outline of suitable processing approaches, on the Coastal Remote Sensing Toolkit website.[5] In each case, you should ensure that you are using an approach that has been tested on the image data you will be using in the environment you will be working.

Image processing and validation: (should not be) a hidden cost

One point we have tried to stress in this chapter is that using remote sensing data does not just involve acquiring an image data set and creating a map. A map of land cover types, water quality, seagrass species, seagrass density, or vegetation communities has significant legal and management implications that demand a clear knowledge of the accuracy of the map product. The maps may be used to decide on zonings for protected areas or set limits for developments, and must be legally

Recipe for success

- Clear definition of the monitoring program's information requirements
- A remote sensing and coastal management person on staff who understands the information needs and what is possible with remote sensing
- A project planning document that sets out the information required, suitable data, required processing approach, validation approach, output product and communication (agreed on by monitoring/management staff)
- Appropriate personnel, hardware, software, and protocols for image processing, if you are to do it inhouse, otherwise a reliable contractor
- Continued, regular, and clear communication between the remote sensing person and the management person who will use the image-based map during the map production and delivery process
- A final complete product package with image-based map, metadata, and validation information in an accessible format for all to use

Obtaining environmental data

213

Table 13.4 Sources of satellite image data.

Data type sensor (platform)	Spatial scale (extent & pixel)	Temporal resolution frequency (time of day)	Archive
Satellite multispectral			
IKONOS	Extremely fine (local) Extent: 10 km max. (east-west)	AM 3 days-pointable	IKONOS/Geoeye *www.geoeye.com/*
Quickbird	Extent: 10-20 km Pixel: 1 m (pan) or 4 m (multi)		Quickbird, see *www.digitalglobe.com/* or Google Earth™
LANDSAT ETM LANDSAT TM	Medium (province/region) Extent: 34,225 km² or 185x185 km Pixel: 15-30 m	AM 16 days AM 16 days	Global Landsat Archive *glcfapp.umiacs.umd.edu:8080/esdi/index. jsp* Global Landsat reef image Archive *oceancolor.gsfc.nasa.gov/cgi/landsat.pl*
SPOT VMI	Coarse (region) Extent: 2,500 km wide Pixel: 1 km	AM 2 days-pointable	SPOT image archive *sirius.spotimage.com*
SeaWiFS (Orbview2 or SEASTAR)	Coarse (region) Extent: 2,200 km wide Pixel: 1 km	AM 1 day	Oceancolor website *oceancolor.gsfc.nasa. gov/*
Satellite hyperspectral			MODIS data can be accessed through the
MODIS (EOS-terra and aqua platforms)	Coarse (region) Extent: 2,048 km wide Pixel: 250, 500, 1,000 m	Daily (Terra=AM and Aqua=PM)	Oceancolor website *oceancolor.gsfc.nasa. gov/*
Hyperion	Medium Extent: 7.5x100 km Pixel: 30 m	AM 16 days (follows ETM)	No archive
MERIS	Coarse (region) Extent: 2,500 km wide Pixel: 300 m	3 days	*envisat.esa.int/*
Airborne laser altimeters			
AAM surveys Optech ALTM 1210 -Profiling laser Enerquest Systems -Scanning laser Bathymetric LIDAT (TENIX LADS, SHOALS)	Extremely fine to fine (local) Extent: 100 km² Sampling intensity: 5,000-10,000 pulses per second. 2-10 samples per 1 m²	User controlled (subject to weather and aircraft availability)	No archive See example from coastal survey for U.S. Army Corp of Engineers *shoals.sam.usace. army.mil/Data/Data_Home.asp*
Airborne SAR			
NASA-AirSAR	Medium (province) Extent: 12 x 120 km Pixel: 10 m	Restricted to research missions November 1996 September 2000 To be announced 2002	*southport.jpl.nasa.gov/*
Satellite SAR			
Radarsat	Medium (province/region) Extent: 100x100 km Pixel: 30 m	AM 3-5 days	Collected since 1995, *www.space.gc.ca/asc/eng/satellites/ radarsat1*
ERS-1/2	Medium (province/region) Extent: 100x100 km Pixel: 10-30 m	AM 35 days	Collected since 1995, *earth.esa.int/ers*

Table 13.4 (continued) Sources of satellite image data.

Data Type Sensor (platform)	Spatial Scale (extent & GRE)	Temporal Resolution Frequency (time of day)	Archive
Satellite SAR			
JERS 1	Medium (province/region) Extent: 75x100 km GRE: 18 m	AM 44 days Ceased operation in 2000	Collected 1992-1998, no CRC archive
ASAR (ENVISAT)	Medium (province) Extent: 100x100 km GRE: 150 m	AM 3-5 days	*envisat.esa.int/*
PALSAR (ALOS)	Fine Medium (province) Extent: 100x100 km GRE: 10–30 m		*www.eorc.jaxa.jp/ALOS/about/palsar.htm*

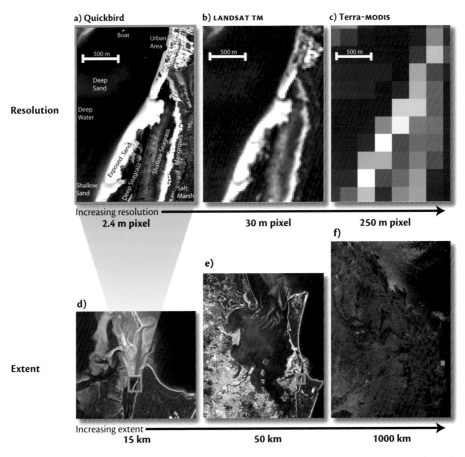

Figure 13.8. These true-color images show the variation in spatial sampling unit (pixel) and aerial coverage (extent) among three commonly used satellite imaging sensors: Quickbird, LANDSAT TM, and Terra-MODIS. Figures a–c show the effects of differences between pixel sizes and resultant spatial resolutions for the same area of water–seagrass–mangrove–urban area in Moreton Bay, Australia. Figures d–f show the section of one image captured by each of the three image sensors. The maximum extent of ground width able to be imaged by each sensor is 16 km (Quickbird), 185 km (LANDSAT TM), and 2000 km (MODIS).

Obtaining environmental data

defendable. If you can find a suitable image–based map that meets all of your requirements in terms of providing the required information at a suitable level of accuracy, then use the existing product. However, if you cannot find a suitable map, you or another party will need to acquire image data, process it to produce a map, and validate the map against reference data to demonstrate its accuracy. Conducting the work internally depends on whether your organization has the capacity and skill to process and validate.

The previous sections have shown the types of biophysical information able to be extracted from image data sets. These maps are the results of extensive image-processing operations developed and tested over time (Figure 13.9). To be able to complete this type of processing, either for implementing processing operations developed by others or for developing your own requires suitable skilled personnel, adequate hardware and image-processing software, and operating protocols. It does take time to develop and implement these approaches, with the amount of time depending on the area to be covered, type of map to be produced, extent of development and validation required, and available resources.

There are people trained to develop and run projects in these areas, with skills from the spatial or geospatial information sciences, geomatics, and remote sensing. Most local-to national-level resource management agencies will have a division dealing with spatial information and data, and there are a number of private companies and non-government agencies who provide these services. There are people out there with the necessary skills and resources!

In all cases, a project plan for the acquisition of image and field data should be established along with the subsequent process for correction, processing, and validation of the data. This document will guide activities within your agency or can be used to define specifications for an external consultant to complete the work. All

Pitfalls to avoid

- Trying to redo or reinvent projects that have already been completed
- Misunderstanding the required pixel size needed to detect your target
- Forgetting to include a validation component for all elements of the project
- Being naïve about contractual obligations—make sure you have the highest quality data
- Forgetting to back up all data
- Overselling your product
- Foregoing field surveys
- Forgetting the value of true color vs. derived images
- Assuming that a map and the field are identical
- Expecting a satellite to work miracles—if you cannot see the bottom, then do not expect a satellite to see it

processing applied to the data should be recorded in an image-processing log to allow quality control and assessment of the process used.

The actual processing of remotely sensed image data to produce maps for coastal monitoring involves several stages once the image data have been acquired. Often, the first stage involves collection of field survey data for calibration of image data and development of the output map at or close to the time of image capture. Once the image data have been captured and delivered, they must first be checked to ensure that they meet the design requirements for coverage and completeness (no missing data), and are not contaminated (by cloud cover, sun glint, turbidity, ocean roughness), and meet other conditions (tide, season). Processing has multiple steps, and each has different options depending on the goals.

The first step is geo-rectification, which involves transforming the image to match with national standards for projection, datum, and coordinates and for spatial data. Once data are in the correct format they can be accurately integrated with other spatial data collected using the same standards. The data set is useless without this type of correction because you cannot integrate it with your field data or other spatial data sets. In some cases, corrections to remove smoke, haze, other atmospheric features and water surface problems (glint) must also be applied. The corrected data set can then be subjected to the required processing algorithm that will convert image pixel values into a value of the biophysical property required.

There are numerous approaches that can used at this point, depending on the required information, type of image, and type of environment you are working in. Readers are referred to various sources for outlines of possible approaches, and their costs.[1,5,17]

Once an image map has been produced, the next stage is validation against some form of reference data; this provides users with some information to determine the overall accuracy and spatial variations in the accuracy of the mapped variable (Figure 13.9).

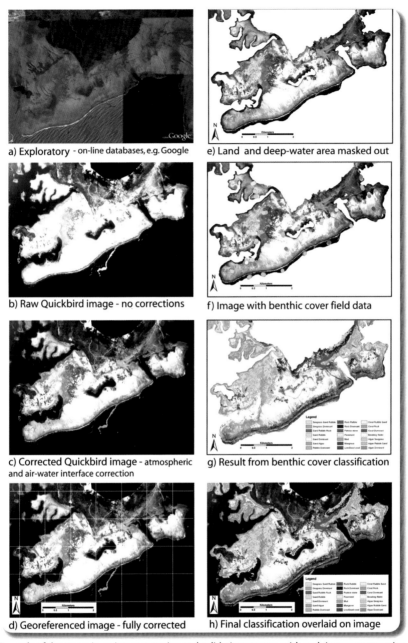

a) Exploratory - on-line databases, e.g. Google

e) Land and deep-water area masked out

b) Raw Quickbird image - no corrections

f) Image with benthic cover field data

c) Corrected Quickbird image - atmospheric and air-water interface correction

g) Result from benthic cover classification

d) Georeferenced image - fully corrected

h) Final classification overlaid on image

Figure 13.9. Example of the stages in an image mapping and validation process, with each image representing output from each step in the processing sequence:
  a) Browse image from Google Earth™ (Landsat ᴛᴍ/Quickbird combination)
  b) Raw Quickbird image with no corrections
  c) Corrected Quickbird image after atmospheric and air–water interface corrections
  d) Georeferenced Quickbird image after atmospheric and air–water interface corrections
  e) Fully corrected image d), with non-reef areas masked out
  f) Shallow water and exposed reef image with calibration and validation field data
  g) Benthic cover map produced by image classification of f)
  h) Benthic cover map overlaid on the original image

Representative effort required for different stages of image processing (Figure 13.9)

- **Select image (a and b):** Image selection involves development of factors that may influence results, including resolution, spectral bands, season (growing, dormant), tide, timeliness, or water clarity (which may be seasonal). The appropriate factors need to be considered for each image under consideration. This may take a day for a simple case of a background image to a week or more, depending on the requirements for new acquisitions for high-resolution data.
- **Atmospheric correction (c):** Atmospheric correction depends on the application. It is relatively straightforward for land applications and may take only a few hours. For water applications, an analyst experienced with the data at hand may take a few hours, but for one working with a new type of data, setting up programs and testing may take days, possibly weeks for hyperspectral data.
- **Georeferencing (d):** Many images can be obtained in georeferenced or nearly georeferenced form, requiring only a simple positional shift (a few hours). If custom georeferencing is required, then acquisition of reference points may add days or weeks to processing.
- **Classification (g):** Classification is an iterative process, and the field data for tuning and validating the classification can be a significant cost. A preliminary classification is necessary before the first field effort. For a small area, such as shown in the figure, a few days may provide sufficient data to tune the classification. A well-designed field experiment may collect all tuning and validation data in one excursion. At least 10 samples per cover type are needed for validation, additional samples for classification, and generally no more than 20 to 50 collected in a day. For a cover map with 10 classes, five days in the field should be planned, with an equivalent number of days in the lab preparing for and post-processing the field data. The classification speed for IKONOS or Quickbird may range from 1 km² per day to 100 km² per day, depending on the resolution, number of classes, and accuracy required. This will include at least two iterations to achieve meaningful accuracies.

How accurate are the data?

For any spatial information to be used within monitoring and management operations, the users of the data must have some indication of how accurate the information is in terms of the attributes mapped and their position. In this context, accuracy is a measure of how close a mapped value is to a reference value considered to be the value on the ground or water. Validation or error and accuracy assessment is an essential part of remote sensing and is conducted by comparing the image-based map against a source of known (or reference) data to provide a quantitative and spatial assessment of the degree to which the mapped biophysical variable matches the "known value" of that feature. This process is widely and incorrectly referred to as "ground truthing." Ground truth imputes an accuracy to the reference data, which is not possible owing to the inherent uncertainties with respect to location, time, or the variable sampled. The accuracy of the validation data set is rarely defined in context of the imagery. For example, chlorophyll concentration from a single bottle is compared to a satellite estimate covering 1km², and road-based visual surveys of forest cover types are used to validate 30m² image pixels.

Design and implementation of a validation procedure for your image-based map is a significant and time-consuming activity in any remote sensing project. The validation process has been neglected too often in past work, resulting in image-based maps with no real assessment of how accurate they are and no details on how they could be improved. This has been one of the main reasons why image-based data sets have not been widely used in operational monitoring and management—lack of information on their accuracy. Given the current wide-spread capacity for field-based survey using GPS and other equipment, this should be changed.

Accuracy assessment is a standard process in remote sensing (Figure 13.10), and techniques have been developed and tested with statistical bases for both thematic maps (e.g., vegetation types) and quantitative maps (e.g., water depth, seagrass biomass).[18-20]

At a minimum, this process should produce one number that indicates the accuracy of the output image-based map against the reference data. At the maximum, it should also provide mapping accuracies for individual classes (if it is a thematic map), a map indicating spatial variation in accuracy levels, and some indication of the precision of the mapped variable, such as the minimum detectable difference in the feature mapped for quantitative maps. Finally, classes with low accuracy need to be examined to assess whether the reference data are reliable enough for meaningful validation.

Why are there not many operational management and assessment programs along the coast using remote sensing?

Based on what we have presented so far in this chapter and the length of time (>30 years) over which we have had aerial photography and coarse to medium spatial resolution satellite image data, there should be a large number of operational management and assessment programs along the coast using remote sensing. There are a few excellent examples of such programs, particularly in western Europe, but there has not been a widespread adoption of these technologies globally. There are a number of possible reasons for this, some of which have been explored in detail,[21] and we encourage readers to look over this reference to see the trials involved in trying to set up satellite image-based monitoring programs for water quality over the past 20 years. Three main factors seem to have played a role in this: 1) the multi-jurisdictional nature of coastal environments, 2) the lack of suitable image data and image-based products, and 3) the lack of reliable quantitative information on the accuracy and cost-effectiveness of remote-sensing–based approaches in comparison to ground-based approaches.

The multi-jurisdictional nature of coastal environments is also compounded by the coastal zone being highly dynamic and at the interface of terrestrial and aquatic environments. Traditionally resource management agencies have focused on terrestrial or aquatic environments, not both. This has resulted in separate data collection and monitoring programs and this has led to a lack of an agreed set of coastal ecosystem health indicators that could be matched to the types of remote sensing information being collected regularly.

Lack of suitable image data and image-based products was a problem until the launches of higher spatial resolution satellite sensors in the early 2000s, and more recently the release of airborne digital photography and LIDAR systems. These systems, together with existing moderate and coarse spatial resolution satellite image data, provide a complete multiscale mapping tool suitable for use from very fine site scales to national and global scales and compatible with scales of information required for legal and monitoring purposes. Web-based and Google Earth™ and Virtual Earth™ platforms have now provided everyone with computer access with the ability to acquire and use remotely sensed data. The previous lack of agreed-upon indicators also meant a lack of standards for data formats, sources, and accuracy.

Lack of reliable quantitative information on the accuracy and cost-effectiveness of remote-sensing–based approaches compared to ground-based approaches has perhaps been the biggest deterrent. This is argued to be responsible for the over-selling of remote sensing and resulting skepticism in the resource management community about the feasibility of using remotely sensed data. We are now in a position to provide realistic and consistent costs of acquisition and processing to convert data into information.

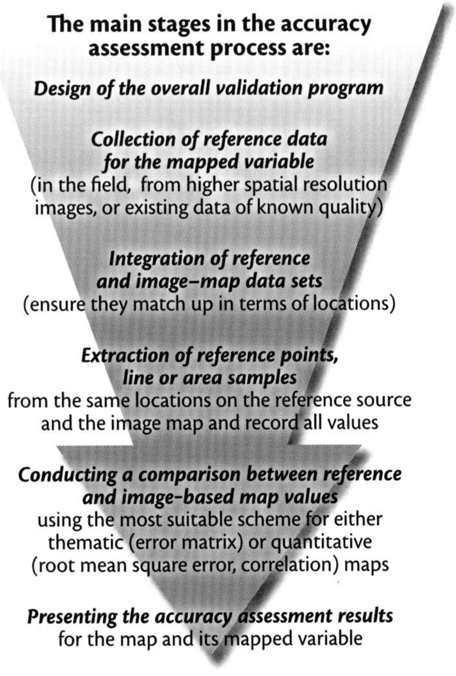

The main stages in the accuracy assessment process are:

Design of the overall validation program

Collection of reference data for the mapped variable
(in the field, from higher spatial resolution images, or existing data of known quality)

Integration of reference and image–map data sets
(ensure they match up in terms of locations)

Extraction of reference points, line or area samples
from the same locations on the reference source and the image map and record all values

Conducting a comparison between reference and image-based map values
using the most suitable scheme for either thematic (error matrix) or quantitative (root mean square error, correlation) maps

Presenting the accuracy assessment results
for the map and its mapped variable

Figure 13.10. The sequence of steps commonly applied when using remotely sensed data to map and monitor environmental features or processes.

Obtaining environmental data

Educating potential users and communicating results

Perhaps the biggest factor explaining why remote sensing has not been widely used in coastal monitoring applications around the world is lack of appropriate communication about what it is, how it works, the resources required to make it work, and the accuracy of the resultant image-based products. Solving this challenge requires input from the remote sensing community and the coastal science and management communities (Figure 13.11). The starting point for addressing such a challenge is a clear commitment to educating potential users about what can be accurately mapped from remotely sensed data in the coastal environment, what resources are required to do this, and how accurate is the output map. Once this has been done for a number of applications, potential users can obtain a realistic assessment for themselves of how remote sensing has and can be used, and they know the process required to transform an image to an image-based map of a relevant biophysical variable.

There are a number of ways to address the communication goal established above, one of which has been to develop online tools (Figure 13.12) that explain the remote sensing process in the coastal zone and then present a number of example applications showing all of the steps involved.[5,22] In each case, these tools try to present which type of biophysical variables can be mapped in an operational sense and then explain the images and resources necessary to complete the operation. In some cases, agencies have developed standard procedures and specifications for the delivery of image-based map products, such as orthophotographs, bathymetry, and vegetation

There are several attributes of a remote sensing project, reflecting the uptake, science, and communication, that make it a successful application:

- Used regularly by one or more agency or company to make decisions
- Integrated into the spatial information workflow of an organization
- Accepted as reliable and accurate under known conditions
- Accessible, along with documentation on how data are produced and validated
- Based on sound science that has been reviewed by managers and scientists
- Communicated to the relevant user and remote sensing community
- Supported by one or more remote sensing and coastal management persons.

cover. These standards should be made public so that potential users can understand where their data were obtained and so that they can build their own similar collection standards. Once the potential user has an understanding of these options *and* they know exactly what information they need, then they are in a position to design an image-based mapping and monitoring project to meet their requirements.

With effective communication, remote sensing could become a very popular tool in the future. Its ability to collect data without having direct contact with that data is ideal when it comes to collecting in the most accurate, natural state. We hope that the table outlining conditions of when to use remote sensing (Table 13.1), as well as the explanation of the tool, will be helpful to you in your coastal assessment program.

Chris Roelfsema

Figure 13.11. Consultation in Fiji with local fishermen to develop habitat maps of their local coastal area (reef and seagrass) from high-spatial resolution satellite images.

Figure 13.12. The flow of information in the remote sensing toolkit, a web-based instructional procedure (*www.gpem.uq.edu.au/CRSSIS-rstoolkit/*) designed to force coastal managers or scientists to specify the information they need (mapping needs table) and to then use this information (scale of map, biophysical variable to map) to select suitable data and image processing techniques.

References

1. Green EP, Mumby PJ, Edwards AJ, Clark CD (2000) Remote sensing handbook for tropical coastal management. UNESCO Publishing, Paris, France
2. Green EP, Mumby PJ, Edwards AJ, Clark CD (2000) Remote sensing handbook for tropical coastal management. UNESCO Publishing, Paris, France
3. Roelfsema CM, Phinn SR, Dennison WC, Dekker AG, Brando VE (2006) Monitoring Toxic Cyano-bacteria *Lyngbya majuscula* in Moreton Bay, Australia by Integrating Satellite Image Data and Field Mapping. Harmful Algae 5:45-56
4. Jensen JR (2007) Remote sensing of the environment: An Earth resource perspective, 2nd ed. Prentice Hall, Upper Saddle River, New Jersey
5. University of Queensland (2009) Coastal remote sensing toolkit. Accessed 30 Jun. http://www.gpem.uq.edu.au/CRSSIS-rstoolkit/
6. Dadouh-Guebas F (2002) The use of remote sensing and GIS in the sustainable management of tropical coastal ecosystems. Environ Dev Sustain 4:93-112
7. Mumby PJ, Skirving W, Strong AE, Hardy JT, LeDrew E, Hochberg EJ, Stumpf RP, David LT (2004) Remote sensing of coral reefs and their physical environment. Mar Pollut Bull 48:219-228
8. Stumpf RP, Frayer ML, Durako MJ, Brock JC (1999) Variations in water clarity and bottom albedo in Florida Bay from 1985 to 1997. Estuaries 22:431-444
9. Phinn S, Menges C, Hill GJE, Stanford M (2000) Optimising remotely sensed solutions for monitoring, modelling and managing coastal environments. Remote Sens Environ 73:117-132
10. Phinn S, Stow D, Franklin J, Mertes L, Michaelsen J (2003) Remotely sensed data for ecosystem analyses: combining hierarchy and scene models. Environ Manage 31:429-441
11. Phinn S, Joyce K, Scarth P, Roelfsema C (2005) The role of integrated information acquisition and management in the analysis of coastal ecosystem change. In: LeDrew E, Richardson, Boston L (eds) Remote sensing of coastal aquatic ecosystem processes. Kluwer Academic Publishers (Springer), New York, New York
12. National Aeronautics and Space Administration (2009) Ocean Color—classic CZCS scenes, Chapter 12. Accessed 30 Jun. disc.sci.gsfc.nasa.gov/oceancolor/additional/science-focus/classic_scenes/12_classics_blooms.shtml
13. Steidinger KA, Haddad KD (1981) Biologic and hydrographic aspects of red tides. BioScience 31:814-819
14. Stumpf RP, Culver ME, Tester PA, Kirkpatrick GJ, Pederson BA, Tomlinson M, Truby E, Ransibrahmanakul V, Hughes K, Soracco M (2003) Monitoring *Karenia brevis* blooms in the Gulf of Mexico using satellite ocean color imagery and other data. Harmful Algae 2:147-160
15. Roelfsema CM, Joyce KE, Phinn SR (2004) Evaluation of benthic survey techniques for validating remotely sensed images of coral reefs. Proc 10th Int Coral Reefs Symp, Int Soc Reef Studies, ReefBase, Penang, Malaysia
16. Stumpf RP, Dunham S, Ojanen L, Richardson A, Wynne T, Holderied K (2005) Characterization and monitoring of temperature, chlorophyll, and light availability patterns in National Marine Sanctuary waters: Final report. NOAA NOS NCCOS CCMA, NOAA Technical Memorandum NOS-NCCOS-13, Silver Spring, Maryland

Obtaining environmental data

17. Mumby PJ, Edwards AJ (2002) Mapping marine environments with IKONOS imagery: Enhanced spatial resolution can deliver greater thematic accuracy. Remote Sens Environ 82:248–257

18. Congalton RG (1991) A review of assessing the accuracy of classifications of remotely sensed data. Remote Sens Environ 37:35–46

19. Congalton R, Green K (1999) Assessing the accuracy of remotely sensed data: Principles and practices. Lewis Publishers, New York, New York

20. Foody GM (2002) Status of land cover classification accuracy assessment. Remote Sens Environ 80:185–201

21. Bukata RP (2005) Satellite monitoring of inland and coastal water quality: Retrospection, introspection and future direction. CRC Press/Taylor and Francis Group, Boca Raton, Florida

22. OEA Technologies (2009) Satellites. Accessed 30 Jun. www.oeatech.com/index.php/oea_tech/satellites/

Further reading

BLUElink Ocean Forecast Products. www.bom.gov.au/oceanography/forecasts/index.shtml

Coastal Change Analysis Program (C-CAP). www.csc.noaa.gov/crs/lca/ccap.html

Great Barrier Reef Marine Park Authority. www.gbrmpa.gov.au/

Millenium Reef Image and Map Archive. imars.marine.usf.edu/corals/index.html or oceancolor.gsfc.nasa.gov/cgi/reefs.pl

NASA MODIS Rapid Response System. rapidfire.sci.gsfc.nasa.gov

National Wetlands Inventory. www.fws.gov/nwi/

NOAA Benthic Habitat Mapping of the Northwestern Hawaiian Islands. ccmaserver.nos.noaa.gov/ecosystems/coralreef/nwhi_mapping.html

NOAA Benthic Habitat Mapping of Florida Coral Reef Ecosystems. ccma.nos.noaa.gov/ecosystems/coralreef/fl_mapping.html

NOAA Coral Reef Watch. coralreefwatch.noaa.gov/

NOAA CoastWatch. coastwatch.noaa.gov/cw_index.html

NOAA Coastal Bathymetry. maps.csc.noaa.gov/TCM/

OROMA. www.brockmann-consult.de/revamp/

Queensland—Coastal Habitat Resource Information System. chrisweb.dpi.qld.gov.au/chris/

SUMMARY

USING AN INTEGRATED APPROACH TO BUILD SCIENTIFIC AND PUBLIC KNOWLEDGE

Ben J. Longstaff, William C. Dennison, and Emily Nauman

Putting it all together

In this book we describe many of the steps and processes associated with establishing and running an effective coastal assessment program. We certainly do not claim to be inclusive of all required elements, but offer what has worked and has been successful for the authors. We acknowledge that success follows from a certain amount of failure, and while trial and error is a necessary process, we try to present some common pitfalls to avoid. Further, each coastal assessment program is different in terms of its physical and biological environments, organizational structure, politics, etc., and these variables need to be considered when implementing some of the concepts espoused in this book. While the individual components are presented as separate chapters, implementing an overall plan or strategy that links and combines multiple elements will lead to the most desirable outcome. Obviously, success is not achieved by any single individual or organization, but requires a community effort with a common vision and approach.

Throughout the book we use a triangle divided into four sections to represent the relationship between research, monitoring, and management, and the effort to turn data into knowledge and application into community engagement. In this final chapter, we summarize the most important elements of each section, and expand upon the conceptual framework by providing a summary figure for each section.

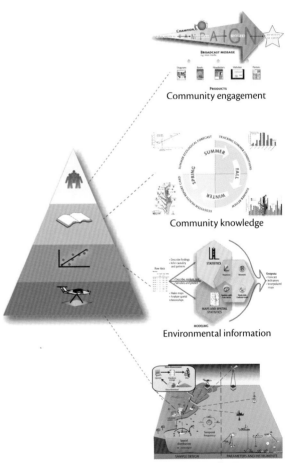

Community engagement

Community knowledge

Environmental information

Data collection

A summary of the four coastal assessment program steps: a conceptual diagram illustrates different ways to obtain data; statistics, modeling, and spatial analysis illustrate analyzing data, an annual cycle of analysis and communication products illustrates building community knowledge; and, leadership and communication illustrate engaging the community.

Community engagement

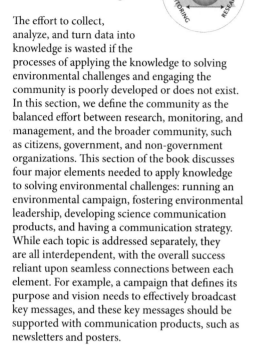

Applying knowledge to solve environmental challenges

The effort to collect, analyze, and turn data into knowledge is wasted if the processes of applying the knowledge to solving environmental challenges and engaging the community is poorly developed or does not exist. In this section, we define the community as the balanced effort between research, monitoring, and management, and the broader community, such as citizens, government, and non-government organizations. This section of the book discusses four major elements needed to apply knowledge to solving environmental challenges: running an environmental campaign, fostering environmental leadership, developing science communication products, and having a communication strategy. While each topic is addressed separately, they are all interdependent, with the overall success reliant upon seamless connections between each element. For example, a campaign that defines its purpose and vision needs to effectively broadcast key messages, and these key messages should be supported with communication products, such as newsletters and posters.

Environmental campaigns

In this book we define an environmental campaign as an organized, collaborative, and strategic process of implementing the changes needed to solve an environmental challenge. The campaign recognizes that solutions are not dependent upon one sector of society alone, such as government, managers, or scientists, but a collective effort where the broader community is engaged. To ensure organized and continued participation, the campaign needs to have an inclusive shared vision that all parties are trying to achieve. This may be as simple as the vision statement used by the South East Queensland Healthy Waterways Partnership: "…our waterways and catchments will be healthy ecosystems supporting the livelihood and lifestyles of the people…".[1] A campaign also needs to follow a staged approach where the overall goal is divided into a series of achievable tasks, and each stage improves upon the past and based on learned experience. It is also important to immediately measure progress, that is, don't spend the first stages in planning alone—take action. As highlighted in the rest of this section, feedback and communication on all aspects of the campaign is essential, requiring a continual supply and array of products and a strategic approach to broadcasting the messages.

Environmental leadership

In addition to forming collaborations and developing a vision, an environmental campaign must recognize the importance of good leadership and foster champions for the cause.

Champions, who may represent different sectors of society and the environmental campaign, tend to have the ability to infuse energy, inspire, and effectively communicate. By combining the passionate efforts of champions with knowledge (e.g., scientists) and the efforts of champions with power (e.g., politicians), it is possible to create the paradigm shifts needed for achieving improved ecosystem health. To illustrate the importance of champions, examples of successful assessment programs that have witnessed paradigm shifts were presented.

A volunteer directing a crowd during a community event.

Science communication products, such as newsletters and posters, have many benefits within an environmental campaign. The first and most obvious benefit is as a tool to help inform and educate the target audience—the effectiveness of the product not only being dictated by the content, but by its layout and presentation. Perhaps a less recognized benefit of a science communication product is the increased understanding and consensus that is built during its preparation, if produced in a collaborative fashion. Not only will a collaborative approach lead to a better product,

Elements needed to engage a community

History shows that the overall success of an environmental campaign is dependent upon one or a few individuals who champion the cause, providing the leadership, dedication, tenacity, and resilience needed to keep the program focused, moving forward, and making a measurable difference.

The overall purpose of the environmental campaign is to take the uninformed to the informed and the informed to the engaged—the premise being that only the engaged will really become sufficiently involved to take the necessary action.

CHAMPION

UNINFORMED → INFORMED → ENGAGED → **CAMPAIGN**

RESULTS/ACTION

BROADCAST MESSAGE
e.g., mass media

Diagrams   Books   Newsletters   Websites   Posters

PRODUCTS

Having a communication strategy allows information and knowledge to be disseminated between each of the different sectors of society, with the products and messages targeted to the specific audience.

it will also result in a product with more credibility than one produced in isolation. As such we often say that the process of preparing a product can be as important as the product itself.

In the past, laying out and designing communication products was the task of specific experts, now with the development of relativity easy to use software, it is now in the realms of most people to produce a quality product.

Communication strategy

An essential element of any environmental campaign is to ensure there is effective communication between the core research, monitoring, and management partnership, and from this partnership to the broader community.

With such differing audiences, information needs to be packaged and delivered in a manner that not only reaches the target audience, but is understandable, informative, and relevant. The mass media, including the internet, is the best vehicle for communicating to a broad audience, but there are certain advantages and disadvantages associated with engaging news media such as television and radio. Products such as ecological report cards are effective communication products as they provide synthesized and easy-to-understand information that targets the broader community, but also provide a framework of analysis and interpretation that facilitates communication between the research, monitoring, and management communities.

Community knowledge

Integrating information to
build practical knowledge

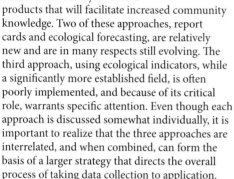

This section discusses three
approaches for directing data
collection and analysis toward
products that will facilitate increased community
knowledge. Two of these approaches, report
cards and ecological forecasting, are relatively
new and are in many respects still evolving. The
third approach, using ecological indicators, while
a significantly more established field, is often
poorly implemented, and because of its critical
role, warrants specific attention. Even though each
approach is discussed somewhat individually, it is
important to realize that the three approaches are
interrelated, and when combined, can form the
basis of a larger strategy that directs the overall
process of taking data collection to application.

A common theme in this section of the book
is the use of conceptual diagrams to help select
appropriate indicators and report card indices.
In summarizing this section we highlight some
of the most important aspects to consider when
producing indicators, report cards, and ecological
forecasts, and then conclude by providing an
example of how the different elements can be
combined.

Ecological indicators

Selecting, developing, and communicating
ecological indicators is perhaps the most
important yet challenging aspect of a coastal
assessment program, and therefore should be given
appropriate effort and resources. In the indicator
chapter we highlight a four-step process to follow
when selecting indicators (conceptualize, select,
develop, and apply/review), and also provide
some selection criteria such as cost effectiveness
and relevance to management. The indicator
development process should also consider the
spatial and temporal resolution required and
the different components of the ecosystem (e.g.,
water quality, habitat, and living resources). In
the same way that the entire restoration program
should be adaptable (i.e., an adaptive management
cycle), the indicator process should also be
adaptable, with indicators periodically reviewed
and, if necessary, revised to ensure they are always
fulfilling the established objective. While indicators
by themselves are effective decision-support and
communication tools, it is important that they are
not used in isolation of other analyses or sources

of information. For example, cause and effect
relationships between state (health) indicators and
pressure indicators should be examined.

Ecological report cards

The most important benefit of producing
ecological report cards is the ability to
communicate a simple and often emotive message
(e.g., the health of a region) to a large audience.
A frequently overlooked aspect is the role they
provide as part of the framework for monitoring
and analysis. A robust and defendable report
card relies on a structure of analysis, synthesis,
and interpretation that should enable the user to
logically explore information at a level of detail
relevant to their needs. Developing and producing
a report card includes four main steps that rely
heavily on the process of selecting appropriate
indicators and ecosystem thresholds. The four
steps are: (1) indicator selection, (2) indicator
development, (3) integration into overarching
indices, and (4) communication.

Scientist explaining an ecological health report card to
peers.

Of course, the main challenges arise in the
details, such as establishing appropriate thresholds
and methods of measuring progress toward a
threshold. Each one of these steps, if not already
resolved during the indicator process, can take
significant effort and resources so that they are
not only scientifically defendable, but have the
support of the local scientific and management
community. While producing, maintaining, and
communicating a report card program can require
some significant time and resources to do it well,
the benefits make it worthwhile. Ecological report

Annual communication cycle

Indicators, report cards, and forecasting can be combined into an overall strategy to build community knowledge. For example, in Chesapeake Bay, each of these components was combined into an annual cycle of analysis and communication aimed at providing timely, synthesized, and geographically-detailed assessments of Bay health.[2] This annual cycle consists of forecasting summer ecological conditions in spring (dissolved oxygen and harmful algal bloom conditions), using indicators to track the actual summer ecological conditions until fall, reporting the summer data and accuracy of the forecast in the fall, and completing the cycle in early spring with the release of an environmental health report card. Overall, the annual cycle engages the community by forcing constant assessment.

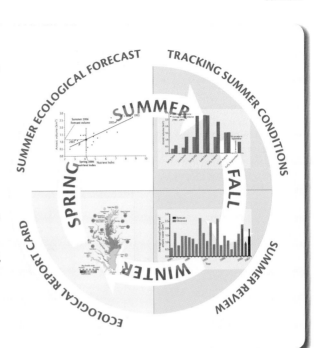

cards have a proven record of not only providing feedback on restoration efforts, but stimulating public and political action, and providing a means of targeting additional resources among others.[3]

Ecological forecasts

Ecological forecasting aims to predict and communicate future ecosystem traits to the broader community. While in some ways forecasting may be seen as an ancillary to the core tasks (e.g., producing indicators and report cards), it must be recognized that there are many benefits to forecasting, and these should be considered when deciding whether or not to proceed. Specific reasons for forecasting include providing resource managers with advanced warning of conditions (therefore giving more time to develop appropriate responses), shifting communication from being reactive to proactive, and fostering interaction at the science-policy interface. One of the common themes identified within this book has been balancing complexity and uncertainty of a product with explanatory power. This theme certainly applies to ecological forecasts, where it is both important for the audience to understand how the forecast was generated and what the forecast results are. To maintain this balance, it is imperative that science, management, and communication teams work together.

Environmental information

Anaylzing data to generate meaningful information

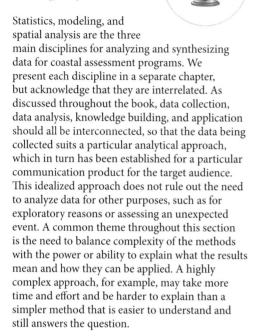

Statistics, modeling, and spatial analysis are the three main disciplines for analyzing and synthesizing data for coastal assessment programs. We present each discipline in a separate chapter, but acknowledge that they are interrelated. As discussed throughout the book, data collection, data analysis, knowledge building, and application should all be interconnected, so that the data being collected suits a particular analytical approach, which in turn has been established for a particular communication product for the target audience. This idealized approach does not rule out the need to analyze data for other purposes, such as for exploratory reasons or assessing an unexpected event. A common theme throughout this section is the need to balance complexity of the methods with the power or ability to explain what the results mean and how they can be applied. A highly complex approach, for example, may take more time and effort and be harder to explain than a simpler method that is easier to understand and still answers the question.

Environmental statistics

Statistics is an essential tool for coastal assessment, with applications ranging from determining optimal sample design to resolving complex research questions. The primary use of statistics for coastal assessment, however, is to describe, and make inferences about, the condition of the ecosystem in response to management actions or other changing variables (e.g., climate). Statistics range from the very simple to the very complex, and it is important to match the complexity of the statistical analysis with the skill set of the analyst or statistician. No matter what the approach or application, statistics synthesize large amounts of data into values that have more meaning and are easier to explain. In other words, it is a process that turns data into information. A coastal assessment program will inevitably have a range of routine statistical analysis requirements that should be determined during design of the field monitoring program. The field sample design should aim to provide sufficient explanatory power and representativeness of the system to answer the questions or aims of the monitoring program. In reality, however, this is rarely the case. Statistical

requirements often demand more than resources can provide, necessitating a balance between statistical power (or result uncertainty), and funding.

Environmental models

Like statistics, environmental models are essential tools for coastal assessment programs. Models can be used to synthesize and analyze data (e.g., explore relationships between system variables), simulate conditions or actions (e.g, run management scenarios), or predict future change (e.g, extrapolate to make ecological forecasts).

NASA

We use spatial analysis to determine our location and the location of natural forces such as hurricanes.

As developing and running a model can require significant resources, selecting an appropriate model is a critical first step. An appropriate model is one that will answer the defined questions or objectives within the required level of error or uncertainty, and within the constraints of available resources. A recent challenge often facing modeling programs is the tendency toward making models more complex than they necessarily need to be. This tendency can result in more resources being used than projected and unnecessary delays in analysis and products. Remember, a carefully formulated simple model may be preferable to a complex model, as it will require less resources and will be easier to understand, manipulate, and communicate to the public. Additionally, in many cases, a simple model will have similar or even less error. This brings us back to the common theme of balancing complexity with understanding. Model selection can be guided by considering

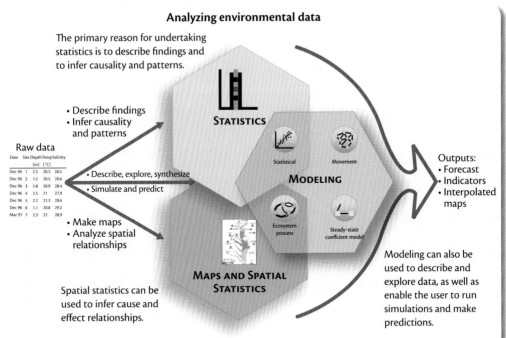

Analyzing environmental data

The primary reason for undertaking statistics is to describe findings and to infer causality and patterns.

- Describe findings
- Infer causality and patterns

Raw data

Date	Site	Depth (m)	Temp (°C)	Salinity
Dec 96	1	2.5	20.3	28.5
Dec 96	2	1.5	20.5	28.6
Dec 96	3	1.8	20.9	28.4
Dec 96	4	2.5	21	27.9
Dec 96	5	2.2	21.3	28.6
Dec 96	6	1.1	20.8	29.2
Mar 97	7	2.3	22	28.9

- Describe, explore, synthesize
- Simulate and predict

- Make maps
- Analyze spatial relationships

STATISTICS

Statistical

Movement

MODELING

Ecosystem process

Steady-state coefficient model

MAPS AND SPATIAL STATISTICS

Spatial statistics can be used to infer cause and effect relationships.

Outputs:
- Forecast
- Indicators
- Interpolated maps

Modeling can also be used to describe and explore data, as well as enable the user to run simulations and make predictions.

The diagram illustrates the overlap in methods that exists between statistics, modeling, and spatial analysis. For example, a simple statistical linear regression can be used as the basis of a predictive model which can then be used to spatially interpolate data between points on a map. In general, all approaches can be used to describe and quantify patterns and to infer cause and effect relationships.

formulation (e.g., statistical vs. mechanistic) and the level of complexity involved. In the modeling chapter, we provide four common types of models with varying formulation and complexity, and provide basic insights into what each model has to offer in terms of spatial, temporal, and functional descriptive capacity. The process of model selection is illustrated by an effort to predict salinity and water flow in the Florida Bay region.

Spatial analysis

Maps and spatial statistics should be a common feature within any coastal assessment program. From a communication standpoint, maps provide a sense of ownership to the audience as they place the information (e.g., condition of a waterway) in relation to the audience's experience of the region (their house, recreation area, etc.). This in turn gives the information more meaning and relevance. From a management and scientific standpoint, maps make spatial features and patterns easy to identify and interpret. For example, maps improve the ability to identify environmental hotspots or

regions that do not comply with environmental goals. For maps to be most useful, attention must be given to presentation, including use of appropriate colors and symbols as well as the removal of extraneous information. Providing maps with continuous surfaces, which do not rely on the user's eye to fill in the blanks, have significant advantages. These surfaces make spatial patterns easier to visualize. However, the spatial interpolation process does require specialist skills and software. The next step in identifying a pattern and suggesting a relationship is to use spatial and GIS analysis to evaluate cause and effect. Spatial analysis requires a series of steps (exploration, in-depth analysis, and product generation) and iterations that rely on a combination of statistical analysis and GIS analysis skills. While spatial analysis requires a significantly more expert skill set than those usually needed to produce maps, the ability to draw statistical relationship between causal factors and effects to the ecosystem is a very powerful tool for managers to use.

Data collection

Gathering relevant data for coastal assessment

This section of the book addresses the practical aspects of collecting data to solve environmental challenges. We emphasize the application of the data because poorly designed and implemented monitoring can result in data that is either unsuitable or poorly suited to the product needs, and therefore may never be used or used to its full potential. Ensuring that any data collected will be used has become more of a concern in recent years because of the 'observation revolution'—a rapid increase in data-generating capacity due to technological advancements. The capacity to analyze, interpret, and communicate this enhanced data stream and the knowledge it generates, seems not to be keeping pace with data. To avoid this potential mismatch between data supply and analysis, decisions dictating data collection should be unequivocally linked to the goals and aims of the coastal assessment program. Also, linkages should be made with the process of turning the data into knowledge and products such as report cards that will feed the overall campaign. Some insights to consider when designing or redefining a monitoring program within an integrated coastal assessment framework are provided in the first chapter of this section. The second two chapters discuss the two main approaches to collecting data within a monitoring program, using either *in situ* instrumentation or remotely sensed data collected largely by satellites and airborne sensors.

Program design

Designing an effective monitoring program is reliant on having clearly-defined and achievable objectives to guide key decisions. These objectives need to be developed in context of the overall campaign and its requirements for products such as indicators and report cards or statistical analyses such as trend analysis or pattern recognition. Conceptual diagrams can play a useful role in helping to design a monitoring program, for example, in assisting partners to define key features, stressors, and pressures. This technique can be used to elucidate appropriate parameters to monitor or to determine relationships that need further research. Sample design needs to consider what to sample, where to sample, and how often to sample. These decisions will depend on factors such as:

- characteristics of the environment being assessed including size, spatial, and temporal variability;
- purpose or objectives of the monitoring (e.g., showing temporal trends or mapping zones); and
- available resources (funding).

Program design benefits from including a data management strategy that assures quality and efficient flow of data from collection through to the final repository. The data management strategy should recognize that management is reliant on the attitudes and habits of everyone interacting with the data (not just data managers), and hence an infrastructure of standards and procedures to guide the process is required.

Following data collection protocols is one aspect of a monitoring program.

In situ measurements

Taking in situ measurements can be as simple and cheap as lowering a Secchi disc through the water column or as complex and costly as establishing and maintaining autonomous, continuous measurement monitoring probes. Choosing an instrument should be based on its suitability for providing data for the intended product or analysis. Factors such as resources and technical support must also be included in the decision process. While many of the 'high-tech' instruments may be tempting to use, it may be the case that a simpler, cheaper, and perhaps more reliable instrument is just as suitable. There are cases in which using 'high-tech' instrumentation is the only option, for example, if you need to collect data remotely, and/or continuously. A reality of continuously deployed in situ instruments is the tendency of the instruments to become biofouled and therefore record erroneous data. While there are many ways to minimize biofouling, routine

Gathering data for coastal assessment

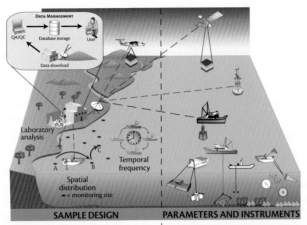

SAMPLE DESIGN	PARAMETERS AND INSTRUMENTS
Ensuring appropriate spatial distribution and temporal frequency is only one step in the process of acquiring high quality data. Equally important is ensuring that quality-assured data management protocols are in place and that data are readily accessible to users in the required time frame.	Based on the overall program requirements, decisions such as what parameters to measure, what precision is required, what size area should be covered, and what instruments and platforms to use, all need to be made.

cleaning and maintenance is generally required to maintain data quality. Clear data management strategies are essential for in situ sensors which, just like remote sensors, have the potential to generate vast quantities of data.

Remote sensing

Remote sensing is becoming an increasingly viable option for monitoring coastal ecosystems, with more and more projects evolving from demonstration or trials to operational use. The primary reason to use remote sensing is the spatial, and to a lesser degree temporal, coverage that is provided. Before embarking on a remote sensing exercise, it is important to match the promise with the reality. The promise is the relative ease of obtaining repeatable, spatially-explicit information and the reality is what can actually be mapped and monitored accurately and reliably—and then at what cost and effort. Quality of information provided depends on factors such as the type of sensor used (e.g., multi-spectral, hyper-spectral etc.), the suitability of the sensor for measuring the defined parameter, the algorithm used to convert a somewhat abstract (e.g., reflected) value to a biophysical property, atmospheric correction, and interfering factors such as bottom reflectance.

The simplest option for applying remote sensing data to coastal monitoring programs is to select existing images and use them in their own form. A more complex option requires acquisition of new image data, integration with field data, processing, and validation. The effort to conduct data processing and validation should not be underestimated, and these tasks require suitably skilled personnel, adequate hardware, image-processing software, and operating protocols. Remote sensing is a useful tool that should be incorporated into many monitoring programs for uses as simple as the visualization of true color images (a use not to be under emphasized) or as complex as the development of highly-processed, field-corrected, and validated data.

Final thoughts

In this handbook, we have tried to provide a roadmap to successful coastal assessment. The hands-on approach articulated in the book should provide guidance to scientists and managers throughout the world's coastal ecosystems on specific aspects of their program. The next few pages list key steps to remember when creating an effective coastal assessment program. Using these techniques will move stakeholders from uninformed and unengaged to informed and engaged, and will lead to involved citizens protecting and restoring coastal ecosystems.

Starting a program

The perfect is the enemy of the good.

—Voltaire

When starting a new program, the most important thing is to DO SOMETHING. No matter how small the initial steps are, it is important to initiate activity. Planning for a new program can occupy long periods of time, but little is actually produced while undergoing a planning process. So it is important to begin producing scientific results as soon as possible, and initiating a pilot program can provide an understanding of the sampling and analytical challenges and the temporal and spatial variability of the ecosystem, and begin to develop the data processing and analysis protocols. At the beginning of a program, it is an opportune time to experiment with different sampling regimes, test various indicators, and develop a nested series of high frequency and high density data collection activities. These initial experiments will provide important information that will help optimize temporal and spatial sampling regimes and lead to appropriate indicator selection. Another aspect of collecting new data is that it invariably leads to new understanding and gives the scientists an opportunity to provide stakeholders with up-to-date information. Initiating programs that include multiple partner agencies and institutions can involve long and difficult negotiations and take many meetings to discuss and establish roles and responsibilities. One way to jump-start this process is to establish an agency/institution partnership, develop an initial collaborative project, and approach other potential partners with the following message: "We are going to conduct this project together, and you are welcome to join us". This contrasts with the approach: "My agency/institution is interested in doing this project and we would like you to help us." The acceptance rate of joining a partnership that is moving forward is higher than when the prospective partner is being asked to help out.

Building a program

Every day you may make progress. Every step may be fruitful. Yet there will stretch out before you an ever-lengthening, ever-ascending, ever-improving path.

—Winston Churchill

Once a program is initiated, a building phase should be developed which leads to an expansion of the stakeholder network and increased

Scientists working together during the building phase of a coastal assessment program.

Integration & Application Network

impacts of the program. This building phase is not necessarily predicated by increased resources (money and people), but should nonetheless have EXPANDED OUTCOMES, which, in turn, often results in increased resources. In order to achieve a broader impact, a key element is to communicate often and widely. All levels of communication are required, from person-to-person, to newsletters, websites, presentations, videos, and conceptual diagrams. Creating communication products leads to a collaborative process, allowing people to build important working relationships. A suite of small frequent communication products (e.g., electronic and paper newsletters), punctuated by large infrequent products (e.g., videos or books) provides both timely updates and leaves a legacy of products which aid in training staff and recruiting new partners. In building an environmental program, the attitude to instill is one of a campaign. As in a political campaign, a small but highly organized team can solicit support through a series of workshops and events in which effective communication principles are employed. A key element is finding, fostering, and nurturing champions who are willing to perform on the campaign trail—scientists willing to provide updates, but also willing to answer questions and listen to stakeholder concerns. Ultimately, it is the quality of the people that dictate the success of the program, not the institutions or program management structures in place.

Reinvigorating a program

When you're finished changing, you're finished.
—Benjamin Franklin

The energy and excitement of starting or building a new program fades over time and it is easy for a program to become stale over time, losing the creative drive that characterized the initial stages. Thus, it is important to consider ways to reinvigorate an established program. The key to maintaining the creative energy is through CONTINUAL CHANGE. The program needs to regularly revisit the shared vision and program objectives to question whether a) the vision and objectives remain valid and b) the projects and activities being conducted adhere to the vision and program objectives. Maintaining the status quo can become the overall goal of a program, so using the peer review approach of having periodic external reviews can help challenge the scientists as well as build credibility and maintain scientific rigor. Often, the internal review or self-analysis that occurs in preparation for an external review is just as valuable as the external review itself. Engagement with stakeholders is aided by providing positive feedback, which can be enhanced by selecting sites and indicators that are responsive to management actions. In this way, stakeholders will be able to celebrate and emulate successes, creating a positive outlook and even if these successes are relatively modest, they create a culture of positive thinking and a "can do" attitude that will prove important in maintaining the energy and excitement throughout the campaign.

Resourcing a program

Lack of money is no obstacle. Lack of an idea is an obstacle.
—Ken Hakuta

It is important to develop SUSTAINABLE FUNDING schemes to support research, monitoring, and management activities. Successful programs attract resources, both in terms of the funding available to support activities and in terms of the personnel available and willingness to work to achieve the goals of the program. The program needs to ask not how to get money, rather how to achieve programmatic objectives. A key funding strategy is to seek leveraging or matching opportunities in which a specific funding source can be used

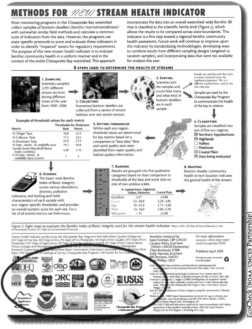

Multiple partners are essential for leveraging resources and information.

to leverage additional funds from different but complementary sources. Pooling resources can also lead to stronger partnerships between agencies and institutions and offer money saving opportunities. Multiple partners provide different institutional attributes that each partner can contribute. For example, an academic institution can supply students working on relevant projects or interning for the program, a resource management agency can supply data analysts in addition to field and laboratory equipment, and a non-governmental organization can supply public outreach capacity and citizen scientists to assist monitoring.

These examples illustrate the advantage of using partnerships to maximize resources. An entrepreneurial approach is often needed and multiple applications for grants required to obtain sufficient funding.

INDEX